The Battle Over
Citizen Lawmaking

The Battle Over Citizen Lawmaking

A Collection of Essays

*An In-depth Review of the Growing Trend
to Regulate the People's Tool of Self-Government:
The Initiative and Referendum Process*

Sponsored by

IRI

INITIATIVE & REFERENDUM INSTITUTE

Edited by M. Dane Waters

Carolina Academic Press
Durham, North Carolina

ISBN 0-89089-968-1
LCCN 00-110008

Carolina Academic Press
700 Kent Street
Durham, North Carolina 27701
Telephone (919) 489-7486
Fax (919) 493-5668
E-mail: cap@cap-press.com
www.cap-press.com

Printed in the United States of America.

Contents

Appendices

What Is the Initiative & Referendum Institute?

In 1998, in recognition of the initiative and referendum process' influence on America, the Initiative & Referendum Institute was founded. The Institute, a 501(c)(3) non-profit non-partisan research and educational organization, is dedicated to educating the citizens about how the initiative and referendum process has been utilized, bringing litigation when necessary to protect it, and in providing information to the citizens so they understand and know how to utilize the process. No other organization does what we do.

The Initiative & Referendum Institute extensively studies the initiative and referendum process and publishes papers and monographs addressing its effect on public policy, citizen participation and its reflection of trends in American thought and culture. We also research and produce a state-by-state guide to the initiative and referendum process that can be used by activists, and we work to educate and update the public on how the process is being utilized across the country. We analyze the relationship between voters and their elected lawmakers and when and why the people turn to initiative and referendum to enact changes in state and local law. Already, the Initiative & Referendum Institute has garnered significant media attention. We have been interviewed or cited by numerous media outlets including, ABC News, Voter News Service, CBS Radio, Pacific Radio Network, CNN, *The Washington Post*, *The New York Times*, *The Chicago Tribune*, Fox News Channel, *The Christian Science Monitor*, The News Hour with Jim Lerher, *The National Journal*, *The Wall Street Journal*, *Governing Magazine*, *USA Today*, Court TV's "Supreme Court Watch" and "Washington Watch," *The Economist*, National Public Radio, *Campaigns and Elections Magazine*, *U.S. News and World Report*, *Congressional Quarterly*, and dozens of other publications, newspapers and radio stations around the world.

The Institute is uniquely qualified to undertake this mission. Comprising the Institute's Board of Directors, Advisory Board and Legal Advisory Board are some of the world's leading authorities on the initiative and referendum process, including prominent scholars; experienced activists—who know the nuts and bolts of the process and its use; skilled attorneys;

and political leaders—including six governors—who have seen first hand the necessity of having a process through which citizens can directly reform their government.

Visit our two award winning websites at **http://www.iandrinstitute.org** and **http://www.ballotwatch.org** for additional information or contact Dane Waters, President of the Initiative & Referendum Institute via email at **mdanewaters@iandrinstitute.org** or by calling 202.429.5539.

Initiative & Referendum Institute
1825 I Street, NW, Suite 400
Washington, DC 20006
Phone: (202) 429-5539
Fax: (202) 986-3001

Acknowledgments

In 1998, the Initiative & Referendum Institute was founded to educate the citizens about the initiative and referendum process. The Institute's success in accomplishing this goal has been possible because of the strong interest of the citizens in this wonderful tool of self-government and due to the strong support of a handful of individuals who believed in this organization in its early days and gave selflessly of their time, energy and financial resources. I would like to personally thank Karen Connell, Jeff Oldham, Angelo Paparella, Bill Piper, Dennis Polhill and Mary Waters who first pushed me to start the Institute and who believed in the goals of the organization. I would also like to thank David Keating for providing hours of advice on how the Institute should operate as well as Paul Jacob and Howie Rich who gave me the opportunity to experience first hand the importance of the initiative and referendum process.

Throughout the last three years numerous people have stepped forward at critical times to help the Institute and to them words of gratitude aren't enough. They include Ed Meese, Governor Kirk Fordice of Mississippi, Wayne Pacelle and Ted Weill.

Additionally, I owe a tremendous debt of gratitude to the contributing authors who made this book possible. They include Anne Campbell, Jennie Drage, Beth Garrett, Liz Gerber, Paul Grant, Paul Jacob, Bill Jones, Kris Kobach, Rob Natelson, Wayne Pacelle, Angelo Paparella, Dennis Polhill, Mads Qvortrup, Peter Schrag, Dan Smith, Don Stenberg and Caroline Tolbert.

Finally, I would like to thank my son Mason, whose love for his father brings joy to me every day and to whom I dedicate this book.

Introduction

Much has been written and spoken about the initiative and referendum process over the years. Many believe, as do I, that much of this rhetoric has been based on misinformation and has been disseminated primarily by people who do not believe in the people's right to self govern as envisioned by our Founding Fathers at the state and federal level. However, one thing that both opponents and proponents of the process agree on is the impact the initiative and referendum process has had on our daily lives.

There is little doubt that in recent years the initiative process has become one of the most important mechanisms for altering and influencing public policy at the local, state and even national level. In the last two years alone, utilizing the initiative process, citizens were heard on affirmative action, educational reform, term limits, tax reform, campaign finance reform, animal protection, drug policy reform and the environment.

But as the authors of this book will make clear, the initiative process has fallen prey to its own success. Lawmakers who have been most affected by this citizen's tool have struck back by imposing new regulations on the process — regulations that can be argued serve no purpose but to deprive the citizens of the only avenue available to them to reign in unresponsive government. Even though it can also be argued that the initiative process is in need of review and possibly reform — state legislators seem to be acting in a vacuum and have not taken the time to truly understand the effects of their attempts at reform.

William Jennings Bryan said it best in 1920 when he stated: "[w]e have the initiative and referendum; do not disturb them. If defects are discovered, correct them and perfect the machinery...make it possible for the people to have what they want...we are the world's teacher in democracy; the world looks to us for an example. We cannot ask others to trust the people unless we are ourselves willing to trust them." This statement couldn't be truer today than it was 80 years ago.

When the initiative process was established, many of the initiative states provided that these reserved powers to the people would be "self-executing." In other initiative states, the legislature was entrusted with creating procedures by which the people could exercise the initiative. Citizen concern about the legislature's efforts to limit initiative rights was the primary reason that in some initiative states, the legislature is specifically instructed to enact laws designed to only facilitate, not hinder, the initiative process.

However, despite the fact that the citizenry adopted the initiative to ensure citizen government, most of the states where the citizens provided that they retain initiative rights have seen the legislature enact legislation that restricts rather than facilitates the use of these powers by the people. The legislatures' regulation of the initiative and referendum have often violated the citizenry's First Amendment rights as articulated by the U.S. Supreme Court in Meyer v. Grant, 486 U.S. 414 (1986)—as pointed out in the chapters by Kris Kobach and Paul Grant. Furthermore, the restrictions imposed on the citizenry are typically not imposed on other individuals seeking to use a state's electoral processes to invoke changes in state government, whether it be through lobbying, legislating, or running for political office.

As Secretary of State Bill Jones of California points out in Chapter 14, states do have a compelling interest in ensuring that all elections, including those on initiatives, are conducted in a non-fraudulent manner. However, if the state legislatures wish to regulate lawmaking by the people they should impose the same restrictions on their own powers. Lobbyists, for example, who seek to have the legislature enact new laws or propose amendments to the state constitution typically have no voter registration or residency requirements imposed on them—but signature collectors for initiatives do. The purported purpose behind legislatively imposed limitations on the citizenry in the initiative process should be viewed skeptically in the absence of evidence of unique voter fraud during these processes.

A variety of legislative enactments in various states demonstrate how the legislatures have reacted to the use of the initiative process. Many argue that their response appears based on self-interest rather than an interest in protecting a system of government where the citizens are an independent branch of government. A review of the various legislatures' responses, many argue, reveals that control of a distinct branch of government, the people, by legislative action is not about fraud but about raw political power.

As the chapters in this book point out, many, if not most, of the regulations on the process were enacted or proposed during the recent wave of term limit, animal protection, tax limitation and campaign finance initiatives enacted by the citizenry. However, legislatures have always vigilantly inhibited the people's right to the initiative and referendum. Regulations imposed on the people's use of these powers have typically been direct responses by the legislature to the people's use of these powers.

Numerous examples could be cited if more space were available. In 1998 and 1999 alone, seven states—Arizona, Idaho, Mississippi, Missouri, Montana, Utah and Wyoming—tightened procedural restrictions on initiatives. These seem extreme when one considers that only 134 laws have been adopted in those states using the initiative process in over eighty years. Since the first statewide initiative on Oregon's ballot in 1904, citizens in the 24 states with the initiative process have placed approximately 1,900 statewide measures on the ballot and have only adopted 787 (41%). In 1996, considered by many to be the "high water mark" for the initiative process, the citizens placed 102 measures on statewide ballots and adopted 45 (44%). In contrast, in 1996, the state legislatures in those same 24 states adopted over 17,000 laws. Furthermore, very few initiatives actually make the ballot. In California, according to political scientist Dave McCuan, only 26% of all initiatives filed have made it to the ballot and only 8% of those filed actually were adopted by the voters.

Additionally, many people try to make the case that new regulations need to be added since, in their minds, the initiative process in this country is unregulated and represents "laws without government." The initiative process in this country is one of the most regulated in the world. The government sets all the rules, including: telling you if you can or can't collect signatures on a specific issue, how many subjects the issue must be limited to, the size and font of the petition you circulate, how many signatures you must collect and from what areas, how long you have to collect signatures and who can and cannot collect those signatures, and the government ultimately decides if your issue can be on the ballot or not.

Regulation has also been proposed, as the chapters of this book will point out, because of concerns regarding the initiative process and the role of money in the process, the competence of voters when making decisions on initiatives, and the role the process has on minority rights. Numerous books addressing these issues have been written by leading academics and can far better address these topics than I can in a few pages. However, in short, many of these concerns seem unfounded and so regulation "addressing" them in turn seems unfounded as well.

For example, Professor Liz Gerber, arguably one of the top political scientists in the country, surveyed 168 different direct legislation campaigns in eight states and found that economic interest groups are "severely limited in their ability to pass new laws by initiative" and that "by contrast, citizen groups with broad-based support and important organization resources can much more effectively use direct legislation to pass new laws." She and Beth Garret discuss this issue in greater detail in Chapter 5.

Additional research by political scientists Todd Donovan, Shaun Bowler, David McCuan, and Ken Fernandez found that while 40% of ALL initiatives on the Californian ballot from 1986-1996 passed, only 14% of initiatives pushed by special interests were adopted. They concluded, "[o]ur data reveals that these are indeed the hardest initiatives to market in California, and that money spent by proponents in this arena is largely wasted." This research complements political scientist Anne Campbell's research on special interest-backed initiatives in Colorado from 1966 to 1994, which found that during those 28 years, only *ONE* initiative pushed by special interests was successful at the ballot box.

Many people are predisposed to believe that money influences elections — it is the conventional wisdom which is why the vast majority of Americans want campaign finance reform — but when it comes to initiative campaigns, the proof does not exist. But, even granting for a moment that money does influence the initiative process, why should the process be abandoned? If the influence of money is the litmus test to abolishing or over-regulating a legislative process, then the normal legislative process controlled by state and federal lawmakers should be abolished and/or stringently regulated as well.

Another argument for regulating and limiting the initiative and referendum process is the claim that the people already have the ability to check government through the existing electoral process and therefore the check and balance created by I&R is not necessary. However, most people who support the initiative process and who utilize the process only use it as a tool to address single issues — issues that their elected officials for whatever reason have chosen not to address. They want, for the most part, to keep a particular elected official and so electing them out of office for failing to deal with one specific issue is considered by many to be an extreme step — far more extreme than allowing the people to make laws on an occasional basis. In 100 years the people have made approximately 800 laws. That is not many considering that an average legislature passes over 1,000 laws a year.

There is no doubt that you can find flaws with citizen lawmaking. No form of legislating is perfect. But adding additional regulations to an already over-regulated process will do nothing — and has done nothing — but increase the cost of utilizing I&R and has precluded most citizens from using this important tool. A tool that the people need access to — a tool the people can use to check government in an era of growing government.

As you can see, the issue of regulation is complex. But one thing that is for certain, the regulation of I&R has generated a deluge of practical questions which thus far have remained either unanswered or have been confined to the pages of specialist journals. This makes it difficult for practitioners and citizens, who need to understand these new regulations and the rationale behind them, to get access to important information and valuable discussions. Regulation raises many questions: philosophical questions about freedom of expression, equality between different groups, legal questions about signature gathering, limits on campaign spending, etc, and political problems about implementing the statutes regulating I&R. This book will attempt to address these issues from the viewpoint of leading scholars, opinion-leaders, journalists, elected officials, activists involved in pushing reform through the initiative process and attorneys that have been involved in fighting these regulations.

The contributors to this book represent both strands in the debate - those that oppose regulation and those that support it. Those that oppose regulation tend to believe that regulations and restrictions challenge—and undermine—the principle of government "by the people." Those that support regulation believe that it ensures the fairness of the outcome, for, as noted philosopher John Rawls writes:

> The liberties protected by the principle of participation lose much of their value whenever those who have greater private means are permitted to use their advantages to control the course of the political debate. For eventually these inequalities will enable those better situated to exercise larger influence over the debate...compensating measures must, then, be taken to preserve the fair value for all of equal political liberties.

This book seeks to enlighten and broaden the debate by adding substance and depth to the discussion. I am quite aware that there are other words on subjects than last words. Yet I do entertain the immodest belief that this collection of essays will provide new departures for the ongoing debate.

M. Dane Waters
President
Initiative & Referendum Institute

The Battle Over
Citizen Lawmaking

Section One

The Evolution of Initiative and Referendum

Before any discussion can take place regarding the regulation of initiative and referendum ("I&R"), one must first understand the reasons for the existence of I&R as well as the necessity of its existence. This Section seeks to provide a fundamental overview of the evolution of I&R. The first chapter by Dennis Polhill will begin the discussion by providing an overview of the evolution of democracy and how "Democracy's Journey" led to the establishment of the initiative and referendum process. The chapter which follows "Democracy's Journey," written by Rob Natelson, will continue this evolutionary track by discussing in greater detail the philosophical underpinnings of I&R and how it is consistent with representative democracy. The final chapter of this section, written by Caroline Tolbert, will discuss how, since its adoption in 1898, the initiative and referendum process has been utilized in the United States.

Let the journey begin. . . .

Chapter 1

Democracy's Journey

By Dennis Polhill

Many historians will argue, and I will agree, that Democracy has its roots in Greek and Roman history. However, for the sake of time and space, I have chosen to begin the discussion of "Democracy's Journey" in the period of English history that immediately preceded the founding of America. This is relevant in my opinion because it is the undemocratic underpinnings of English governance during this period of time that lead to the push for freedom in America and eventually the adoption of initiative and referendum.

Historical Backdrop

The dominant form of government throughout all of human existence has been Kings. Sometimes called Caesar, Czar, Pharaoh, Caliph, Emperor, Kaiser, or Chief, the system was the same. One man determined all aspects of life for all of the people. Because "the King was the law" fairness and consistency were no more than occasionally dreamt ideals. Individual rights existed only to the extent that the King granted them. Because Kings were granted their power to rule from God, the King's eldest son typically became the next King.

As society grew larger, it was increasingly difficult for Kings to oversee an enlarging geography. As a result the system of Feudalism, using lesser Kings called barons, earls, and lords evolved. To administer the increasing number of items requiring the attention of the King, the corps of advisors in service to the King grew larger, more bureaucratic and more corrupt. Together the King, the barons, earls, lords, and their advisors, made up society's ruling class, called the aristocracy. Slavery was common and non-slaves were not much better off. The role of commoners or serfs in this caste system was to work and to pay tribute.

Island Feudalism Leads to Laws

England was somewhat insulated from the more frequent Feudalistic conflicts of mainland Europe. Thus, internal domestic concerns reached center stage sooner. The natural tension between the King and his barons, earls and lords came to a head in 1215. A collection of barons had mutinied, defeating the King's army. The Magna Carta was then drafted and defined Feudalistic Rights in 63 written articles. The single revolutionary notion achieved by the Magna Carta was that there should be limitations upon the absolute power of the King. The Magna Carta was a necessary step, but more time would be needed to invent democracy.

The Magna Carta did more to help the barons than the commoners. It reorganized the judicial system; it abolished tax assessments without consent; it standardized penalties for felonies; and trials were to be conducted according to strict rules of procedure. Although the Pope voided the Magna Carta, it was reissued in 1217. In 1258, again over taxation, the barons revolted, forcing the Baronial Council to become permanent. The permanent Baronial Council was the first vestige of the House of Lords of Parliament. The Magna Carta was modified and confirmed by Parliament in 1297.

Conflict over the divine right of Kings versus limitations on his powers continued for centuries. In the 17th century, religious fragmentation and persecution, and the lack of individual liberties, fueled internal turmoil and emigration to the New World. Royal abuses had become so extreme that in 1628 Parliament passed the Petition of Rights. The Petition enumerated abuses and asked that they cease. The King responded by forcing Parliament to adjourn and imprisoning parliamentary leaders. An eleven years religious war against the Scots forced the King to convene Parliament to raise taxes. Unfriendly to the idea, Parliament was immediately adjourned and a new Parliament convened in 1640. But the new Parliament was even less friendly to the King and quickly arrested and executed one of the King's closest advisors for treason, emphasizing the view that the King and his advisors were not above the law.

Soon after, a national referendum was proposed on the abolition of the monarchy and the House of Lords. The House of Commons was created which would be elected by universal male suffrage but limited by a bill of rights. However, the King refused to cooperate and was convicted of violating his coronation oath by attacking the people's liberties, and was publicly beheaded in 1649. Parliament took unilateral control of government under the dictatorial leadership of Oliver Cromwell. The state-preferred religion changed, but religious persecution continued. Parliament was purged and Cromwell cruelly suppressed the Irish and Scots. Soon, the Commonwealth began to crumble. Upon Cromwell's death, his son proved too weak to maintain control and so the son of the beheaded King was asked to return in 1660 and the Monarchy was restored.

John Locke

Events during this period influenced the thinking of John Locke, arguably the foremost political thinker of all times. Locke was born in 1632 and was educated at Oxford University. After teaching briefly, he became a physician. Uncomfortable with the restoration of the monarchy, Locke went to France in 1675. He returned in 1679 only to discover religious persecution as rampant as ever, and returned to the Continent until 1689. He was a philosophical empiricalist emphasizing the importance of experience and experimentation in the pursuit of knowledge. His two most important writings, *Essay Concerning Human Understanding* and *Two Treatises of Government* were written in 1690. Locke attacked the theory of divine right of Kings and argued that sovereignty resided with the people, not the state. The state was limited by civil and "natural" law. It was government's duty to protect natural rights, such as life, liberty, property, and religious freedom. He advocated checks and balances via three branches of government and separation of church and state. Locke held that revolution was not only a natural right, but also an obligation.

The contest for supremacy between the King and Parliament continued after Cromwell's death. Finally the divine right of Kings ended with the Glorious Revolution in 1688. In a Parliamentary vote, the Crown was taken from James II and offered to William and Mary conditioned upon a written Declaration of Rights, which enumerated rights in similar fashion to what was to become the Bill of Rights in the U.S. Constitution.

Evolution of Sovereignty

During this period, John Locke introduced the next revolutionary notion: that the people were sovereign, not the King. The King-by-proxy government of the American colonies, proved both ineffective and largely irrelevant to the increasingly self-reliant colonists.

Locke's ideas soon took hold in the American colonies. Thomas Jefferson, a reader of Locke, based many of his beliefs on Locke's theories, which can easily be seen in his writings. A perfect example is Jefferson's belief that "[t]he people…are the only sure reliance for the preservation of our liberty." It's that principal, that one simple statement, that best summarizes not only Jefferson's and Locke's beliefs, but also the beliefs that America was founded upon.

The Evolution of Initiative and Referendum in the United States

It wasn't long before the American colonies had tired of the undemocratic governance by the Crown and soon gained their independence. Then came the tough job of designing a system of government that would recognize the sovereignty of the people while creating a strong government that would insure the stability of a newly formed country. Even though many historians believe initiative and referendum was a subject of discussion, it was left out of the original constitution—as was women's suffrage and the abolishment of slavery.

However, Jefferson was a strong and vocal advocate of the referendum process, which in his view recognized the people to be the sovereign. Whereas the King of England spoke of his power to govern being derived from God, Jefferson knew that those chosen to represent the citizenry as envisioned in a republican form of government were only empowered by the people.

James Madison, as did Jefferson, knew too well the possibility that in a republic, those chosen to rule can and would on occasion become consumed with their power and take actions not consistent with the Constitution—actions that represented their self-interest and not the interest of the people. For this reason, a series of checks-and-balances were placed in the U.S. Constitution in order to right the errors caused when elected representatives chose to rule unconstitutionally or in their own self-interest. Not only did the Founding Fathers create these checks-and-balances by one branch of government over the next, they created a provision in Article V of the Constitution that allowed the people the right to make change and/or restore our Constitution absent action by the Government. Unfortunately this process still relied on some form of action by those in power and therefore can be argued as being unusable by the citizenry since it has never been utilized in over 200 years.

The Founding Fathers at the state level created republican governments on a smaller scale that mirrored that of the Federal Government. In these constitutions a series of checks-and-balances were created to take into account the possible abuse of power by elected representatives and to protect the people from an out of control government—when and if that were to happen. But what the citizens began to realize in the late 1800s was that no matter what checks-and-balances existed, the people had no direct ability to reign in an out-of-touch government or government paralyzed by inaction.

Then came the Populist Party of the 1890s. Its members had become outraged that moneyed special interest groups controlled government, and that the people had no ability to break this control. They soon began to propose a comprehensive platform of political reforms. They advocated women's suffrage, secret ballots, direct election of U.S. Senators, primary elections and initiative and referendum. Difficult as it would be to envision modern political systems without these reforms, they were considered quite extreme changes in the 1890s.

Perhaps the most revolutionary Populist reform was initiative and popular referendum. These forms of initiative and referendum, as well as the already established legislative referendum—which Jefferson championed in the late 1700s—acknowledged that the authority to legislate and govern was delegated by the people and reaffirmed that the people were the only true sovereign—as Jefferson and Locke had envisioned. They rightfully believed that government without the consent of the governed was tyranny and because authority, but not responsibility, can be delegated, a mechanism to un-delegate, when appropriate, was a proper check on the process of legislating.

It should be noted and emphasized that the move to establish initiative and referendum was not a movement to change our system of government or abolish representative government—but to enhance it. Our Founding Fathers at the state and federal levels created wonderful documents, but they were documents based on compromise. They realized that they would need to be changed which is why they created a mechanism to alter them when necessary. The system of checks and balances were created as a theoretical system based on how to check the power of one branch of government with another—but it was an unproven system. As time progressed, the citizens discovered that this theoretical system of checks and balances at the state and federal level worked—but not good enough—for their were times when elected officials chose not to act in the people's best interest. For this reason, the Populists/Progressives strove to strengthen the system of checks and balances on government at the state level and advocated the initiative and referendum process. Additionally it must be remembered that we have two tiers of Founding Fathers in this country—those at the federal level and those at the state level. The Founding Fathers of Oklahoma and Alaska, for example, chose to put initiative and referendum in their states' original constitutions. It would be wrong in my opinion to pass judgment that the Founding Fathers at the state level were in some way inferior to our Founding Fathers at the federal level.

In 1897, Nebraska became the first state to allow cities to place initiative and referendum in their charters. One year later, the Populists adopted methods from the 1848 Swiss Constitution and successfully amended them into the South Dakota Constitution. On November 5, 1898, South Dakota became the first state to adopt statewide initiative and popular referendum. Oregon followed in 1902 when Oregon voters approved initiative and popular referendum by an 11-to-1 margin. Other states soon followed. In 1906 Montana voters approved an initiative and popular referendum amendment proposed by the state legislature. Oklahoma became the first state to provide for the initiative and popular referendum in its original constitution in 1907. Maine and Michigan passed initiative and popular referendum amendments in 1908.

In 1911 California placed initiative and popular referendum in their constitution. Other states were to follow—but even with popular support in many states, the elected class refused the will of the people and did not enact this popular reform. In Texas, for example, the people actually had the opportunity to vote for initiative and popular referendum in 1914, but voted it down because the amendment proposed by the legislature would have required that signatures be gathered from 20% of the registered voters in the state—a number twice as large as what was required in any other state. The proponents for initiative and popular referendum felt it was more important to get a useable process than one that would have maintained the status quo and provided no benefit to the citizenry. However, the legislature used this defeat as an excuse to claim that initiative and popular referendum was not wanted by the people and therefore effectively killed the movement in Texas.

Eventually, between 1898 and 1918, 24 states adopted initiative or popular referendum—mostly in the West. The expansion of initiative and popular referendum in the West fit more with the Westerners belief of populism—that the people should rule the elected and not allow the elected to rule the people. Unfortunately in the East and South this was not the case. Those that were in power were opposed to the expansion of initiative and popular referendum because they were concerned that blacks and immigrants would use the process to enact reforms that were not consistent with the beliefs of the ruling class.

In 1959, when Alaska became a state, the citizens had adopted the power of initiative and popular referendum. Then in 1972, Floridians adopted statewide initiative. Mississippians in 1992 restored initiative and referendum to their constitution, 70 years after the state Supreme Court invalidated the election creating the process. Mississippi became the newest and last state to get this valuable tool.

The credit for the establishment of initiative and popular referendum in this country belongs with the Progressives. They worked steadily to dismantle the political machines and bosses that controlled American politics by pushing reforms eliminating the influence the special interest had on political parties and the government. Their goal, as is that of today's proponents of the initiative and popular referendum, is to ensure that elected officials remain accountable to the electorate.

Conclusion

The evolution from tyranny to democracy has been a long and difficult road—a road that is never ending. But as you can see, the evolution of initiative and referendum is not contrary to the evolution of representative democracy—but an enhancement to it. The two are designed to work hand-in-hand with each other. The following chapter by Rob Natelson specifically addresses this issue.

The long journey for democracy that began with the Magna Carta is far from finished. Though its future form may be unclear today, we can be certain that democracy will increase and that initiative and referendum will play a role in determining future democratic systems.

Initiative and Referendum Historical Timeline[1]

1775   In his proposed 1775 Virginia state constitution, Thomas Jefferson includes a requirement that the constitution must be approved by the voters in a statewide referendum before it can take effect. Unfortunately, because he was hundred of miles from Virginia at the time attending the Continental Congress, delegates to the Virginia Convention did not receive the proposal until after the convention was already over.

1776   Georgia delegates gather in Savannah to draft their state's constitution. The constitution includes a provision that would allow amendments whenever a majority of voters in each county signed petitions calling for a convention, but the provision is never invoked.

1778   Massachusetts becomes the first state to hold a statewide legislative referendum to adopt its constitution. The voters reject it by a five-to-one margin, forcing the legislature to rewrite its proposal.

1792   New Hampshire becomes the second state to hold a statewide legislative referendum to adopt its constitution.

1830   Voters in Virginia demand the power to veto amendments to their state constitution and are given it.

1834   Alabama, Connecticut, Georgia, Maine, Mississippi, New York, North Carolina, and Rhode Island adopt provisions preventing their state constitutions from being amended without the approval of the voters.

1848   The Swiss Constitution includes provisions for initiative and popular referendum.

1857   Congress requires that voters must approve all state constitutions proposed after 1857.

1885   Father Robert Haire, a priest and labor activist from Aberdeen, South Dakota, and Benjamin Urner, a newspaper publisher from New Jersey become the first Americans to propose giving the people statewide initiative and popular referendum power.

1897   Nebraska becomes the first state to allow its cities to use initiative and popular referendum.

1898   South Dakota becomes the first state to adopt statewide initiative and popular referendum.

1900   Utah becomes the second state to adopt statewide initiative and popular referendum.

---

1. This information compiled from research contained in David Schmidt's *Citizen Lawmakers* and from independent research conducted by the Initiative & Referendum Institute.

1901 The Illinois legislature creates a statewide nonbinding advisory initiative process.

1902 Oregon becomes the third state to adopt statewide initiative and popular referendum. In Illinois, using a statewide nonbinding advisory initiative process, citizens place an advisory question on the ballot asking whether or not Illinois should adopt a real initiative and referendum process—voters say yes, but the legislature ignores them.

1904 Oregon is the first state to place a statewide initiative on the ballot. In Missouri, voters defeat a measure that would have established statewide initiative and popular referendum.

1905 Nevada adopts statewide popular referendum only.

1906 Montana adopts statewide initiative and popular referendum. Delaware voters approve an advisory referendum put on the ballot by the state legislature, asking whether they want the initiative process—but the legislature ignores the mandate.

1907 Oklahoma becomes the first state to provide for statewide initiative and popular referendum in its original constitution.

1908 Michigan and Maine adopt statewide initiative and popular referendum. Unfortunately, Michigan's initiative procedures are so difficult that, under them, citizens are unable to place a single initiative on the ballot. Missouri adopts statewide initiative and popular referendum.

1910 Arkansas and Colorado adopt statewide initiative and popular referendum. Kentucky adopts statewide popular referendum. Illinois voters again approve a citizen-initiated nonbinding advisory question in support of statewide initiative and popular referendum—and the legislature again ignores them.

1911 Arizona and California adopt statewide initiative and popular referendum. New Mexico adopts only statewide popular referendum.

1912 Idaho, Nebraska, Ohio and Washington adopt statewide initiative and popular referendum. Nevada adopts a statewide initiative process, complementing its statewide popular referendum process adopted in 1905. A majority of Wyoming voters voting on a constitutional amendment to adopt statewide initiative and popular referendum approve the amendment; but Wyoming's constitution requires that all amendments also receive a majority vote of all voters voting in the election, regardless of whether or not they vote on the actual amendment itself—so the measure fails. A majority of Mississippi voters voting on a constitutional amendment to adopt statewide initiative and popular referendum also approve the amendment; but, like Wyoming, a constitutional requirement that all amendments also receive a majority vote of all voters voting in the election, defeats the measure.

1913 Michigan initiative and popular referendum supporters lobby the legislature to pass amendments simplifying its statewide initiative and popular referendum process, a process so difficult that it is unusable. The legislature passes the amendments and voters approve them.

1914 Mississippi and North Dakota adopt statewide initiative and popular referendum. Wisconsin and Texas voters defeat measures creating a statewide initiative and popular referendum process. A majority of Minnesota voters voting on a constitutional amendment to adopt statewide initiative and popular referendum approve the amendment; but Minnesota's constitution requires that all amendments also receive a majority vote of all voters voting in the election, regardless of whether or not they vote on the actual amendment itself—so the measure fails.

1915 Maryland adopts popular referendum.

1916 A majority of Minnesota voters voting on a constitutional amendment to adopt statewide initiative and popular referendum again approve the amendment; but the Minnesota constitution's requirement that all amendments also receive a majority vote of all voters voting in the election, regardless of whether or not they vote on the actual amendment itself—again dooms the measure.

1918 Massachusetts adopts statewide initiative and popular referendum. North Dakotans vote and approve a more lenient initiative process. The amendment passed by the North Dakota legislature and adopted by the voters in 1914 had such strict procedures that no initiatives qualified for the ballot in the following election, so initiative proponents put an initiative on the 1918 ballot to ease the procedures.

1922 The Mississippi Supreme Court overturns Mississippi's initiative and popular referendum process.

1956 Alaska adopts statewide initiative and popular referendum as part of its new constitution.

1968 Wyoming adopts statewide initiative and popular referendum.

1970 Illinois adopts a very limited initiative process.

1972 Florida adopts statewide initiative.

1977 *Hardie v. Eu* is decided by the California Supreme Court which finds unconstitutional the Political Reform Act's cap on expenditures for qualifying ballot measures since it violates the First Amendment of the U.S. Constitution. The District of Columbia adopts initiative and popular referendum. The U.S. Supreme

Court rules in *First National Bank of Boston v. Bellotti* that state laws prohibiting or limiting corporate contributions or spending in initiative campaigns violates the First and Fourteenth Amendment.

1980 For the third time, a majority of Minnesota voters voting on a constitutional amendment to adopt statewide initiative and popular referendum approve the measure; but for the third time the Minnesota constitution's requirement that all amendments also receive a majority vote of all voters voting in the election, regardless of whether or not they vote on the actual amendment itself dooms the measure. The U.S. Supreme Court rules in *Pruneyard Shopping Center v. Robins* that state constitutional provisions that permit political activity at a privately- owned shopping center does not violate federal constitutional private property rights of owner.

1981 The U.S. Supreme Court rules in *Citizens Against Rent Control v. Berkeley* that a California city's ordinance to impose a limit on contributions to committees formed to support or oppose ballot measures violates the First Amendment.

1986 Rhode Island voters defeat a measure establishing statewide initiative and popular referendum.

1988 The U.S. Supreme Court rules in *Meyer v. Grant* that states cannot prohibit paid signature gathering, saying that initiative petitions are protected political speech.

1992 Mississippi adopts statewide initiative for the second time.

1996 Rhode Island voters approve a nonbinding advisory question put on the ballot by the legislature asking if they would like to have a statewide initiative and popular referendum process — but the legislature ignores them.

1998 The Initiative & Referendum Institute is formed to study and defend the I&R process on the 100 year anniversary of the adoption of the statewide initiative and popular referendum process in America

1999 The Minnesota House of Representatives approves a constitutional amendment that would establish a statewide initiative and popular referendum process. The U.S. Supreme Court declares in *Buckley v. American Constitutional Law Foundation* that, among other things, states cannot require that petition circulators be registered voters.

2000 The Minnesota Senate kills the initiative and referendum bill passed by the House the year before. The Initiative & Referendum Institute files suit against the U.S. Postal Service's 1998 prohibition on collecting signatures on initiative petitions on postal property.

Chapter 2

Initiative and Referendum and the Republican Form of Government

By Robert G. Natelson

I. Introduction

A recurrent issue in discussions of the initiative and referendum ("I&R") process has been whether, and to what extent, I&R violates that portion of Article IV, Section 4 of the United States Constitution providing that the United States shall guarantee every state a "republican form of government" — a provision commonly called the Guarantee Clause.[1]

The issue arises because opponents of I&R argue that to be "republican," the people must enact laws *exclusively* through their representatives rather than directly. Those opponents draw a sharp distinction between republican and democratic government, and maintain that direct democracy is inconsistent with the republican form. They argue that the courts should invalidate all, or many, laws and constitutional amendments enacted through I&R.

In this paper, I examine the historical record and show that opponents of initiative and referendum are clearly wrong on this point. Although one of the Framers — Madison — expressed a personal preference for a wholly representative form, all of the Framers who spoke on the issue, including Madison, acknowledged that direct democracy could be a major, even a dominant, part of a republican government.

I further suggest that a principal reason modern writers have so misunderstood the Framers' views on this subject has been the failure of modern "educators" to properly impart the precious Greco-Roman tradition so central to the thought of the Founders.

---

1. U.S. Const., Art. IV, Section 4 states: "The United States shall guarantee to every State in this Union a Republican Form of Government, and shall protect each of them against invasion; and on Application of the Legislature, or of the Executive (when the Legislature cannot be convened) against domestic Violence."

II. The Case Law

The issue of whether Oregon's I&R system violated the Guarantee Clause arose before the U.S. Supreme Court in 1912 in *Pacific States Tel. & Tel. Co. v. Oregon*.[2] However, the court sidestepped the issue by holding that whether a state had a republican form of government is a political question, and therefore non-justiciable. The court was motivated in part by reluctance to conclude that adoption of the initiative and referendum destroyed all government republican in form in Oregon. "This being so, the contention, if held to be sound, would necessarily affect the validity, not only of the particular statute which is before us, but of every other statute passed in Oregon since the adoption of the initiative and referendum."[3] Any such determination should, the court concluded, be made by Congress. This seemed to settle the issue at the federal level.

At the state level, the Oregon Supreme Court already had sustained I&R against a Guarantee Clause attack in 1903.[4] The court held:

> The purpose of this provision of the Constitution is to protect the people of the several states against aristocratic and monarchical invasions, and against insurrections and domestic violence, and to prevent them from abolishing a republican form of government. Cooley, Const. Lim. (7th Ed.) 45; 2 Story, Const. (5th Ed.) § 1815. But it does not forbid them from amending or changing their Constitution in any way they may see fit, so long as none of these results is accomplished. No particular style of government is designated in the Constitution as republican, nor is its exact form in any way prescribed.[5]

The court acknowledged that James Madison had described republican government as representative,[6] but stated:

> Now, the initiative and referendum amendment does not abolish or destroy the republican form of government, or substitute another in its place. The representative character of the government still remains. The people have simply reserved to themselves a larger share of legislative power, but they have not overthrown the republican form of the government, or substituted another in its place. The government

---

2. 223 U.S. 118 (1912).

3. 223 U.S. at 139.

4. Kadderly v. City of Portland, 44 Or. 118, 74 P. 710 (1903).

5. Id., 44 Or. at 144-45, 74 P. at 719.

6. The meaning of Madison's comments is explored infra at notes 37-55 and accompanying text.

is still divided into the legislative, executive, and judicial departments, the duties of which are discharged by representatives selected by the people. Under this amendment, it is true, the people may exercise a legislative power, and may, in effect, veto or defeat bills passed and approved by the Legislature and the Governor; but the legislative and executive departments are not destroyed, nor are their powers or authority materially curtailed.[7]

Three years later, the California Supreme Court upheld a *local* initiative law against a Guarantee Clause challenge[8] while implying that similar measures on the state level would be constitutional as well.[9] In 1909, the Washington Supreme Court considered the same issue, with the same result.[10] In fact, the Washington court did not think the question of representative government was relevant at all to the question of whether a form of government was republican:

> . . . it can scarcely be contended that this plan is inconsistent with a republican form of government, the central idea of which is a government by the people. Whether the expression of the will of the people be made directly by their own acts or through representatives chosen by them is not material. The important consideration is a full expression.[11]

Almost uniformly, other state courts have followed these early decisions and have held that I&R is consistent with republican government.[12] This effectively determines that republicanism and democracy are not

---

7. Id., 44 Or. at 145-46, 74 P. at 720.

8. In re Pfahler, 150 Cal. 71, 88 P. 270 (1906).

9. The court stated: In saying this, we do not wish to be understood as intimating that the people of a state may not reserve the supervisory control as to general state legislation afforded by the initiative and referendum, without violating this provision of the federal Constitution. Id. at 150 Cal. at 77, 88 P. at 273.

10. Hartig v. City of Seattle, 53 Wash. 432, 102 P. 408 (1909).

11. Id., 53 Wash. at 435, 102 P. at 409.

12. Cagle v. Qualified Electors of Winston Co., 470 So.2d 1208 (Ala. 1985); Margolis v. District Court, 638 P.2d 297 (Colo. 1981); McKee v. City of Louisville, 200 Colo. 525, 616 P.2d 969 (1980); Bernzen v. City of Boulder, 186 Colo. 81, 525 P.2d 416 (1974); Amador Valley Joint Union High Sch. Dist. v. State Bd. of Equalization, 22 Cal.3d 208, 237, 149 Cal. Rptr. 239, 583 P.2d 1281 (1978) (two thirds vote to raise local taxes); Westerberg v. Andrus, 114 Idaho 401, 757 P.2d 664 (1988); State of Oregon v. Montez, 309 Or. 564, 789 P.2d 1352 (1989); State of Washington v. Davis, 133 Wash.2d 187, 943 P.2d 283 (1997); State ex rel. Billingston v. Sinclair, 28 Wash. 2d 575, 183 P.2d 813 (1947). See also cases cited infra note 15.

mutually exclusive categories. Some courts have gone further, ruling that I&R is a fundamental part of republican government.[13]

Nevertheless, political interest groups discontented with I&R or with the results of particular ballot measures have continued aggressively to contend that whether a state has a republican form of government is a justiciable issue in *state* court and that I&R either entirely or in specific cases violates the Guarantee Clause. Indeed, I&R opponents intensified this line of argument during the 1990s.[14] Although the courts continue to reject it,[15] to my knowledge they have not judged it so frivolous as to justify imposition of sanctions on those raising it.

III. Examining The Anti-I&R "Guarantee Clause" Argument

A. The Basis of the Argument

Opponents of I&R base their argument almost entirely on the supposed view of the Constitution's Framers that republicanism and democracy were wholly mutually exclusive categories.[16] A few commentators support this view, also appealing to the historical record.[17] Interestingly enough, the

---

13. The Colorado courts take this position. See, e.g., Bernzen v. Boulder, 186 Colo. 81, 525 P.2d 416 (1974) (viewing recall, as well as initiative and referendum, as fundamental rights of a republican form of government which the people have reserved unto themselves). See also Margolis v. District Court, 638 P.2d 297 (Colo. 1981); McKee v. City of Louisville, 200 Colo. 525, 616 P.2d 969 (1980).

14. Infra note 15.

15. E.g., Santa Clara County v. Guardino, 11 Cal. 4th 220, 45 Cal. Rptr. 2d 207 (1995) (contention not reached); In re Initiative Petition No. 364, 930 P.2d 186 (Okla. 1996) (Guarantee Clause not justiciable, although court must consider possible Congressional action in judging effect of initiative); In re Initiative Petition No. 348, 820 P.2d 772 (Okla. 1991) (upholding mandatory referendum on tax increases because representative government remains, although restricted); State of Oregon ex rel. Huddleston v. Sawyer, 324 Or. 597, 932 P.2d 1145 (1997) (Guarantee Clause not justiciable); Lowe v. Keisling, 130 Or.App. 1, 882 P.2d 91 (1994) (same); State of Washington v. Davis, 133 Wash.2d 187, 943 P.2d 283 (1997). In addition, the plaintiffs raised the issue at the trial level in a case in which I was a prevailing defendant, Nicholson v. Cooney, 265 Mont. 406, 877 P.2d 486 (1994) (sustaining petition referendum) and the American Civil Liberties Union raised it as amicus in Marshall v. State of Montana, 1999 MT 33, 975 P.2d 325 (striking down on other grounds a constitutional initiative to require public votes on tax increases).

16. See infra notes 17-22 and accompanying text.

17. See, e.g., Rogers & Faigman, infra, "References" (all initiatives are unconstitutional).

commentary in response has not fully investigated these historical claims. For this reason, I believe, some of the rejoinders have been merely tepid; one of the best known of these rejoining writers states merely that the Guarantee Clause argument is "not proven."[18]

According to the opponents of I&R, the Framers' understanding was that no government is "republican" unless it relies on institutions *wholly* representative. Therefore, the argument goes, institutions of direct democracy[19] disqualify a state from having a republican form of government.

The opponents' historical case has several props. The first is the Framers' known antipathy to excessive democracy and their corresponding preference for checks and balances.[20] Another is Madison's personal preference for republics purely representative.[21] A third consists of a few fragments, primarily from the writings of Hamilton and Madison that, when selectively (and sometimes deceptively) excerpted, seem to exclude institutions of direct democracy from republican governments.[22]

---

18. Amar, infra, "References."

19. I&R supporters sometimes reject the term direct democracy. See, e.g., Waters, infra, "References," at 6. I use the term here to include I&R because it has the feature of direct citizen, rather than representative, lawmaking.

20. E.g. Rogers & Faigman, infra, "References," at 1060 ("Indeed, some historians contend that the delegates at the Constitutional Convention were more concerned about an excess of populism in the state governments than they were about the weakness of the Articles of Confederation.").

21. See, e.g., THE FEDERALIST, No. 63.

22. See, e.g., Rogers & Faigman, infra, "References," in which a few ambiguous quotations from Madison and one from Hamilton are characterized as "a consensus among the Framers: a republican form of government was seen as the best 'safeguard against the tyranny of [majoritarian] passions'...[r]epresentative decisionmaking was considered so critical that it was not only instituted at the federal level but guaranteed at the state level." Id. at 1060-61. Some opponents of I&R have made arguments bordering on—or slipping over into—deception. See, e.g, infra note 78 (ACLU brief). See also Graves, infra, "References," which states, "A growing body of opinion holds that the initiative process in California and other states violates the Guarantee Clause of the United States Constitution.... A considerable amount of historical literature supports this theory..." Id. at 1305. But the "considerable amount of historical literature" footnoted consists only of three numbers of The Federalist, one of which (No. 9) is actually contra because while it identifies representation as good, it acknowledges it to be a "wholly new discover[y]," and refers to ancient states with popular assemblies as "republics"); the second of which (No. 10) is ambiguous (discussed infra at notes 37-56 and accompanying text); and the third of which (No. 51) does not deal at all with the issue of whether republican government must be wholly representative.

The same article also alleges that Minor v. Happersett, 88 U.S. 162 (1874) "concluded that the term 'Republican'...meant representative government," although in fact, Minor held only that the 13 original states were republican although they did not give women

B. Flaws in the Argument

For reasons set forth below, the Framers would have viewed as absurd the notion that a government is disqualified as a republic if it is not wholly representative. That notion seems plausible to some today only because those examining the issue seem to have overlooked two points:

1. The Framers *preferences* for republican government did not fully determine their *definition* of republican government; but on the contrary,
2. They specifically and repeatedly classified as "republican" various governments that they themselves specifically and repeatedly acknowledged featured significant, even dominant, institutions of direct democracy.

1. Framers' Disapproval Does Not Prove Prohibition

The first overlooked point is that the Framers *preferences* for republican government did not fully determine their *definition* of republican government. This would seem obvious from the historical record: There were all sorts of things the Framers wanted that the Constitution did not prescribe, and there were all sorts of things they detested that the Constitution did not proscribe. For example, many Framers believed that paper money was evil, [23] but the Constitution specifically banned only the state governments, not the national government, from "emit[ing] Bills of Credit.[24] It is, in other words, an inadmissible leap to conclude that because some of the Framers disliked democracy they intended the Guarantee clause to abolish it.

There had to be a certain amount of latitude in the Guarantee Clause, if only because, as prominent historian Forrest McDonald has observed, "...though the Framers shared the commitment [to republicanism] in the

---

the franchise. The article further alleges that in re Pfahler, 150 Cal. 71, 88 P. 270 (1906) "distinguished, under the Guarantee Clause, between allowable direct democracy at the local or municipal level of government and the representative democracy required at the state level," 31 Loy. L.A. L. Rev. 1305, neglecting to note that the court also strongly intimated that direct democracy also was valid at the state level—as that court subsequently has ruled. See, e.g., Amador Valley Joint Union High Sch. Dist. v. State Bd. of Equalization, 22 Cal.3d 208, 237, 149 Cal. Rptr. 239, 583 P.2d 1281 (1978).

23. See e.g., the comments of Charles C. Pinckney, Elbridge Gerry, and James Madison in Madison, Notes, infra, "References," at 73, 78, 86 & 143-44) See also Storing, infra, "References," at 180 & 181 ("Brutus").

24. U.S. Const., Art. I, Section 10.

abstract, they were far from agreed as to what republicanism meant, apart from the absence of hereditary monarchy and hereditary aristocracy."[25] If anything, Professor McDonald's observation overstates the level of agreement.[26] So it is not surprising that when James Madison, the Framer most often relied on by I&R opponents, addressed the Guarantee Clause, he offered no suggestion that it was targeted at democracy, much as excess democracy was a concern. Madison saw the Clause as serving almost exactly the opposite purpose: to "defend the system against aristocratic or monarchical innovations."[27] Other prominent Framers, including Edmund Randolph,[28] who introduced the Virginia Plan, and Nathaniel Gorham,[29] who chaired the Committee of the Whole, expressed similar sentiments while discussing the Guarantee Clause.[30]

To be sure, in 1787, government in all thirteen states was wholly representative at the state level (although New England towns governed themselves through town meetings). But no one suggested this must remain unchanged. Madison for one liked the wholly representative system, but he also recognized that the Constitution did not require adherence to existing forms:

> As long, therefore, as the existing republican forms are continued by the states, they are guaranteed by the federal constitution. *Whenever the states may choose to substitute other republican forms, they have a right to do so and to claim the federal guaranty for the latter.*[31]

Thus, despite his strong views on what kind of republican institutions would work best, Madison considered the class of permissible alternatives under the Guarantee Clause to be broader than his particular preferences. His tolerance in this respect was shared by Hamilton: While Hamilton

---

25. McDonald, infra, "References," at 5. See also Cooper, infra, "References," at 245-46.

26. For example, John Adams (for one) classified even England as a republic, hereditary monarchy and aristocracy withal, because in England one branch of Parliament represented the people. Adams, infra, "References," at 70.

27. THE FEDERALIST, infra, "References," No. 43.

28. Farrand, infra, "References," at I.206.

29. Farrand, infra, "References," at II.48.

30. Cf. comments by Tench Coxe, Kurland & Lerner, infra, "References," at 561 (Guarantee Clause designed to protect against kings and nobles), and by Hamilton: "As long as offices are open to all men, and no constitutional rank is established, it is pure republicanism." Farrand, infra, "References," at I.432 (as reported by Robert Yates).

31. THE FEDERALIST, infra, "References," No. 43 (emphasis added).

favored a constitution far more "high toned" than what eventually was adopted,[32] he viewed the final draft—and other options—as republican.[33]

2. The Framers' Own Statements Prove Permission

The foregoing shows that the Framers' dislike for direct democracy does not prove that their Constitution abolished it. The second and more important overlooked point is that their understanding of republican government clearly *permitted* institutions of direct democracy. To see why this is so, one must examine their writings and those of their Anti-Federalist adversaries in the context of what they understood of Greek and Roman history.

To an extent not comprehended by modern Americans, the culture of the Framers' time was informed by the classical Greco-Roman heritage.[34] During the Framers' generation, many educated men learned ancient Greek. All educated people studied and used Latin.[35] All were steeped in the history and literature of the ancient Mediterranean world. This heritage affected their understanding of many things, including their views on government. Among the many influential classical authors were Polybius (*c.*200–*post* 118 B.C.), the expatriate Greek historian of the Roman Republic; Titus Livius ("Livy") (59 B.C.–A.D. 17 or 64 B.C.–A.D. 12), the Augustan-era Latin historian; and Marcus Tullius Cicero (106–43 B.C.), the republican statesman, orator, and philosopher.[36]

Consider the passage in *The Federalist* No. 10 (Madison) often cited[37] for the claim that I&R is inconsistent with republican government:

> …a pure democracy [is] a society consisting of a small number of citizens, who assemble and administer the government in person…
>
> A republic [is] a government in which the scheme of representation takes place…Let us examine the points in which it varies from pure democracy…
>
> The two great points of difference between a democracy and a republic are: first, the delegation of the government, in the latter to a small number of citizens elected by the rest; secondly, the greater

---

32. See Madison, Notes, infra, "References," at 129-39.

33. See Farrand, infra, "References," at I.432 (Hamilton as reported by Yates: "As long as offices are open to all men, and no constitutional rank is established, it is pure republicanism.")

34. For the profound debt the Framers owed to classical literature and history, see McDonald, infra, "References"; Wills, infra, "References."

35. McDonald, infra, "References," at xi.

36. McDonald, infra, "References," at 67-68. The debates at the constitutional convention were filled with classical ideas. See, e.g., Farrand, infra, "References," at I.308 (Hamilton cites Aristotle and Cicero); id. at I.449 (Madison cites Plutarch).

37. See, e.g., Rogers & Faigman, infra, "References," at 1059.

number of citizens and greater sphere of country over which the latter may be extended.[38]

Those arguing that I&R violates the Guarantee Clause interpret this passage as meaning that republican government requires institutions *wholly* representative. Yet the passage is susceptible of another meaning: that to be a republic requires only that the government have *some* representative institution—so that it is not a "pure democracy" in which "a small number of citizens...assemble and administer the government in person."

One reason to reject the first interpretation, in which free governments consist only of pure democracies and purely representative republics, is that it is too restrictive. It leaves no place on the spectrum for governments that feature both representative institutions and directly democratic institutions. For example, today every American state except Delaware authorizes some form of the initiative, the referendum, or both,[39] and no state is "administered solely and in person by the entire citizenry." This would leave the second interpretation—that only some representative institution is necessary for a republic—standing by mere process of elimination.

But there is more: The Framers' other writings, read by the light of the classical heritage, demonstrates that the second interpretation is what Madison had in mind.

One way to determine this is to identify the specific polities the Framers and their contemporaries called "republican," determine what they knew or thought they knew about the governments of those polities, and then apply the constructional rule of *ejusdem generis* to determine what they meant when they said that each American state must have a "republican form of government."

Fortunately, the writings of the Framers and their Anti-Federalist opponents contain a fair number of examples of governments they considered

---

38. See also THE FEDERALIST, infra, "References," No. 39: ("...we may define a republic to be, or at least bestow that name on, a government which derives all its powers directly or indirectly from the great body of the people, and is administered by persons holding their offices during pleasure for a limited period, or during good behavior.") To my knowledge, those claiming that the Guarantee Clause requires exclusively representative lawmaking have overlooked another passage that would seem to assist them: A comment in the first paper by "Brutus," an Anti-Federalist New Yorker who may well have been Robert Yates, a convention delegate. See Storing, infra, "References," at 103. The comment reads: In a free republic, although all laws are derived from the consent of the people, yet the people do not declare their consent by themselves in person, but by representatives, chosen by them. Id. at 114.

39. Twenty-four states allow initiatives, 24 allow referenda on citizen petition, and 49 provide for legislative referenda. Waters, infra, "References," at 5-6.

to be in the republican form. There does not seem to have been serious dispute about most of the governments on the list.[40]

For example, in *Federalist No. 63*, Madison listed five republics: Sparta, Carthage, Rome, Athens, and Crete. In *The Federalist No. 6*, Hamilton tells us, "Sparta, Athens, Rome, and Carthage were all republics..."[41] In one of his Anti-Federalist papers, "Brutus"—likely Robert Yates, a constitutional convention delegate from New York—states that Rome and the various "Grecian states" were republics.[42] Anti-Federalist author "Agrippa" (John Winthrop of Massachusetts) identifies Carthage, Rome, and the ancient Greek states as republics.[43] The Anti-Federalist "Federal Farmer" refers to the "republics of Greece."[44]

Now, most, if not all, of these republics featured prominent institutions of direct democracy. Indeed, some of them featured more direct democracy than even the most fervent I&R advocate could wish for. Thus, all laws adopted in Sparta had to be approved by an assembly of citizens—in other words, all laws, not just a few, were subject to a form of referendum.[45] Athens was even more democratic: The assembly of all citizens over 18 both approved and initiated laws.[46]

Rome was on almost everyone's list of republics, and the ideals and constitution of the Roman Republic were uniquely influential among the Framers.[47] By the term *Roman Republic* we mean the various forms of government prevailing after the end of the kingship (traditional date: 510 or 509 B.C.) until creation of the empire (27 B.C.). Stretching over nearly five centuries, this was one of the longest-lived republics in the history of the world.

Sovereignty in the *Res Publica Populi Romani* was, as the name indicates, in the *populus Romanus*—the whole body of citizens[48] acting through

---

40. The major area of dispute is that John Adams included certain hereditary monarchies on his list of republics. Other Framers would have excluded all hereditary monarchies. See supra note 25 and accompanying text. For our purposes, this difference is not relevant.

41. Cf. Hamilton, THE FEDERALIST, infra, "References," No. 70 (Rome described as a republic).

42. Storing, infra, "References," at 113 & 158 (Rome was a "free republic").

43. Id. at 230.

44. Id. at 89.

45. OCD, infra, "References," at 79 (Sparta) & 272 (Rome).

46. Id. at 376-77.

47. McDonald, infra, "References," contains extensive discussions of the impact of Roman Republican ideals on the Framers. See, e.g., pp. 67-68.

48. There are innumerable books discussing the structure of Roman government. For a scholarly survey, see OCD, infra, "References," at 272. For focus on the republic at its height, see Dudley, infra, "References," at 37-39. A classic book-length treatment is Greenidge, infra, "References."

their four popular assemblies. All citizens could participate directly in those assemblies; they were not representative institutions. Major legislation was enacted directly by those assemblies on recommendation of either the presiding magistrate or the senate.[49] The assemblies also had the power to declare war, and one of these, the *comitia centuriata,* could hear certain judicial appeals. They also elected magistrates to exercise the executive power (such as consuls and aediles), magistrates to represent the people's interest against the senate (tribunes), treasury officials (quaestors), and judges (praetors).

Each of the four assemblies had different (although sometimes overlapping) jurisdiction. To be sure, the voting rules for each were different. In the *comitia centuriata,* for example, the rules were stacked in favor of the nobility. In the *concilium plebis,* the nobility was excluded entirely. The critical point, however, is that citizens voted on legislation themselves, not through representatives.

Of course, the fact that ancient republics included direct democracy would not be relevant to interpretation of the Guarantee Clause if the Founders were ignorant of that fact. But the Founders knew it very well. As noted above,[50] the histories of Polybius and Livy and the writings of Cicero were standard fare in the education of the day.

From Polybius in particular the Framers came to respect the notion of a "mixed" constitution—one containing monarchical, aristocratic, and democratic elements.[51] The Roman republic was "mixed" in this sense but also in the sense that some decisions were made by direct democracy while others were made by delegates. Like other ancient writers, Polybius discoursed on the power of the popular assemblies.[52] In his popular survey of the Roman Constitution, he wrote that if one focused on the awesome power of the popular assemblies, "from this point of view one could reasonably argue that the people have the greatest share of power in the government, and that the constitution is a democracy."[53]

With this information at hand, there is no way the Framers could have repeatedly acknowledged that Rome and other ancient states were republics while believing that republics had to be wholly representative. On the contrary, the Framers had quite another problem. Anti-Federalists claimed the

---

49. Greenidge, infra, "References," at 238-60 summarizes the power of the popular assemblies.

50. Supra notes 34-36 and accompanying text.

51. Polybius, infra, "References," at 312-15.

52. To be sure, many modern historians tend to focus on the power of the senate, see, e.g., Dudley, infra, "References," at 38-39, but modern historians were not what the Framers were reading.

53. Polybius, infra, "References," at 315.

new constitution would be so remote from the people that it was a prescription for monarchy.[54] Federalists had to demonstrate that it was republican even though it did not contain institutions of direct democracy.

Madison explored the question in *Federalist No. 63*. After first classifying Sparta, Carthage, Rome, Athens, and Crete as republics, Madison argued that all had representative institutions *in addition to* their directly-democratic ones—that none were "pure democracies." Because the federal constitution also authorized representative institutions, the federal constitution was also republican.[55] A point underlying Madison's argument appears to be that pure democracy is an unattainable ideal, and that all free governments of any consequence are republics because they all feature *some* degree of representation.

Hamilton, too, understood that republics could include prominent institutions of direct democracy. In *The Federalist No. 34*, Hamilton referred to two of the Assemblies of the Roman Republic, the *Comitia Centuriata* and the *Comitia Tributa*, where the Roman people directly voted on laws, judicial decisions, and other matters.[56]

Prior discussions of this Guarantee Clause issue have tended to center mostly on Madison and Hamilton's views as expressed in *The Federalist*. This is far too narrow a scope. Both Hamilton and Madison demonstrated in the convention debates their familiarity with classical sources.[57] Edmund Randolph and Nathaniel Gorham—far more influential drafters than Hamilton—weighed in with their own views on the purpose of Guarantee Clause, a purpose that had nothing to do with excluding direct democracy.[58] Various Anti-Federalist writers listed examples of governments they considered republican.[59]

---

54. See, e.g., Storing, infra, "References," at 308 (Patrick Henry) ("Besides the expenses of maintaining the Senate and other House in as much splendor as they please, there is to be a great and mighty President, with very extensive powers; the powers of a King."

55. THE FEDERALIST, infra, "References," No. 63 ("The true distinction between these and the American governments lies in the total exclusion of the people in their collective capacity from any share in the latter and not in the total exclusion of the representatives of the people from the administration of the former." [emphasis in original]). Madison then states his preference for the purely representative form of republic, but as noted above there is no suggestion the Constitution imposes that preference on the states.

56. Actually, there were four assemblies of citizens, each apportioned under different principles and serving different purposes. OCD, infra, "References," at 272.

57. E.g. Farrand, infra, "References," at I.308 (Hamilton cites Aristotle and Cicero); id. at I.449 (Madison cites Plutarch).

58. Supra notes 28-32 and accompanying text.

59. Supra notes 42-44 and accompanying text.

In addition, the views of John Adams form an important, and neglected part of history of the Guarantee Clause. Adams was in London during the Constitutional Convention, but his spirit haunted the delegates nonetheless: Shortly before the Convention opened, the first volume of his encyclopedia was published: *A Defence of the Constitutions of Government of the United States* (i.e., the state constitutions). It was a collection of historical writings and an overview of governmental structures throughout history, supplemented by Adams' own commentary. Apparently, the volume was well thumbed and heavily relied on by the delegates in Philadelphia that summer.[60]

Following Cicero, Adams defined a republic as any government ruled in accordance with laws for the benefit of the people. He further stated (quoting Cicero) that *res publica res est populus*: "the republic is the affair of the people."[61]

Adams maintained that for a republic to be well governed, it should feature checks and balances—legislative, executive, and judicial branches, and elements of monarchy, aristocracy and democracy. He reproduced in his volume Polybius' essay on the excellence of the Roman constitution, including its monarchical, aristocratic, and directly democratic parts.[62]

As an advocate of mixed government, Adams opposed unchecked democracy just as he opposed unchecked aristocracy or monarchy. But far from arguing that republics had to be wholly representative, he specifically cited example after example of republics with direct citizen lawmaking. Among these were some from the ancient world, including:

- The Roman Republic, with its popular assemblies enjoying lawmaking power;[63]
- The Carthaginian Republic, which he labeled "the most democratical republic of antiquity"[64] because any one senator could send any measure directly to the people for resolution;[65]

---

60. Rossiter, infra, "References," at 66; Bowen, infra, "References," at 11.

61. Adams, infra, "References," at xxi-xxii.

One can translate the Latin phrase *res publica* in a variety of ways, most of which capture the basic idea communicated to the classically-trained minds of the Framers: the people's affair; popular government; the people's (or popular) state. New York Times humorist Russell Baker, admittedly no Framer, once suggested: "the public thing."

62. Adams, infra, "References," at 171-75. See also THE FEDERALIST No. 63 (Madison cites Polybius).

63. Adams, infra, "References," at 348 (listing three of the four assemblies, and noting the independent lawmaking power of the plebeians).

64. Id. at 214.

65. Id. at 213.

- The Athenian Republic;[66] and
- Laecedaemon (Sparta), which although classified as an "aristocratic republic," still gave citizens the direct power to vote "yes" or "no" on proposed laws in the style of the modern referendum.[67]

Adams' work was distinctive in that he discussed contemporary as well as ancient examples. These included San Marino, whose democratic assembly (the *arengo*) admittedly had withered,[68] but also:

- The Grisons, which placed "sovereignty in the commons;"[69]
- The Swiss canton of Underwald, where sovereignty rested in an assembly of all males 15 years of age or older;[70]
- The Swiss canton of Glaris, where a similarly constituted assembly laid taxes, made law and peace, and ratified all laws;[71] and
- The Swiss canton of Zug, where a similarly constituted assembly enacted laws.[72]

The available evidence demonstrates, therefore, that the Framers did not believe that republican government had to be purely representative. They did believe that republican government can contain significant elements of direct democracy. Their views are reflected in case law sustaining I&R against Guarantee Clause challenges on the ground that I&R merely restricts, but does not abolish, representative government.[73]

The Founders' debt to classical wisdom offers yet another insight into their views on democracy. To the Founders, pure democracy meant only one thing: all free male citizens gathering together in a single body, governing without the checks and balances of the mixed constitution. Much of the evil in that form of democracy arose from the fact that a concentrated gath-

---

66. Id. at 260-85.

67. Id. at 254.

68. Id. at 11.

69. Id. at 21.

70. Id. at 26.

71. Id. at 29-30.

72. Id. at 31. In later volumes of the same work, Adams cited further cases, e.g., Neuchatel, a "monarchical republic" in which "[t]he legislative authority resides conjunctively in the prince, the council of state, and the town or people, each of which has a negative. John Adams, A Defence of the Constitutions of Government of the United States of America (1787), Vol. 2, at 450.

73. E.g. In re Initiative Petition No. 348, 820 P.2d 772 (Okla. 1991); Amador Valley Joint Union High Sch. Dist. v. State Bd. of Equalization, 22 Cal.3d 208, 149 Cal. Rptr. 239, 583 P.2d 1281 (1978); Kadderly v. City of Portland, 44 Or. 118, 144, 74 P. 710, 719 (1903).

ering of thousands of citizens could become emotional and act like a mob. Both classical literature[74] and the Framers[75] resorted to metaphors of waves and storms to depict the results.

Obviously, the modern initiative or referendum election has little in common with that sort of democracy. Modern I&R is subject to various checks and balances provided by a mixed constitution: burdensome petitioning or legislative pre-approval; lengthy political campaigns, and judicial review. On election day, people vote in dispersed localities with little of the physical immediacy or "turbulence"[76] of the ancient forum. This difference would have been quite important to Madison and Hamilton.[77] See also *The Federalist* No. 68 (Hamilton cites as a principal advantage of the electoral college system that each state's electors will vote in separate locations so that "this detached and divided situation will expose them much less to heats and ferments...").

IV. Conclusion

The continued pressing of Guarantee Clause arguments against I&R in defiance of unanimous historical and legal authority results in delay, vexation, and a waste of judicial and other resources. The courts should put those arguments to rest finally and forthwith and, if necessary, impose appropriate sanctions on the parties who persist in raising them.

The usual source for Guarantee Clause arguments is *The Federalist,* so one wonders how such arguments could ever become current, given that one can ascertain the truth by examining that source more closely. Unfortunately, lawyers and judges do not always examine the text of documents cited to them, which gives an advantage to unscrupulous brief writers.[78]

---

74. E.g., Virgil, infra, "References," at 1.148-1.150 (comparing a storm at sea with a mob).

75. E.g. Hamilton, THE FEDERALIST, infra, "References," No. 9 ("If they exhibit occasional calms, these only serve as short-lived contrasts to the furious storms that are to succeed.")

76. THE FEDERALIST, infra, "References," No. 10 (Madison) uses the word turbulence from the Latin noun *turba* to mean a disturbance in a crowd of people.

77. See, e.g., THE FEDERALIST, No. 63: It may be suggested that a people spread over an extensive region cannot, like the crowded inhabitants of a small district, be subject to the infection of violent passions or to the danger of combining in pursuit of unjust measures. I am far from denying that this is a distinction of peculiar importance. I have, on the contrary, endeavored in a former paper to show that it is one of the principle recommendations of a confederated republic.

78. A good example is the amicus brief filed by the American Civil Liberties Union in Marshall v. State of Montana, 1999 MT 33, 975 P.2d 325. The brief misleadingly extract-

Modern lawyers and judges are more apt to be misled on this score because most now lack the fundamental classical knowledge every Framer enjoyed. During the 20th century — and especially during the last four decades — Americans became more and more disconnected from the classical heritage that had enriched the Western World for two millennia.[79] The decision of many "educators" to abandon responsibility for transmitting that heritage was largely to blame. Unlike educators in Europe, they were able to get away with it: Americans' curiosity is not constantly triggered by surrounding physical remains from classical times.

In my view, the decision to downplay the classical tradition has inflicted great damage on our society. One of the costs is radical misinterpretation of our own legal institutions.[80] When the legal institution in point is the U.S. Constitution, the price is particularly steep — both because of the importance of the subject matter and because of the difficulty those ignorant of the classical tradition have in understanding the language of the men who wrote, debated, and approved the Constitution.[81] The language of the Framers — even central words like *republic* — is intelligible only to those who have reclaimed the heritage unknown to so many.

References

Adams, John Adams, A DEFENCE OF THE CONSTITUTIONS OF GOVERN- MENT OF THE UNITED STATES OF AMERICA (1787), Vol. 1 ("Adams").

Amar, Akhil R., The Central Meaning of Republican Government: Popular Sovereignty, Majority Rule, and the Denominator Problem, 65 U. COLO. L. REV. 749 (1994) ("Amar").

---

ed portions of THE FEDERALIST, No. 63 to suggest that republican government must be wholly representative. Actually, that number of THE FEDERALIST is devoted largely to demonstrating that certain ancient governments were republics even though they were not wholly representative! See supra note 55 and accompanying text.

79. A measure of this is the devastating drop in the number of American students studying high school Latin. From a peak of 702,000 in 1962, enrollment plummeted to only 150,000 in 1976. Editorial, Latin Gains a New Life, ST. PETERSBURG TIMES, 12/6/87, p.2D. Since that time, there has been a slow resurgence—to 164,000 in 1990 and 189,000 in 1994. Pop Ousts Classics to Give Latin a New Life, DAILY TELEGRAPH, 11/28/98, p.18.

80. I have commented on this phenomenon before. See Natelson, Peyote, infra, "References," and Natelson, Comments, infra, "References."

81. On the Latinate English of the Framers, see, e.g., Wills, infra, "References," at 93; McDonald, infra, "References," passim.

Bowen, Catherine Drinker, MIRACLE AT PHILADELPHIA (1966) ("Bowen").

Cooper, John F., The Citizen Initiative Petition to Amend State Constitutions: A Concept Whose Time Has Passed, or a Vigorous Component of Participatory Democracy at the State Level? 28 N.M. L. REV. 227 (1998) ("Cooper").

Farrand, Max (ed.), THE RECORDS OF THE FEDERAL CONVENTION OF 1787 (1937) ("Farrand").

THE FEDERALIST PAPERS (Clinton Rossiter, ed.) ("THE FEDERALIST")

Graves, Ernest L., The Guarantee Clause in California: State Constitutional Limits on Initiatives Changing the California Constitution, 31 LOY. L.A. L. REV. 1305 (1998) ("Graves").

Greenidge, A.H.J., ROMAN PUBLIC LIFE (Cooper Square, ed., 1970) ("Greenidge").

Kurland, Philip B. & Ralph Lerner (eds.), THE FOUNDERS' CONSTITUTION, vol. 4 (1987) ("Kurland & Lerner").

Madison, James, NOTES OF DEBATES IN THE FEDERAL CONVENTION OF 1787 (Adrienne Koch, ed., 1966) ("Madison, Notes").

McDonald, Forrest, NOVUS ORDO SECLORUM: THE INTELLECTUAL ORIGINS OF THE CONSTITUTION (1985) ("McDonald").

Natelson, Robert G., Peyote, "Multiculturalism" and the Caricature of the West, 52 MONT. L. REV. 453 (1991) ("Natelson, Peyote").

———, Comments on the Historiography of Condominium: The Myth of Roman Origin, 12 OKLA. CITY L. REV. 17 (1987) ("Natelson, Comments").

OXFORD CLASSICAL DICTIONARY (1970) ("OCD").

Polybius, THE RISE OF THE ROMAN EMPIRE (Penguin edition, Betty Radice, tr., 1979) ("Polybius").

Rossiter, Clinton, 1787: THE GRAND CONVENTION (1966) ("Rossiter").

Storing, Herbert J. Storing (ed.), THE ANTI-FEDERALIST (1981) ("Storing").

Rogers, Catherine A. & David L. Faigman, "And to the Republic for Which It Stands:" Guaranteeing a Republican Form of Government, 23 HASTINGS CONST. L.Q. 1057 (1996) ("Rogers & Faigman").

Vergilius Maro, Publius, Aeneidos (Oxford edition) ("Virgil").

Waters, M. Dane, A Century of Citizen Lawmaking: An American Experiment in Self-Governance in A CENTURY OF CITIZEN LAWMAKING: INITIATIVE AND REFERENDUM IN AMERICA (Conference notes, 1999) ("Waters").

Wills, Garry, INVENTING AMERICA: JEFFERSON'S DECLARATION OF INDEPENDENCE (1979) ("Wills").

Chapter 3

Public Policy and Direct Democracy in the Twentieth Century: The More Things Change, the More They Stay the Same

By Caroline J. Tolbert

Introduction

The year 1998 marked the 100th anniversary of the initiative process in the United States. First adopted in the frontier state of South Dakota in 1898, the process has spread to almost half the states—and has become a major focus of political discourse in the most populous state, California. Over the past century ballot initiatives have touched on some of the most important political issues from women's suffrage, the direction election of US senators and prohibition to more recently, term limits for elected officials, tax limitations and ending affirmative action.

Twenty-four states provide for the initiative process, which allows groups (citizens and economic) outside of the formal institutions of government to draft their own laws, then petition to have citizens vote directly on the proposals in a statewide election (Magleby 1984; Gerber 1999).[1] Progressive reformers secured passage of direct democracy provisions in legislatures and constitutional conventions in nineteen states during the first two decades of the 20th century. Over the past 100 years, the politics of direct democracy has evolved beyond the scope of imagination, giving rise to an initiative industry—paid petition gatherers, consultants, slate ballots,

---

1. In the initiative process, an interest group drafts a proposition and qualifies it for the ballot by collecting a specified number of voter signatures. If the measure qualifies, it is placed on the election ballot for a popular vote. In the indirect initiative, a group drafts and qualifies a proposition, than submits it to the legislature for consideration. If the legislature passes the measure, then it become law. Otherwise, the policy is placed on the ballot and the voters decide whether it passes or fails.

multi-media campaigns, pollsters — and multimillion dollar campaigns (Magleby and Patterson 1998). In the latest phase in California politics, ballot initiatives have eclipsed the candidates running for office (Schrag 1998). In 1998, despite an open contest for governor and a close-fought Senate election, the amount spend on statewide offices in California was dwarfed by spending on ballot initiatives, which surpassed $140 million. Recent research, however, finds that big spending on initiative campaigns does not necessarily lead to success at the ballot box. Rather citizen groups, as compared to economic groups, continue to be the greatest beneficiaries of the initiative process (cf. Gerber 1999).

Governance is a primary focus of many ballot measures (cf. Tolbert 1998). There have been non-partisan issues such as the blanket primary, approved in 1996, that allows California voters to choose among candidates from all parties in the primary. Californians and voters from twenty other states have imposed term limits on state legislatures. California and Arizona voters may face propositions that would transfer the task of congressional redistricting that will occur after the 2000 census from state legislators to independent commissions. Initiatives at the turn of the twenty-first century are as diverse as the electorate that supports them. One of the best ways to evaluate the initiative process is to examine the types of public policies that have been adopted by this process over time.

The Need for Regulating the Initiative Process?

Critics of direct democracy make many arguments including that special interest groups with money control the process. A way to evaluate this claim is to examine the diversity of public policies, and thus the diversity of interest groups, that participate in the process. Another criticism is that the process has had a destructive impact on representative institutions of government, especially state legislatures (Schrag 1998; Rosenthal 1997). During the 1990s twenty-one states adopted legislative term limits restricting the number of consecutive terms state lawmakers could serve in office, the majority via referenda. Many argue term limits weaken the legislative branch in comparison to powerful interest groups and the bureaucracy who are not tenured, as well as serve to transfer additional power to the executive branch (Benjamin and Malbin 1992; Rosenthal 1997). Since the late 1970s, tax limitations have also been a frequent subject of ballot propositions. Tax limitations, such as supermajority rules for tax increases and voter approval of tax increases, constrain the authority of legislatures over fiscal policy and diminish their ability to respond to citizen demands (Rosenthal 1997; Schrag 1998).

California has historically been a leader in use of the initiative process, with more initiatives qualifying for the ballot than in any other state besides Oregon. In California the initiative process has become the driving engine for policy decisions. California voters alone considered over 60 initiatives placed on the ballot via citizen petition in the 1990s, many of which fundamentally reshaped the state's social services and governmental structures.

An argument has been made that increased use of direct democracy coincides with the beginning of a dramatic decline in the state's social services (Schrag 1998). California's public schools for example were ranked first in the nation during the early 1970s in terms of test scores, but by the 1990s had fallen to 48th in nation, ahead of only New Mexico and Mississippi. Not only did tax limitation, Proposition 13, create severe fiscal limitations, but in the last two decades California has experienced increasing social costs resulting from growing immigrant populations. The initiative process is a majoritarian mechanism of decision-making, operating to deliver governmental services to those who vote (white, middle class) and deny social services to those who vote in lower numbers (the poor and minorities). Critics argue policymaking via direct democracy has had profound and negative impacts on the state of California, especially for the state's growing social and political minorities (Schrag 1998; cf. Chavez 1998, Hero 1998).

But would the deterioration of California's social services have occurred even if the initiative process was not available? Could the decline in the state's social services be a function of fluctuating economic conditions, ideological/partisan politics, growing racial/ethnic diversity, increased immigration, low turnout rates for nonwhites or a combination of all these factors? Is the initiative process in California and across the states "the problem," or merely a vehicle for the preferences of state electorates and larger socioeconomic trends occurring at the end of the twentieth century? Two important question are: (1) Does the initiative process today operate as it has throughout the twentieth century in terms of the diversity of interest group participation? (2) Does the initiative process today operate as it has throughout the twentieth century to reform representative governments when they fail to act, or is the process a vehicle to weaken and/or replace representative democracy with a pure (direct) democracy?

While answers to these questions are not easy, the first question can be addressed by examining the types of policies placed on election ballots across the twenty-four states with the initiative process during the Progressive era (1900-1920) and the contemporary period (1980-1996). This provides one evaluation of interest group participation in the process. Only by examining historical trends, do we have a "yard-stick" with which to evaluate current initiative policies. Data on the number and type of initiatives appearing on state election ballots from 1904-1996 is from the Initiative & Referendum Institute, Washington, DC.

Direct Democracy Policy Making

Scholars and elected officials are increasingly concerned with the lack of citizen participation in the policy making process. Schneider and Ingram (1998) lament that the structure and design of contemporary public policy *discourages* active citizen participation—i.e. public policies are not designed to foster citizen participation. Osborne and Gaebler (1992) contend Americans are increasingly frustrated with impersonal and Byzantine bureaucracies created for an industrial era. Scholars have long sought appropriate mechanisms for maximizing civic participation (Fishkin 1991; Barber 1984). Peters (1996) suggests twenty-first century governments are likely to be more participatory, with "flatter" public sector organizations that encourage employee and citizen participation in decision making. This participatory trend in policy making is evident world wide.

In the US context, states with the initiative process have a built-in mechanism for increasing citizen participation in politics and policy making. Groups (citizens and economic) can place a policy question on the state ballot through the petition process without delays or legislative intermediaries. State legislatures under direct legislation threats are also more likely to adopt the proposed legislation (Gerber 1996, 1999). The initiative process, or the threat of a pending or circulating initiative, is often necessary to translate citizen preferences into policy, especially over the resistance of powerful economic interests, such as the tobacco or car insurance industry. The process is often used to adopt policies resisted by elected officials, corporate interests and established political parties, but supported by a majority of the public. Examples are endless, ranging from term limits, campaign finance reform to health care reform.

In terms of *substantive* public policy, citizens have passed initiatives over the last two decades ending affirmative action and bilingual education, banning smoking in public buildings, legalizing doctor assisted suicide and medical marijuana, earmarking taxes for environmental protection, overhauling criminal sentencing laws and have attempted to pass legislation in many other areas, including regulating the health insurance industry (Bowler, Donovan and Tolbert 1998; Bowler and Donovan 1998; Cronin 1989; Gerber 1996, 1999; Gamble 1996; Lascher, et al. 1996; Magleby 1984; Schrag 1998; Smith 1998; Tolbert and Hero 1996). In terms of *procedural* policy, citizens have passed initiatives to limit campaign finance contributions and expenditures of candidates as well as to require public financing of candidates. They have altered the institutions of representative government by approving term limits on elected officials and requiring a supermajority of the legislature to raise taxes (Rosenthal 1997; Schrag 1998; Smith 1998; Tolbert 1998). State ballot initiatives have been used to adopt conservative policies, such as tax limitations, as well as liberal policies, such as legalization of medical marijuana.

Procedural Policy and Citizen Participation

During the early twentieth century and today, frequent usage of direct democracy is associated with attempts to reform and update political institutions. While the initiative process has been used to adopt a range of public policies, its most important application may be in the area of "governance policy," that changes the procedures and operation of representative democracy (Tolbert 1998). Governance policies are procedural policies that change the internal rules of the game that public officials must follow in such areas as elections, levying taxes or governmental resources. Governance policy is an aspect of public policy that has received less attention than traditional substantive policies, such as health, welfare, education or other expenditure policies. Governance policy, unlike traditional distributive and regulatory policy, redistributes power within institutions and thus reforms the institutions of representative government at the local, state and national level. Governance policies not only modify the actions of elected officials, but the very fabric of representative government.

Examples of historical (Progressive era) governance policies include provisions for direct democracy (initiative, referendum and recall), direct election of US senators, direct primary, home rule for municipalities, secret ballot, women's suffrage and many other procedural policies adopted during the Progressive era (1890-1917). Examples of contemporary governance policies (1980s and 1990s) include legislative term limits, two-thirds vote of the legislature to raise taxes, campaign finance reform, nonpartisan primaries, voting by mail, and legislative redistricting laws. These policies have a prominent procedural component and change the rules elected officials must follow. The resurgence in use of the initiative process in the late twentieth century, and preference for procedural reforms has long-term impacts for the operation of state, local and the federal government.

Governance policies themselves can restructure political institutions to increase citizen participation in politics or "expand the scope of conflict" (Schattschneider 1960). Recent research suggests states with the initiative process have higher voter turnout over the last three decades than states without this process, even after controlling for other factors (Tolbert, Grummell & Smith 2001). Legislative term limits require more frequent open-seat competitive elections. Tax limitations requiring voter approval of tax and spending increases require more frequent voter referenda. California's new blanket or nonpartisan primary aims to increase voter turnout and the success of minor or third party candidates. Similarly, early twentieth century governance policies functioned to increase civic participation, via expanding suffrage to women, or allowing citizens to directly elect US senators rather than state legislatures.

Socioeconomic Change and the Cyclical Pattern in Direct Democracy Use

Paralleling the turn of the twentieth century, a distinguishing feature of politics in the late twentieth century is a pervasive sense of public distrust, frustration and alienation with government that is perceived as corrupt (Craig 1996; Citrin 1996). The late twentieth century is a transformational period in the history of American politics — an era of rapidly changing information technologies and global marketplaces. Reform of political institutions necessarily lags between socioeconomic change (Skowronek 1982). This lag in reform of our political institutions has led to unprecedented levels of voter distrust of government and elected officials.

The argument developed here is that frequent use of direct democracy may serve to adapt political institutions to changing social and economic conditions. Both the very early and very late decades of the twentieth century were distinguished by rapid economic and social (demographic) change (Dodd 1991, 1993, 1995). During the late 1800s and early 1900s America shifted from an agrarian society based on farming to an industrial economy. A political response to this socioeconomic change was the Progressive movement (1890-1917). Scholars widely consider the rise of the Populist and later Progressive movements to be a political response to rapid economic and social change (Goodwyn 1978; Hofstadter 1955; Hayes 1957, 1964, 1965; Pollack 1992; Peffer 1992). During the 1980s and 1990s America has experienced another dramatic transformation from an industrial economy to one based on information technology (Peters 1996). This research suggests a new progressivism may be on the horizon (cf. Dionne 1996).

While the Progressives are commonly remembered for lobbying for the passage of direct democracy provisions (initiative, referendum and recall) at the state level, what is less well understood is that once these mechanisms were in place, the Progressives relied on the initiative process to adopt much of their reform agenda. The Progressives most important innovation may have been to use the initiative process as a catalyst for political and social reform. According to Schmidt, "In the initiative process the Progressives created a perpetual reform machine that not only continues to be a vehicle for political change, but is increasing in its usefulness to reformers more than three-quarters of a century after it first gained widespread acceptance" (1989, pg. 15). Progressive political reforms reshaped American democracy both substantively and procedurally, and were critical in adapting government institutions for a new industrial economy.

Examination of historical usage of direct democracy in the states corresponds with increased efforts at social and political reform. Use of the initiative process appears to follow a cyclical pattern in American politics, with frequent usage of the process in the first and last two decades of the twentieth century. Figure 1 shows the total number of initiatives appearing on state election ballots in the 24 states that permit the process, from 1904 through 1998 for every two-year election cycle. Figure 2 shows a six-year moving average of the number of initiatives per year on state election ballots to emphasize the trend line. Use of the initiative process was dramatic during the early years of its existence during the Progressive era: "Between 1910 and 1919 a record setting 269 measures went to a vote, of which 98 were approved" (Magleby 1994, 229). The initiative process was used only sparingly during most of the middle decades of the twentieth century (1940-1960) and has risen dramatically since the late 1970s.

Since the mid-1970s the initiative was "rediscovered" with a resurgence in the use of the process. The passage of California's Proposition 13 property tax limitations in 1978 (Sear and Citrin 1982) sparked a renewed interest in direct democracy in the states and gave rise to a tax revolt that rolled eastward all the way to Washington, DC. It also breathed new life into the idea of circumventing elected officials and state legislatures to make laws. The last two decades have witnessed an unprecedented number of ballot initiatives across the states, many demanding a greater role for the public in issues of governance. In the 1990s, over 300 statewide initiatives qualified for the ballot. Only during the Progressive era did use of the initiative process rival the current political era (Price 1975; Schmidt 1989; Cronin 1989; Magleby 1994). California now has dozens of ballot measures every even-numbered year, some in the spring and more in the fall. Ballot initiatives now dominate media headlines, shape candidate elections and national party politics (Chavez 1998).

The Subject Matter of Ballot Initiatives Then and Now

Tables 1 and 2 analyze the peaks from Figures 1 and 2 by presenting a breakdown of the subject matter of initiatives appearing on state election ballots from 1900-1920 (Table 1) and the current period of 1980-1996 (Table 2). There are strong parallels between the general subject matter of initiatives during the current period and the first two decades of the twentieth century. In both periods governance or political reform and taxation

Figure 1: Raw Frequency of Initiative Use in the States

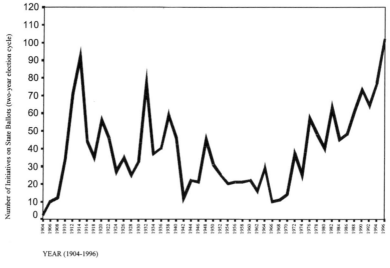

YEAR (1904-1996)

Source: raw data from the Initiative and Referendum Institutue

Washington, DC. Analysis by author.

Figure 2: Smoothed Frequency of Initiative Use in the States

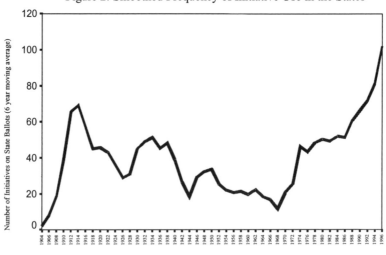

YEAR (1904-1996)

Source: raw data from the Initiative and Referendum Institute

Washington, DC. Analysis by Author.

Table 1. Subject Matter of Initiatives Appearing
on State Ballots 1900-1920

Tax, Revenue, Spending and Bond Issues	78	22%
Government Reform	128	36%
Social Policy	52	15%
Environmental Policy Land Acquisition	17	5%
Labor	20	6%
Education	9	3%
Crime	12	3%
Other	34	10%
Total	350	100%

are the most common topics of state ballot initiatives. In the twenty-year period from 1900-1920, 350 initiatives qualified for the ballot in the nineteen states that provided for direct democracy. Governmental reform was the most common subject matter during this period, comprising 36% of all initiatives. Fiscal policy (taxation, spending and bond issues) was the second most common subject matter, accounting for 22% of the total.

During the sixteen-year period of 1980-1996, a record 570 initiatives appeared on statewide ballots. Of this total, 22% dealt with issues of taxation, spending and bonds, exactly the same proportion as during the Progressive era. Fifteen percent of initiatives dealt with social policy during the Progressive era (1900-1920), roughly the same percent (17.5%) focused on social policy during the contemporary period. The issues have evolved of course from prohibition, women's pensions and child labor to abortion and health care reform. Ballot measures focusing on governmental reform

Table 2. Subject Matter of Initiatives Appearing
on State Ballots 1980-1996

Tax, Revenue, Spending and Bond Issues	125	22%
Government Reform	131	23%
Social Policy	105	17.5%
Environmental Policy Land Acquisition	80	13.5%
Labor	15	3%
Education	18	3%
Crime	18	3%
Other	61	11%
Total	572	100%

accounted for 23% of the total in the contemporary period, down slightly from the 36% during the historical period. Of the 131 governmental reform initiatives appearing on statewide ballots from 1980-1996, 50 (or 39%) dealt with legislative term limits. Environmental policy is a more prominent issue in the current period, accounting for 13.5% of all ballot measures, up from 5% during the Progressive era. Ballot measures concerning education policy accounted for exactly the same proportion of total initiatives during the Progressive era and contemporary period—3%. Similarly, 3% of ballot measures focused on crime policy during both time periods. Labor issues, however, were clearly a more important policy issue during the Progressive era (6% of the total), than today (3% of total). The overall passage rate for initiatives from 1900-1920 was 43%, and has increased modestly to 47% for the period 1980-1996.

In terms of the diversity of public policy issues appearing on state election ballots, the data suggests that the initiative process continues to operate much as the founder's of the process intended. The diversity of policy issues is only matched by the diversity of interest groups that use the process. While state initiative agendas have been subject to an evolutionary process, historically and today the process creates a venue for substantive reform in the area of social policy, environmental policy, crime (abolition and prison labor to strict sentencing laws) and education policy (normal schools to school choice). But its most important impact may be in the area of procedural policy, such as taxation (poll tax to property tax) and political reform (direct election of US senators to term limits). The ideology of the American electorate has swung from liberal to conservative to liberal or vice versus, depending on the policy area over time. The public policies produced by the initiative process mirror these underlying ideological shifts.

Substantive Historical Policy

During the Progressive era, the initiative process was used to adopt a wide range of social policies opposed by business interests that dominated state legislatures. Many policies first adopted via ballot initiative diffused across the states and were later adopted at the national level. State level women's suffrage initiatives at the turn of the twentieth century, for example, paved the way for the Nineteenth Amendment to the U.S. Constitution granting women universal suffrage. Progressive era policies adopted by ballot initiatives included the eight-hour workday for women, child labor laws, prohibition, mother's pensions, women's suffrage, environmental legislation, and the creation of normal schools, but the movement's most important contribution was in the area of procedural reform.

Procedural Historical Policy

Progressives advanced a series of procedural policies that can be commonly referred to as *governance policies*. Since governance policies change the rules under which governments operate, they had long-term consequences, changing the landscape of American politics for the next century. Progressive reformers succeeded in passing ballot initiatives aimed at making government more honest, efficient, and responsive. From 1904-1984, voters approved 58 initiatives in the areas of political reform and government organization (Schmidt 1989, p. 15). Progressive era political reforms included the Australian (or long) ballot, home rule for local governments and municipalities, civil service, secret ballot, manager-council system, non-partisan local elections, legislative redistricting, direct primary, direct election of US Senators, women's suffrage, and the initiative, referendum and recall (Schmidt 1989).

The initiative process was first used to establish the nomination of candidates through primary elections in Arkansas, Maine, Montana, Oregon and South Dakota. Voters in Oregon first passed an initiative creating the direct election of US Senators, which later became known as the "Oregon model" for similar legislation adopted across the states. Direct election of US Senator initiatives were also passed early on in Arizona, Arkansas and North Dakota.

Home rule for municipalities was first adopted via initiatives in Colorado and Oregon, and permanent voter registration, instead of requiring voters to re-register every election by initiatives in California and Washington. A 1912 Arizona initiative required reapportionment of the lower house of the state legislature based on population, more than half a century before the US Supreme Court rule this method of reapportionment mandatory. Five other states passed reapportionment initiatives (Arizona, Arkansas, California, Colorado and Washington). Successful women's suffrage initiatives in Arizona and Oregon helped pave the way for passage of the national suffrage amendment nine years later (Schmidt 1989, pp. 17-19). In each case, voter adoption of the political reform established the popularity of the policy, which later gained acceptance by state legislatures. In many cases, the initiative process was used to "jump start" the political reform process.

Contemporary Substantive Policy

Ballot initiatives dealing with social policy in the last two decades reflect both conservative and liberal ideologies of state electorates. State referenda have regulated abortions (Gerber 1996), while others have raised taxes on cigarettes with revenues dedicated to prevention and social services. A California initiative capped class sizes at twenty students in public K-12 schools, while pending ballot measures in California and Washington would guarantee cost-of-living salary based on inflation for public school teachers. "School Choice" initiatives have been defeated by voters in a number of states; under this policy, parents would receive a voucher that could be used to pay for private or parochial school tuition if they chose not to attend the public schools. Voucher policies were on the ballot in California and Michigan in 2000 and were defeated. In the past twenty years, California voters have adopted a series of social policy initiatives with direct and sometimes adverse consequences for the state's growing minority population, including ending social services to illegal immigrants (primarily Latinos) and their children (1994), ending affirmative action (1996) and ending bilingual education (1998). Research suggests in certain contexts, high racial ethnic/diversity combined with frequent usage of the initiative process, may lead to policy outcomes with detrimental consequences for minority groups (Tolbert and Hero forthcoming).

Other ballot measures echo the Progressive's legacy of expanding the welfare state. Beginning in 1994, the year that also witnessed President Clinton's failed effort at federal health care reform, ballot initiatives have become an increasingly important venue for health policy reform. Proposition 186 (1994) would have created a universal health insurance system for the state of California. Propositions 214 and 216 (1996), also California ballot measures, would have regulated the health insurance industry. Even though none of the more radical or comprehensive health policy initiatives have been adopted by voters, they have sparked considerable public discourse on health reform and have, in some instances, been met with action by state legislatures previously unwilling to act on health reform measures. To date, there have been four types of health related state ballot initiatives: those calling for some form of single payer universal coverage; those calling for regulation of managed care industry and HMOs; those involved with so-called "right to die" legislation; and those involved with the medical use of marijuana. Progressive reformers relied on the initiative process to regulate the railroads that had an iron-hold on state legislatures. In the twenty-first century the initiative process may be the only way to regulate the health insurance industry, given its influence over state legislatures.

Statewide initiatives in 2000 continue to reflect the diversity of interest groups that rely on the process. Environmental legislation requiring that "growth pay its way" through excise taxes on new development to control urban sprawl will likely appear on ballots in Colorado and Arizona. Massachusetts and Washington state ballot measures propose to create a universal health care system for the state. Initiatives to end bilingual education programs will appear on the ballot in Arizona while defense on marriage laws are on the ballot in numerous other states.

Contemporary Procedural Policy

Table 3 shows state adoption of a series of governance policies introduced by activists from the left and the right of the political spectrum[2]. There are many examples of contemporary procedural policies, but the most prominent are legislative term limits. Since 1990 when legislative limits were first adopted by initiatives in California, Colorado and Oklahoma, term limits have been adopted in twenty-one states. However, term limit provisions in three states—Massachusetts, Nebraska and Washington—were invalidated by the state supreme court. Of contemporary governance policies, none have had as direct an effect on legislative institutions as term limits (Benjamin and Malbin 1992).

Thirteen states have constitutional provisions requiring a "supermajority" or a two-thirds vote of the legislature to raise all taxes. Rather than targeting a certain tax (property tax or poll tax), supermajority rules and voter approval requirements to enact or increase taxes are procedural policies that restrict the authority of state lawmaker over taxation and spending (Tolbert 1998). Arkansas was the first state to adopt supermajority rules for tax increases in 1934. Arkansas voters approved a constitutional amendment that requires a two-thirds vote to increase "the rate for property, excise privilege, or personal taxes now levied" (Stansel 1994; Mackey 1993). In 1992, four states (Arizona, Colorado, Oklahoma, Washington) enacted initiatives requiring tax increases to be approved by a margin larger than a simple majority of both houses. Oregon, Missouri and South Dakota were the latest states to require a supermajority vote for tax increases in 1996. Colorado was one of the first states in the nation to require voter approval of all tax increases adopted by the state legislature, county governments or municipalities. Voters in Arizona, Washington and Oklahoma adopted similar measures.

In the last three decades, campaign finance reform has been an active area for legislation at the state level. Recent state efforts at reforming campaign finances have focused on lowering contribution limits, increasing disclosure requirements and public financing of campaigns. The most sweeping state reforms in recent years are commonly referred to as "clean elections" that provide for public financing of political campaigns. First passed by Maine voters in 1996 by initiative, clean election measures were adopted by the Vermont legislature in 1997 and by voters in Arizona and Massachusetts

---

2. Raw data is from the National Conference of State Legislatures, Denver, Colorado and is current as of July 1999.

Table 3. State Political Reforms

State	Initiatives per year (average) 1970–92	Term Limits	2/3 Vote Legislature for Tax Increases	Voter Approval Tax Increases	Complete Open Primary All Types	Blanket Primary	Very Low Contribution Limits	Public Financing Campaign	Voting by Mail 2000 Elections
Alabama	.00								
Alaska	.95				X	X			
Arizona	1.25	X	X	X	X			X	
Arkansas	.75	X	X				X		
California	4.10	X	X		X	X	X		
Colorado	2.05	X	X	X			X		
Connecticut	.00								
Delaware	.00		X						
Florida	.60	X	X		X				
Georgia	.00								
Hawaii	.00				X				
Idaho	.40	X			X				
Illinois	.50								
Indiana	.00								
Iowa	.00								
Kansas	.00								
Kentucky	.00								
Louisiana	.00	X	X		X	X			
Maine	1.00	X						X	
Maryland	.00								
Massachusetts	1.25	X						X	
Michigan	.80	X			X				
Minnesota	.00				X				
Mississippi	.00		X						

State	Value								
Missouri	1.35	X	X		X		X		
Montana	1.25	X			X		X		
Nebraska	.40	X							
Nevada	.55	X	X						
New Hampshire	.00								
New Jersey	.00								
New Mexico	.00								
New York	.00								
N. Carolina	.00								
N. Dakota	1.45	X	X		X				
Ohio	1.10	X	X						
Oklahoma	.45	X	X	X					
Oregon	2.95	X	X	X		X	X		X
Pennsylvania	.00								
Rhode Island	.00								
S. Carolina	.00								
S. Dakota	1.05	X	X		X				
Tennessee	.00								
Texas	.00								
Utah	.55	X			X				
Vermont	.00								
Virginia	.00								
Washington	1.65	X	X	X	X	X	X		
W. Virginia	.00								
Wisconsin	.00								
Wyoming	.15	X							
Total	.53 (mean)	21	14	4	16	4	6	4	1
% of Total		42	28	8	32	8	12	8	2

Source: Raw data on state adoption of political reforms from the National Conference of State Legislatures, Denver, CO.

via initiatives in 1998. These reforms stimulate that candidates must first raise a certain amount in small contributions from individuals ($1500 for example) before qualifying for public campaign funds. In all four states, once a candidate qualifies, he is prohibited from receiving any additional private contributions (Drage 1999).

Very low contribution limits is another state innovation in campaign finance reform that has been adopted in six states. In 1994, voters in Missouri, Montana and Oregon passed citizen initiatives that set limits as low as $100 on individual contributions to legislative candidates. Arkansas, California and Colorado followed in 1996, passing initiatives setting similar limits. The courts have voided all of these measures, with the exception of laws in Colorado and Montana, arguing the limits are too low to allow meaningful participation in constitutionally protected speech and association (Drage 1999). Nevertheless, low contribution limits are an important political reform.

Reform of election systems (primaries) is another area that has received growing attention in the 1990s. California voters, for example, adopted an initiative in 1996 creating a blanket or nonpartisan primary (which was struck down by the U.S. Supreme Court in 2000). Prior to this reform, California's 1.5 million independent voters were excluded from voting in primary elections at all, as well as all minor party voters. Only registered Republicans could vote in the Republican primary and registered Democrats in the Democratic primary. Closed primary systems favor the election of party hard-liners, over moderates; discourages minority or third party candidates; and decreases voter turnout in elections.

California's blanket or nonpartisan primary allowed all persons who were entitled to vote in primary elections, including those not affiliated with a political party, to vote for any candidate (major or minor party) regardless of the candidate's political party affiliation. All candidates from both major political parties and minor parties are presented on one slate (or blanket) ballot. Voters can pick and choose the candidates of their preference. The candidate with the highest number of votes from each party is the party's nominee in the general election. Washington, Alaska and Louisiana have blanket or nonpartisan primaries similar to California's system. Blanket or nonpartisan primaries, like the direct election of US senators, weakens the role of state political parties, while increasing citizen participation in the electoral process.

Sixteen states, including the four with blanket primaries, have completely open primaries. These election systems allow any person who is registered as an independent or with no party preference or is registered to a party that is not represented on the ballot (minor party) to vote in the primary election of the major political parties. A voter is not required to state party preferences and is usually given two ballots. Voters must choose one party once in the polling boot), but their choice is private. Arizona voters adopted an initiative in 1998 creating an open primary, and Florida voters adopted a modified open primary the same year.

The most innovative political reform discussed here is Oregon's voters' passage of a 1998 initiative requiring voting by mail in the biennial primary and general elections. The law requires a vote by mail for the 2000 elections. Prior to this law, voters could vote by going to the polling place on election day or by some form of absentee voting, including permanent absentee or single-election absentee. The initiative eliminates polling places for primary and general elections. Voters will return their ballots by mail or drop them off at designated sites. County government expenditures are estimated to be reduced each primary and general election year by $3,021,709.

Conclusion: A Diversity of Policies Reflecting a Diversity of Interest Groups

The rise in state use of direct democracy and associated adoption of social and political reforms may coincide with critical junctions in our political history. Increased use of direct democracy may function to adapt political institutions to changing socioeconomic conditions. At the turn of the twentieth century, Progressives used the initiative process to adopt substantive and procedural policies to meet the demands of an industrial economy. Today, the initiative process is once again being used to adopt substantive and procedural public policies to meet the demands of a technological economy. Progressive era reforms shaped our political system for 100 years. Current initiative reforms will likely also have profound impacts on our political system.

The initiative process has always been regulated and continues to be regulated in terms of rules setting petition requirements, geographical distribution requirements and time period to gather signatures to qualify an initiative for the ballot (Tolbert, Lowenstein and Donovan 1998). There are strong parallels not only in the total number of initiatives appearing on state ballots during the Progressive era and today, but also in the general categories of public policy. There are striking similarities in the proportion of total ballot measures devoted to governmental reform, taxation and spending, and social policy during the early and late twentieth century. In terms of the diversity of public policy issues (and thus the diversity of interest group participation in the process), this analysis suggests that the initiative process continues to operate as the founder's intended.

It is more difficult to answer the second question, whether the initiative process continues to operate to reform representative institutions of government when they fail to act, or to weaken or replace our system of representative government with a pure direct democracy. As Progressivism reached its high-water mark, national leaders endorsed the cause, including Theodore Roosevelt: "I believe in the Initiative and Referendum, which should be used not to destroy representative government, but to correct it whenever it becomes misrepresentative."

While ballot initiatives are sometimes not the most reasoned or balanced solution to policy problems available, given the experimental nature of states politics (50 jurisdictions) they often allow for innovative solutions to intractable public problems. Given the scope of this essay, it is impossible to evaluate the magnitude of individual ballot measures or their relative impact on the institutions of representative government. The labels used to categorize the subject matter of initiative policies are necessarily very broad. Nevertheless, Progressive era initiatives creating the civil service, granting women universal suffrage, prohibiting the sale of alcohol, and allowing for the direct election of U.S. senators were no more radical given their historical context, than current initiatives taxing cigarettes, limiting the tenure of state legislatures, legalizing gambling, allowing voting by mail, creating nonpartisan primaries or ending affirmative action. The diversity in the policies produced by state provisions for direct democracy is the beauty of the process, reflecting the diversity of groups that use the process. Historically and today, state ballot measures reflect the issues of great importance to a majority of Americans.

References

Barber, Benjamin R. 1984. *Strong Democracy: Participatory Politics for a New Age*. Berkeley: University of California.

Baumgartner, Frank R., and Bryan D. Jones. 1993. *Agendas and Instability in American Politics*. Chicago: University of Chicago Press.

Benjamin, Gerald, and Michael J. Malbin (eds.). 1992. *Limiting Legislative Terms*. Washington, DC: Congressional Quarterly Press.

Bowler, Shaun, Todd Donovan, and Caroline Tolbert (eds.). 1998. *Citizens as Legislators: Direct Democracy in the United States*. Columbus: Ohio State University Press.

————, and Todd Donovan. 1998. *Demanding Choices: Opinion, Voting and Direct Democracy*. Ann Arbor: University of Michigan Press.

Cain, Bruce. 1992. "Voting Rights and Democratic Theory: Toward a Color-Blind Society?" in *Controversies in Minority Voting*, edited by Bernard Grofman and Chandler Davidson. Washington, DC: Brookings Institution.

Chavez, Lydia. 1998. *The Color Bind: California's Battle to End Affirmative Action*. Berkeley: University of California Press.

Citrin, Jack. 1996. "Who's the Boss? Direct Democracy and Popular Control of Government," in *Broken Contract? Changing Relationship between Americans and Their Government*, edited by Stephen C. Craig. Boulder, CO: Westview Press.

Craig, Stephen C. 1996. "The Angry Voter: Politics and Popular Discontent in the 1990s," in *Broken Contract? Changing Relationship Between Americans and Their Government*, edited by Stephen C. Craig. Boulder, CO: Westview Press.

Cronin, Thomas. 1989. *Direct Democracy: The Politics of Initiative, Referendum, and Recall*. Cambridge, MA: Harvard University Press.

Dionne, E.J., Jr. 1996. *They Only Look Dead: Why Progressives Will Dominate the New Political Era*. New York: Simon and Schuster.

Dodd, Lawrence C. 1991. "Congress, the Presidency, and the American Experience: A Transformational Perspective," in *Divided Democracy: Cooperation and Conflict Between the President and Congress*, edited by James A. Thurber. Washington DC: Congressional Quarterly Press.

———. 1993. "Transformational Politics." in *The Dynamics of American Politics: Approaches and Interpretations*, edited by Lawrence Dodd and Calvin Jillson. Boulder, CO: Westview Press.

———. 1995. "The New American Politics: Reflections on the Early 1990s," in *The New American Politics*, edited by Byron D. Jones. Boulder, CO: Westview Press.

Drage, Jennifer. 1999. "Campaign Finance Reform," *National Conference of State Legislatures Leg. Brief*, vol. 7, no. 25 (June/July).

Dye, Thomas R. 1981. *Politics, Economics, and the Public: Policy Outcomes in the American States*. Chicago, IL: Rand McNally.

Fishkin, James S. 1991. *Democracy and Deliberation: New Direction for Democratic Reform*. New Haven, CT: Yale University Press.

Gerber, Elisabeth R. 1996. "Legislative Response to the Threat of Popular Initiatives," *American Journal of Political Science*, 40(1): 99-128.

———. 1999. *The Populist Paradox: Interest Group Influence and the Promise of Direct Legislation*. Princeton, NJ: Princeton University Press.

Goodwyn, Lawrence. 1978. *Democratic Promise: The Populist Moment in America*. Oxford University Press.

Hayes, Samuel P. 1964. "The Politics of Reform in Municipal Government in the Progressive Era," *Pacific Northwest Quarterly*, 55: 157-69.

Hays, Samuel. 1965. "The Social Analysis of American Political History: 1880-1920," *Political Science Quarterly*, 373-394.

Hero, Rodney E. 1998. *Faces of Inequality: Social Diversity in American Politics*. New York: Oxford University Press.

Hofstadter, Richard. 1963. *The Progressive Movement, 1900-1915*. Englewood Cliffs: Prentice-Hall.

Key, V.O., Jr. 1949. *Southern Politics—In State and Nation*. Knoxville: University of Tennessee Press.

Lascher, Edward, M. Hagen, and S. Rochlin. 1996. "Gun behind the Door? Ballot Initiatives, States Policies and Public Opinion," *Journal of Politics* 58: 760-75.

Mackey, Scott. R. 1993. "Constitutional Restrictions on Legislative Tax Powers." *National Conference of State Legislatures*, vol. 1, no. 29.

Magleby, David B. 1984. Direct Legislation: Voting on Ballot Propositions in the United States. Baltimore: John Hopkins University Press.

———. 1994. "Direct Legislation in the American States." in *Referendums around the World: The Growing Use of Direct Democracy*. Edited by David Butler and Austin Ranney, AEI Press.

———, and K.D. Patterson. 1998. "Consultants and Direct Democracy," *PS: Political Science and Politics*, 31(2): 160-169.

Mishel, Lawrence, Jared Bernstein, and John Schmitt. 1999. *The State of Working America 1998-99*. Ithica, NY: ILS Press.

Neal, Tommy. (1993) "The Voter Initiative," *National Conference of State Legislatures*, no. 38.

Osborne, David, and Ted Gaebler. 1992. *Reinventing Government: How the Entrepreneurial Spirit is Transforming the Public Sector*. Reading, MA: Addison-Wesley.

Peffer, William A. 1992. *Populism: Its Rise and Fall*. University of Kansas Press.

Peters, Guy E. 1996 *The Future of Governing: Four Emerging Models*. Lawrence, KS: Kansas University Press.

Pollack, Norman. 1962. *The Populist Response to Industrial America: Midwestern Populist Thought*. Cambridge, MA: Harvard University Press.

Price, Charles M. 1975. "The Initiative: A Comparative State Analysis and Reassessment of a Western Phenomenon," *Western Political Quarterly*, 28: 243-62.

Rosenthal, Alan. 1997. *The Decline of Representative Democracy: Process, Participation and Power in State Legislatures*. Washington, DC: CQ Press.

Schattschneider, E.E. 1960, 1975. *The Semi Sovereign People: A Realist's View of Democracy in America*. Hinsdale, IL: Dryden Press.

Schmidt, David D. 1989. *Citizen Lawmakers: The Ballot Initiative Revolution*. Philadelphia, PA: Temple University Press.

Schneider, Anne Larason, and Helen Ingram. 1997. *Policy Design for Democracy*. Lawrence: University Press of Kansas.

Schrag, Peter. 1998. *Paradise Lost: California's Experience, America's Future*. New York: The New York Press.

Sears, David O., and Jack Citrin. 1982. *Tax Revolt: Something for Nothing in California*. Cambridge, MA: Harvard University Press.

Skowronek, Stephen. 1982. *Building the New American State: The Expansion of National Adaptive Capacities, 1877-1920*. Cambridge: Cambridge University Press.

Smith, Daniel A. 1998. *Tax Crusaders and the Politics of Direct Democracy*. New York: Rutledge.

Tolbert, Caroline J., and Rodney E. Hero. 1996. "Race/Ethnicity and Direct Democracy: An Analysis of California's Illegal Immigration Initiative," *Journal of Politics* 58: 806-18.

Tolbert, Caroline J. 1998. "Changing the Rules for State Legislatures: Direct Democracy and Governance Policy," in *Citizens as Legislators: Direct Democracy in the United States*. Columbus: Ohio State University Press.

Tolbert, Caroline, Daniel Lowenstein, and Todd Donovan. 1998. "Election Law and Rules for Using Initiatives," in *Citizens as Legislators: Direct Democracy in the United States*. Columbus: Ohio State University Press.

Tolbert, Caroline J., John Grummell, and Dan Smith. Forthcoming 2001. "The Effects of Ballot Initiatives on Voter Turnout in the American States," *American Politics Quarterly*.

Tolbert, Caroline J., and Rodney E. Hero. Forthcoming 2001. "Direct Democracy, Racial/Ethnic Diversity and Social Policy," *Political Research Quarterly*.

Section Two

The Impetus for and Impact of Regulation: Interest Groups and Initiative and Referendum

Now that we have a basic understanding of how and why the initiative and referendum process was established as well as how it has been used, we should continue our discussion by looking at why the regulation of the process has increased over the last several years and the tangible impact those regulations have caused. This section includes academic studies by Dan Smith in Chapter 4 and Liz Gerber and Beth Garrett in Chapter 5 on the role "special interests" have played in utilizing the I&R process, if their involvement has "corrupted" the process, and whether "special interest" involvement warrants increased regulation.

Their chapters are then followed by the observations of two individuals whose groups have utilized the I&R process substantially over the last few years. Paul Jacob, of the term limits movement, and Wayne Pacelle, of the animal protection movement, will give their thoughts on how regulation has impacted their efforts at reform as well as provide candid comments on how their activities have been the impetus for many of the new regulations.

Following the discussion on the impact of regulation on groups wishing to utilize the process, we will hear from Angelo Paparella who will give insight into how the regulations and restrictions on the process impact the companies that are on the frontlines helping the citizens utilize I&R.

This section will then conclude with an in-depth review by Anne Campbell of the U.S. Air Force Academy on one of the most troublesome regulations of the I&R process — the single subject requirement — and the impact this regulation has had on the use of the I&R process.

Chapter 4

Special Interests and Direct Democracy: An Historical Glance

By Daniel A. Smith

There is a growing concern among many proponents of direct democracy that special interests have come to dominate the process of initiative and referendum. Taking a cursory look at the enormous sums of money spent on ballot measures, it is not difficult to arrive at this conclusion. In 1998 alone, ballot committees spent nearly $400 million promoting and opposing ballot measures (both initiative and referendum) in 44 states (Initiative & Referendum Institute, 1998). Large and small states alike, regardless of the number of measures on their ballots, experienced high expenditure levels on ballot measures during the 1990s. With particular respect to the "citizen" initiative, a disproportionate amount of money spent on ballot campaigns in the twenty-four states that permit the process comes from special interests — corporations, labor unions, agricultural interests, and professional associations. Whether promoting or opposing ballot measures, special interests today are key players in initiative politics.

This essay examines the historical role of special interests in initiative and referendum ballot contests in the American states. Most scholars agree that special interest money today plays a major role in ballot initiative campaigns, especially when groups are trying to qualify their measures for the ballot (Garrett, 1999). The jury is still out, however, as to the causal nexus between campaign contributions and expenditures on ballot measures and subsequent success (Braunstein, 1999; Gerber, 1999; Smith, 2001). Sidestepping this important question, this essay instead focuses on the unfolding of special interests in the process of direct democracy over time. As such, it calls into question some of the assumptions that scholars, journalists, and practitioners often make about how "populist" or "grassroots" the process once was during the beginning of the 20th century.

The understanding of special interest involvement in early ballot campaigns has serious implications for the current debate over the merits of direct democracy. While some early ballot campaigns were certainly "grassroots" and "populist," many in fact were not. Since so much of the current debate concerning the practice of the initiative and referendum hinges

59

on the belief that direct democracy was somehow purer in its incipient stage, a fuller historical understanding of early ballot campaigns is critically important.

After this historical overview of the role of special interests in initiative and referendum ballot campaigns, the essay considers a few attempts by states to regulate the involvement of special interests in the process of direct democracy. Although they have a goal of returning direct democracy to the people, most state regulations of interest group activity have been struck down by the courts as infringing on First Amendment rights. As a result of a series of judicial rulings, states largely have been unable to restrict the involvement of special interests in ballot campaigns. If in the future, however, states were to become more successful in curtailing the role of special interests in ballot campaigns, some current developments in ballot campaigns suggest there may be severe unintended consequences resulting from any increase in the state regulation of the process. The essay concludes by examining some of these current developments by special interests in direct democracy campaigns.

The Current Lament

There is common perception among supporters of direct democracy that during the first half of the century citizen interests — rather than special interests — dominated the process of initiative and referendum. Advocates of direct democracy, with little empirical evidence to support their claims, frequently assert that eighty years ago citizens successfully utilized the two populist mechanisms to circumvent or counteract state legislatures or elected officials who were held captive by special interests. As David Schmidt (1989: 25-26) writes, citizens used the tools of direct democracy as "a safeguard against the concentration of political power in the hands of a few." Although little empirical evidence is compiled in support of their claims, there is a strong yearning among supporters of direct democracy for the earlier, purer days when the process was allegedly more "grassroots" and "populist" and less tainted by special interests.

Scholars and journalists alike hold California up as an example of how far the process of direct democracy has fallen from its supposedly unadulterated olden days. The editorial board of the *Los Angeles Times* (1998) commented that in California, "well-heeled special interests," are able to "write their own wishes into state law or the Constitution." This concern about the process certainly seems to ring true. In 1998, for example, special interests spent more money fighting for and against the 21 ballot measures in California than in all of the other states combined. While the spending level by groups sponsoring and opposing ballot measures in California is not necessarily representative of ballot campaigns in other states, it does shed light on the role of interest groups in the initiative and referendum process. In 1998, issue committees in California spent nearly $250 million on 12 general election and nine primary ballot measures, approximately the same amount spent by all the political candidates running for the California General Assembly and statewide offices, and more than the combined total or "soft money" raised by the national Republican and Democratic parties during the 1997-98 election cycle (Morain, 1999a; Common Cause, 1999). The quarter billion dollars spent on the 21 ballot measures broke several state records, including the previous spending record of $141 million, set just two years earlier. Furthermore, a record $88.6 million was spent on a single November 1998 ballot measure, Proposition 5. The successful measure, sponsored by Native American tribes, allowed Indians to operate casinos on their reservations. Indian tribes anteed up an impressive $63.2 million in support of the tribal gaming measure, with Nevada casino operators and organized labor in California spending $25.4 million to oppose the measure. The San Manuel Tribe alone spent $27.8 million promoting the measure, and Mirage Resorts, Circus Circus Enterprises, and Hilton Hotels all spent in excess of $6 million opposing the measure (California Voter Foundation, 1998).

California special interests were heavily involved in several other recent ballot measure contests. In the November ballot contest, electric companies spent $38.1 million in their successful effort to defeat Proposition 9, a measure that would have deregulated the electric utility industry. Edison International/Southern California Edison and Pacific Gas and Electric each contributed more than $17 million to defeat the measure, sponsored by several consumer and public interest groups. Tobacco companies drained $29.7 million from their corporate coffers (including nearly $21 million from Philip Morris and $5 million from Brown and Williamson) in their failed bid to defeat Proposition 10, a measure raising taxes on cigarettes by 50 cents a pack to pay for early childhood education and health programs. The California Teachers Association spent $6.8 million in their successful effort to defeat Proposition 8, Pete Wilson's education reform measure promoting accountability of teachers in the public schools, and spent a total of $20 million on ballot measures in 1998 (California Voter Foundation, 1998; Morain, 1999b).

Less populous states too have witnessed a dramatic rise in spending on ballot measures by special interests. In Colorado, issue committees supporting and opposing eleven ballot measures spent in excess of $10 million in 1998. The amount easily surpassed the previous spending record on ballot measures of $8.8 million set in 1994. The privately owned Stockman Water Company—the sole financial backer of two Colorado initiatives, Amendments 15 and 16—spent in excess of $1 million, only to see both measures badly defeated by the voters. In addition, Colorado billionaire Phil Anschutz—a railroad and mining magnate and the principal sharehold-er of Quest Communications—contributed $402,500 of the $425,282 (95%) raised by the successful proponents of Amendment 14, an initia-tive placing severe environmental regulations on large, corporate hog farms. The National Education Association contributed $685,000 of the $1.1 million raised by the opponents of Colorado's Amendment 17, a private school tax credit program defeated by the voters in 1998. In Montana, corporate interests opposed to Initiative 122, a 1996 measure that would have required tougher water treatment standards in mine operations, spent nearly $9 per vote to defeat the measure (Billings, 1998). In Nebraska, AT&T spent $5.3 million in its successful campaign to defeat a single 1998 initiative that would have lowered long-distance access charges (Cordes, 1999). During the decade of the 1990s, the sugar industry in Florida con-tributed over $10 million to issue committees supporting successful ini-tiatives capping state taxes and spending and thwarting efforts to clean up the Everglades (Smith, 1998b; Florida Secretary of State, 1998). These are only a few of the numerous examples of the involvement of special interests in the initiative process.

Numerous commentators have noted how the practice of direct democ-racy today appears to be distinctly different from that of yesteryear. The heavy involvement of special interests these days seems to run counter to the populist-sounding story preached by proponents of direct democracy. Present day champions of the initiative and referendum frequently claim that when states began adopting these plebescitary mechanisms nearly a century ago, they had the effect of minimizing the role of special interests. The mechanisms of direct democracy, proponents assert, made it possible in the past for "the people" to circumvent intransigent state legislatures beholden to special interests by allowing citizens to propose and vote on public policies directly.

But today, special interest influences—these commentators argue—seem to be undermining the once-populist tools of initiative and referen-dum. Rather than citizen groups utilizing the initiative and referendum process, it is now the special interests themselves that are dominating the process of direct democracy. By paying for the collection of signatures and by spending hundreds of thousands or even millions of dollars on thirty-second TV and radio soundbites, direct mailings, and print advertising, special interests have allegedly debased the once hallowed process.

Lamenting the loss of purity of these populist tools, some journalists and scholars write fondly of the earlier, more sacrosanct past. For exam-ple, journalist Peter Schrag (1998: 195) observes that in California, "the people's remedy," specifically the initiative, is being used by "'the inter-ests'—the insurance industry, the tobacco companies, the trial lawyers, public employee unions." These special interests "are themselves running and/or bankrolling ballot measures to advance their economic agendas," Schrag contends, with other states inevitably following California's lead. Political scientist David McCuan and his co-authors (McCuan, et al. 1998: 55-56) note how there is a common perception that almost all initiative campaigns today are run by highly paid professionals:

> [A] major cause of dismay for contemporary supporters of the initiative process has been the perceived decline in its amateur status. From this perspective, what was once the province of good government amateurs has recently been taken over, and possibly subverted, by big-money special interests and their hired-gun campaign firms. In consequence…supporters bemoan its lost 'innocence' and newfound professionalism.

Embedded in these commentaries of how special interests today are dominating the process of direct democracy is the implication that special interest groups and professionals were somehow not as prominent during the early days of initiative and referendum.

Historical Backdrop of Special Interests and Ballot Measures

Unfortunately, there is very little scholarly research documenting exactly who was behind early ballot measures or how initial campaigns were actually conducted. Unlike more recent scholarly studies (Gerber, 1999; Smith, 1998a; Cronin, 1989; Magleby, 1994), earlier scholarly research does not delve into the particularities of how initiative and referendum campaigns were run; nor do they investigate the political and economic motivations of the financial supporters and opponents of the measures (see Beard, 1912; Munro, 1912; Wilcox, 1912; Barnett, 1915; Cushman, 1916; Cottrell, 1939). A few recent historical studies, though, are beginning to directly challenge what Richard Ellis (1999) calls the "mythic narrative" of citizen-dominated initiative and referendums at the turn-of-the century. Ellis argues that there "was no enduring golden age" in Oregon and California. Similarly, Smith and Lubinski (n.d.) challenge the prevailing perception of how early ballot measure campaigns were untainted by special interests. Their archival research uncovers the active presence of special interests in Colorado from the inaugural 1912 election onward. With this historical research, it is gradually becoming clearer that since the earliest days of the initiative and referendum, special interests regularly have tried to manipulate the process to advance or defeat ballot measures in which they have a stake.

Interestingly, early proponents of the initiative and referendum occasionally admitted that special interests would try to influence the outcomes of ballot measure. Writing in 1912, Professor Delos Wilcox (1912: 103), an avid supporter of the initiative, stated that he fully "expected" that "the people...will have to rebuke not only public service corporations [utilities] seeking to get favors from them, but also many other kinds of special interests having a pecuniary stake in legislation proposed by themselves." Wilcox noted that "school-teachers," "letter-carriers, or the policemen," "brewers" and "labor unions" would in all likelihood try to use the initiative to offer "some legislation for their own benefit or for the advancement of their pet ideas." Not surprisingly, these special interests were eager to use the initiative and popular referendum to advance or protect their own private agendas. Due to their considerable financial resources, these interests were able to overcome a series of collective action hurdles facing citizens and public interest groups. The historical record suggests that the initiative as practiced in the states, even in its formative years, was not dominated by "grassroots" operations run by "amateurs" and "citizen" groups.

With respect to spending on ballot initiatives and referendums, levels of campaign spending by special interests on ballot measures is nothing new. Special interests, since at least the 1910s, have *always* played an important, if not a decisive role in the process of direct democracy. Despite the good intentions of the original reformers, the systematic lack of restrictions on campaign contributions and expenditures of ballot measures has concentrated an immense amount of power in the hands of a few well-financed interests. While state campaign finance records dealing with the initiative and referendum are scarce, the existing documents do suggest that large spending by special interests was a large part of the process.

In South Dakota in 1910, for example, 11 out of 12 ballot propositions were rejected by the voters. Historian Charles Beard (1912: 49) submits that the defeat of the measures—which included a popular referendum invoked by the railroads to overturn a law requiring electric headlights for locomotives and a referendum regulating embalmers—was directly attributable to the "activity of certain parties, especially interested in the defeat of one or two propositions, who filled the newspapers with advertisements and plastered the fences with billboards advising the electors to 'Vote No.'" In Oregon, substantial expenditures were also made by rival fishing interests during the months leading up to the June 1908 election. Upstream and downstream fisherman each placed an initiative on the ballot that would effectively eradicate the other's right to fish for salmon on the Columbia River (Cushman, 1916; Beard, 1912; Eaton, 1912; Bowler and Donovan, 1998: 118-128). Ellis (1999: 12) documents how special interest money was so rampant in Oregon ballot measures that the state's newspapers frequently editorialized how the initiative process was becoming corrupted. The Eugene *Register* penned in 1913 that "Any person with sufficient money knows that he can get any kind of legislation on the ballot." Furthermore, the Portland *Oregonian* noted, "The corporation, the 'vested interest' or 'big business,' when it takes a hand in law making, dips into a well-filled cash box and never misses the money."

In many of the states permitting direct democracy it is quite difficult (if not altogether impossible) to acquire early records documenting the campaign activity of special interests. Many of the contribution and expenditure records of early ballot issue committees that are requisite today were either not required or have been discarded by state governments. In Colorado, for example, state records from early campaigns do not exist, but there is extensive newspaper coverage of special interest activity in the first statewide ballot election of 1912. That year, citizens cast their vote on 32 ballot measures:
20 initiatives (eleven statutes and nine constitutional amendments) and six popular referendums, placed on the ballot by various organizations; and six compulsory referendums (five constitutional and one statutory), placed on the ballot by the legislature.

According to Smith and Lubinski (n.d.), the most prominent example of special interest activity in these early campaigns was a statutory referendum promoted by a land speculator, Newman Erb, who had purchased land surrounding James Peak with the hopes of having a tunnel drilled through the peak connecting Denver with Salt Lake City and the rest of the West. In addition, there were several initiatives and popular referendum on the ballot that year, including a pair of utilities bills and two versions of an eight-hour workday law for miners. In each case a citizen's group sponsored one measure while the competing counter-measure was drawn up by utility companies and mining companies, respectively. By the 1920s, Colorado special interests were hiring lawyers to draft petitions, paying solicitors up to 3 cents a name for collecting signatures on petitions, and routinely spending more than $25,000 to promote or oppose ballot initiatives (City Club of Denver, 1927).

Evidence of early special interest ballot measure activity in California is similarly quite striking. A California Senate committee issued a report in 1923 that unearthed "startlingly large expenditures in [ballot initiative] campaigns" (McCuan, et al., 1998: 57). The committee reported that an excess of $1 million was spent on seven measures on the 1922 ballot. In an effort to defeat the Water and Power Act, proponents and their opponents (led by the powerful Pacific Gas and Electric Company) spent over $660,000. By the 1930s, the process of direct democracy in California was becoming even more centralized and capital-intensive (Key, 1936; Cottrell, 1939; Kelley, 1956; Crouch, 1950; McCuan, et al., 1998). Clem Whitaker and Leone Baxter, a husband and wife team, were the leaders of this "industrialization" of the initiative process. Whitaker and Baxter joined forces in 1933 to work as campaign managers for candidates and ballot initiatives. The two public relations specialists experimented with radio and television ads, direct mail solicitation, and the use of "gimmicks" in their ballot campaigns (Kelley, 1956: 39-66). A few years later, Whitaker & Baxter's Campaigns, Inc. were running as many as five or six ballot campaigns per election (McCuan, et al., 1998: 59). In 1936, special interests spent $1.2 million fighting for and against a referendum taxing chain stores, and groups battling an initiative on a retirement life payment proposal spent almost $1 million (Crouch, 1950: 32). In the 1950s, Whitaker and Baxter were hired by Pacific Telegraph and Telephone, Standard Oil, Pacific Gas and Electric, and Southern Pacific Railroad, who collectively had raised $3.45 million to fight Proposition Four, an oil conservation initiative (Pritchell, 1958: 287; Heard, 1960, 95). The precedent for high amounts of money spent on ballot measures by special interests is deeply rooted in the history of California as well as in other states.

State Regulation of Special Interest Activity

While the involvement of special interests in direct democracy seems relatively untrammeled today, is it any different from the early days of the process? While the level of activity is perhaps different in scale, it certainly is not anything new. Special interests have attempted to use the process to their advantage whenever possible. With this history in mind, what is to be done? Will it ever be possible to devolve direct democracy to "the people," as Populists and Progressives originally intended?

Efforts to regulate the role of special interests in the process of direct democracy is currently underfoot in several states (Drage, 1999). This is nothing new. Since the early 1900s, states allowing the initiative and referendum have tried to check the activity of special interests in a variety of ways. Two regulations in particular bear mentioning. As early as the 1940s, several states passed laws prohibiting payment to circulators to collect signatures in order to qualify measures for the ballot (Grant, 1996). These laws were intended to purify the initiative and referendum process by forcing special interests to use volunteers to circulate petitions. The United States Supreme Court in its 1988 decision, *Meyer v. Grant*, overturned these laws by unanimously striking down Colorado's ban on paid signature gatherers. Beginning as early as the 1910s, quite a few states tried to eliminate corporate expenditures on ballot measures. By the early 1970s, in fact, nearly half of the states permitting direct democracy had some form of limitations on either the campaign contributions or expenditures of ballot issue committees (Shockley, 1980: 8). In 1974, for example, voters in California passed Proposition 9, the Political Reform Act. The initiative limited the spending by issue committees sponsoring or opposing ballot measures to $1.2 million each. Montana had a law dating back to 1912 banning corporate spending on ballot campaigns (Winkler, 1998: 140). By the mid-1970s, though, the state laws in California and Montana and most other states were found to be unconstitutional by the courts. With its 1978 decision, *First National Bank of Boston v. Bellotti*, the Supreme Court weighed in on the matter, and invalidated Massachusetts's limits on corporate contributions to ballot measures on First Amendment grounds.

It is important to note that prior to being struck down by the courts, these state regulations had relatively minor success in mitigating the role of special interests. It is highly unlikely, therefore, that any current legislative attempts to rein in the influence of special interests — even if they could pass constitutional muster — would have much success either. The reason for this is fairly straightforward. One way or another, special interest money will find its way into the process of direct democracy. As such, there are good reasons not to try to restrict special interest money in the process, as increased state regulation may produce some severe unintended consequences.

Take, for example, the current involvement in ballot campaigns by some non-profit, 501(c)(3) organizations and some "educational" committees. These organizations, which do not have to list their donors (and in the case of 501(c)(3) organizations, may receive unlimited, tax deductible contributions from their benefactors), are legally eligible to participate in ballot measure campaigns (Colvin and Finley, 1996). It is possible, then, for special interests to make unregulated and anonymous contributions to initiative and referendum campaigns by funneling their money through these non-profit or "educational" organizations serving as conduits.

A case in point is the role of Grover Norquist's non-profit and "nonpartisan" organization, Americans for Tax Reform. ATR was behind several statewide ballot campaigns in the late 1990s. There is substantial evidence that the Republican National Committee transferred more than $4.5 million to Norquist's ATR in 1996 for the explicit purpose of promoting conservative ballot measures (Smith, 1998c; Levin, 1997). As it turns out, Norquist did funnel a substantial amount of this money to issue groups in California, Colorado, and Oregon to promote conservative initiatives, including anti-tax, right to work, and "paycheck protection" ballot measures. In 1996, ATR contributed $509,500 to Bill Sizemore's group, Oregon Taxpayers United, to promote a tax limitation measure, and in 1998, it provided $441,000 to the Campaign Reform Initiative in California, the sponsoring group of Proposition 226, the paycheck protection measure (Smith, 1998c; California Secretary of State, 1998).

Similarly, in 1998 in Colorado, the libertarian-leaning Independence Institute, which is formally registered as a nonprofit 501(c)(3) group, laundered campaign contributions to the issue committee backing Amendment 17, a tax credit program to help parents offset the cost of sending their children to private schools. Steve Schuck — who served simultaneously as the Chairman of the Independence Institute and the director of Coloradans for School Choice, the political committee that sponsored Amendment 17 — freely admitted to the press that he intentionally routed campaign contributions through the non-profit Institute. According to Schuck, this scheme had real benefits, as "The contributor gets the advantage of passing the money through a tax-deductible organization," and that the donors to the institute can remain anonymous (McPhee, 1998).

Conclusion

Although it may come as a surprise to some observers, special interests have played a major role in direct democracy ballot measures since the turn of the 20th century. For nearly 100 years, vested interests have tried to influence the process of initiative and referendum in the American states. While by no means have these groups always been successful in their endeavors, special interests have not been shy about trying to use the process of direct democracy to their own advantage. There is little indication that they will voluntarily lessen their involvement in the initiative and referendum process in the future.

Regulatory actions by the states, many of which have been overturned in the courts, have done little to curb the activity of special interests. But such legislation, even if it were to be upheld as constitutional, likely would do little to eliminate the influence of special interests in the process of direct democracy. The recent (and growing) practice by special interests of funneling contributions through nonpartisan or "educational" organizations (or even making their own "independent expenditures" for or against a ballot measure) is likely to become more common in direct democracy campaigns. These ballot campaign practices, which are perfectly legal, provide special interests with tax-deductible incentives as well as anonymity.

Direct Democracy emerged in the late 19th century out of a widespread popular concern of moneyed special interests controlling the legislative process. Ironically, due to protections afforded under the First Amendment, the relatively unregulated process of direct democracy has catered to special interests just as much as it has to citizen groups. While it is impossible to predict what the 21st century holds for the initiative and referendum, it appears fairly certain that special interests will continue to have a hand in shaping the process.

References

Barnett, James. 1915. *The Operation of the Initiative, Referendum, and Recall in Oregon.* New York: MacMillan Co.

Beard, Charles. 1912. "Introduction." In Charles Beard and Birl Shultz, *Documents on the State-wide Initiative, Referendum and Recall.* New York: MacMillan Co.

Bowler, Shaun, and Todd Donovan. 1998. *Demanding Choices.* Ann Arbor: University of Michigan Press.

Billings, Erin. 1998. "Big bucks couldn't sway state voters." *Missoulian* (December 6). Available: missoulian.com/archives.

Braunstein, Richard. 1999. "Big Money and Ballot Issues: Do Voters Care Where the Money Comes From?" Paper prepared for presentation at the 1999 Western Political Science Association Meeting, Seattle, Washington (March).

California Secretary of State. 1998. "Late Contributions and Independent Expenditures." Primary Election. Available: ss.ca.gov/prd/bmprimary98.

California Voter Foundation. 1998. "Top Ten Contributors." Available: calvoter.org/98general/followthemoney/topten1.html.

City Club of Denver. 1927. "Direct Legislation in Colorado." Denver: Eames Brothers.

Colorado Secretary of State. 1998. "Report of Contributions and Expenditures." (July 1–December 31).

Colvin, Gregory and Lowell Finley. 1996. "Seize the Initiative." Washington, DC: The Alliance for Justice.

Common Cause. 1999. "National Parties Raise $193 Million in Soft Money during 1997–1998 Election Cycle." Available: commoncause.org/publications/020399.htm.

Cordes, Henry. 1999. "Initiative 414 Spending Set Record." *Omaha World-Herald* (January 7).

Cottrell, Edwin. 1939. "Twenty Five Years of Direct Legislation in California. *Public Opinion Quarterly* (January): 30-45.

Cronin, Thomas. 1989. *Direct Democracy: The Politics of Initiative, Referendum, and Recall.* Cambridge: Harvard University Press.

Crouch, Winston. 1950. *The Initiative and Referendum in California.* Los Angeles: The Haynes Foundation.

Cushman, Robert. 1916. "Recent Experience with the Initiative and Referendum." *American Political Science Review* (August) 10: 532-39.

Drage, Jennie. 1999. "1999 Initiative & Referendum Legislation." National Conference of State Legislatures. Briefing notes prepared for the 1999 Initiative & Referendum Institute Conference, Washington, DC (May).

Eaton, Allen. 1912. *The Oregon System*. Chicago: McClurg and Co.

Ellis, Richard. 1999. "The Myth of the Golden Age of the Initiative and Referendum." Paper prepared for presentation at the 1999 Pacific Northwest Political Science Association Meeting, Eugene, Oregon (October).

Florida Secretary of State. 1998. "Florida Campaign Finance Database." Available: election.dos.state.fl.us/campfin/cfindb.shtml.

Garrett, Elizabeth. 1997. "Perspective on Direct Democracy: Who Directs Direct Democracy?" *University of Chicago Law School Roundtable*, 4: 17-36.

Gerber, Elisabeth. 1999. *The Populist Paradox: Interest Group Influence and the Promise of Direct Legislation*. Princeton: Princeton University Press.

Grant, Paul. 1996. "Citizen Initiatives under Attack in Colorado." Independence Institute. Available: iandrinstitute.org/indepth/document6/.

Heard, Alexander. 1960. *The Costs of Democracy*. Chapel Hill: University of North Carolina Press.

Initiative & Referendum Institute. 1998. "Revised Overview of Statewide Initiatives, Popular Referendum and Legislative Referendum on the 1998 Election Ballot." Available: iandrinstitute.org/updates.

Kelley, Stanley. 1956. *Professional Public Relations and Political Power*. Baltimore: The Johns Hopkins University Press.

Key, V.O. 1936. "Publicity of Campaign Expenditures on Issues in California." *American Political Science Review*, 4: 713-723.

Levin, Carl. 1997. "Incomplete Hearings from the Senate Campaign Finance Investigation." Congressional Record. 105th Congress, 1st Session (November 10). Available: senate.gov/~levin/floor/111097a.htm.

Los Angeles Times. 1998. "Initiatives: Use and Abuse" (April 19).

Magleby, David. 1994. "Direct Legislation in the American States." In David Butler and Austin Ranney, eds., *Referendums around the World*. Washington, DC: American Enterprise Institute.

McCuan, David, et al. 1998. "California's Political Warriors: Campaign Professionals and the Initiative Process." In Shaun Bowler, Todd Donovan, and Caroline Tolbert, eds., *Citizens as Legislators: Direct*

Democracy in the United States. Columbus: Ohio State University Press, pp. 55-79.

McPhee, Mike. 1998. "Schuck IRS violations alleged." *Denver Post* (September 2).

Morain, Dan. 1999a. "Wealth Buys Access to State Politics." *Los Angeles Times* (April 18).

———. 1999b. "Governor Race Set Spending Record." *Los Angeles Times* (February 4).

Munro, William, ed. 1912. *The Initiative, Referendum, and Recall.* New York: Appleton and Co.

Pritchell, Robert. 1958. "The Influence of Professional Campaign Management Firms in Partisan Elections in California." *Western Political Quarterly,* 11: 278-300.

Schmidt, David. 1989. *Citizen Lawmakers: The Ballot Initiative Revolution.* Philadelphia: Temple University Press.

Schrag, Peter. 1998. *Paradise Lost: California's Experience, America's Future.* New York: New Press.

Shockley, John. 1980. *The Initiative Process in Colorado Politics: An Assessment.* Bureau of Governmental Research and Service, University of Colorado.

Smith, Daniel. 2001. "Campaign Financing of Ballot Initiatives in the American States." In Larry Sabato et al., *Dangerous Democracy? The Battle over Ballot Initiatives in America.*

———. 1998a. *Tax Crusaders and the Politics of Direct Democracy.* New York: Rutledge.

———. 1998b. "Unmasking the Tax Crusaders." *State Government News,* 41, 2 (March): 18-21.

———. 1998c. "The Legacy of Howard Jarvis and Proposition 13? 1996 Tax Limitation Initiatives in the American States." Paper Presented at the Annual Meeting of the Western Political Science Association, Los Angeles, CA (March).

———, and Joseph Lubinski. n.d. "The 'Golden Era' of Direct Democracy? Evidence from the Colorado Election of 1912." University of Denver. Unpublished manuscript.

Wilcox, Delos. 1912. *Government by All the People.* New York: MacMillan Co.

Winkler, Adam. 1998. "Beyond Bellotti." *Loyola of Los Angeles Law Review,* 32: 133-220.

Chapter 5

Money in the Initiative and Referendum Process: Evidence of Its Effects and Prospects for Reform

By Elizabeth Garrett and Elisabeth R. Gerber [*]

Several chapters in this volume have documented the increasing use of initiatives and referendums in many states. They have also shown that as policy advocates more frequently appeal directly to citizens, they have devoted larger and larger sums to direct legislation campaigns. In 1998, for example, issue committees across the country spent nearly $400 million promoting and opposing measures on ballots in 44 states,[1] up from the $117 million spent in 21 states in 1992.[2] In California alone, an estimated $256 million was spent in 1998 by groups in campaigns concerning ballot questions.[3] These figures are, by any measure, substantial, and they have intensified concerns that well-funded organized interests unduly influence the initiative and referendum process.[4]

As suggestive as these recent numbers might be, however, evaluating claims that money disproportionately influences direct democracy is difficult because arguments about the nature and extent of this influence are

* We thank Alina McLauchlan and Paul Skiermont for research assistance.

1. Initiative & Referendum Institute, Revised Overview of Statewide Initiatives, Popular Referendum and Legislative Referendum on the 1998 Election Ballot (1998). See also Elisabeth R. Gerber, *The Populist Paradox: Interest Group Influence and the Promise of Direct Legislation* 5 (1999) (detailing growth of spending in 1980s and 1990s).

2. David B. Magleby, Let the Voters Decide? An Assessment of the Initiative and Referendum Process, 66 U. Colo. L. Rev. 13, 30 (1995).

3. See California Secretary of State, Financing California's Statewide Ballot Measures on the November 3, 1998 General Election Ballot: Campaign Receipts and Expenditures Through December 31, 1998 at http://www.ss.ca.gov/prd/bmprimary98_final/bmprimary 98_final_mainpage.htm.

4. See, e.g., Richard Briffault, Ballot Propositions and Campaign Finance Reform, 1 NYU. J. Legis. & Pub. Pol'y 41, 43-44 (1997); John S. Shockley, Direct Democracy, Campaign Finance, and the Courts: Can Corruption, Undue Influence, and Declining Voter Confidence be Found? 39 U. Miami L. Rev. 377, 392-395 (1985).

often imprecise and couched in ideologically charged rhetoric. One claim is that moneyed interests involved in direct democracy will resort to fraud more frequently than will groups that rely on volunteers.[5] This argument has been advanced by reformers who seek to restrict expenditures in issue campaigns.[6] However, no empirical evidence has been produced to support the assertion of fraud.[7] Furthermore, there is good reason to doubt this claim, even in the absence of hard empirical evidence, because professionals in the initiative industry have incentives to avoid questionable or illegal tactics that will tarnish their reputations in the campaign consultancy marketplace.

A second concern is that the same sorts of quid pro quo corruption and the appearance of such corruption—the traditional justifications for regulation of campaign finance in candidate elections[8]—may also be present in the context of direct democracy. The Supreme Court has generally maintained that direct democracy is inherently free of quid pro quo corruption and has therefore been hostile to laws regulating contributions to and expenditures in issue campaigns. The justices have reasoned that in elections on initiatives and referendums, there are no candidates who can dispense favors to wealthy interests in return for contributions.[9] This reasoning may be overly simplistic, however. Candidates for office increasingly use ballot questions as part of their campaigns.[10] For example, in 1974, California gubernatorial candidate Jerry Brown backed initiatives on campaign finance and lobbying reform to underscore his commitment to clean government.[11] In a different political climate, California Governor Pete Wilson supported an initiative curtailing state-provided services for illegal aliens.[12] Candidates who coordinate their campaigns with ballot questions are no doubt grateful for the resources of groups that pay for petition drives, advertisements, and other electoral strategies. One could argue

---

5. See, e.g., Tort and Insurance Practice Section of the American Bar Association, *The Challenge of Direct Democracy in a Republic: Report and Recommendation of the Task Force on Initiatives and Referenda* 57 (1992).

6. See Buckley v. American Constitutional Law Found., Inc., 119 S.Ct. 636, 647-648 (1999); Meyer v. Grant, 486 U.S. 414, 425-26 (1988).

7. See Meyer v. Grant, 486 at 425-426.

8. See Buckley v. Valeo, 424 U.S. 1, 26-29 (1976) (per curiam).

9. See First Nat'l Bank of Boston v. Bellotti, 435 U.S. 765, 790 (1978).

10. Stephen Nicholson, *Rethinking Voting Behavior: Agenda, Priming and Spillover Effects in U.S. Elections*, Doctoral dissertation, Department of Political Science, University of California, Davis (1998).

11. David D. Schmidt, *Citizen Lawmakers: The Ballot Initiative Revolution* 28 (1989).

12. Peter Schrag, *Paradise Lost: California's Experience, America's Future* 225-34 (1998).

that this relationship comes close to the kind of quid pro quo corruption sufficient to justify regulation in the candidate election arena.

A third concern is that the involvement of wealthy interests in the direct legislation process may distort political outcomes. Critics who make this assertion fear that well-funded interests, who often dominate the traditional legislative arena, also exert substantial influence over initiatives and referendums. This attack highlights a potential paradox: instruments of direct democracy were established to provide outsider groups access to lawmaking in a world where well-funded entrenched interests, like the railroads, controlled the agenda in state legislatures.[13] The progressive and populist ideals that gave rise to initiatives and referendums are potentially undermined if interests with clout in the legislative branch also disproportionately influence direct lawmaking.[14]

Those who argue about the influence of money over direct legislation outcomes tend to focus on two distinct stages of the process. One set of critics is concerned about the effects of money in the qualification stage.[15] These critics argue that money spent during qualification undermines the grassroots nature of the process. They contend that when interests can use money in place of volunteers to collect signatures, it becomes less obvious that the measures they promote have the broad-based popular support that meeting a substantial signature threshold is supposed to indicate.[16] They also argue that qualifying measures for the ballot carries important advantages, even if the measures ultimately fail, and interests that can qualify their measures strictly by virtue of their financial resources disproportionately benefit from these advantages.

A second set of critics is concerned about the effects of money in direct legislation campaigns. These critics contend that by spending large sums to promote or defeat ballot measures, wealthy interest groups can affect what issues win and what issues lose on election day.[17] Along similar lines, some argue that the dominance of money crowds out certain interests from the process. They contend that when some interests spend a lot of money

---

13. See Elisabeth R. Gerber, supra note 1, at 4-5.

14. See Bruce E. Cain & Kenneth Miller, "The Populist Legacy: Initiatives and the Undermining of Representative Government," Working paper, Institute of Governmental Studies, Berkeley, CA (nd.).

15. See Daniel Hays Lowenstein & Robert M. Stern, The First Amendment and Paid Initiative Petition Circulators: A Dissenting View and a Proposal, 17 HASTINGS CONST. L.Q. 175 (1989); Elizabeth Garrett, Money, Agenda Setting, and Direct Democracy, 77 TEX. L. REV. 1845 (1999).

16. See Daniel Hays Lowenstein & Robert M. Stern, supra note 15, at 199.

17. See Special Interest Spending; Laws for Sale, L.A. TIMES, Oct. 28, 1998 at 6. See also Richard Briffault, supra note 4, at 54-56; John S. Shockley, supra note 4, at 393-400.

in an initiative or referendum campaign, other interests must follow suit. Those who cannot raise comparable sums cannot make their positions heard and thus cannot compete.

In this chapter, we consider evidence regarding the validity of some of these claims. Specifically, we focus on concerns about the influence of money over direct legislation outcomes. We first review existing empirical evidence about money in the qualification and campaign stages of the direct legislation process. This brief review concludes that while the dominance of money in the qualification process may in fact have some impact on the types of measures that make it to the ballot and the types of interests that can promote their objectives through ballot initiatives, its effects on election outcomes are quite limited. We then present some new evidence from recent direct legislation campaigns in California to show that while the amount of money being spent in direct legislation campaigns has increased dramatically in recent years, its effects are still limited. We end by discussing the implications of these results for proposed reforms.

Evidence: Money and Qualification

One of the most striking recent developments in direct legislation in states across the country is the nearly universal reliance on professional signature gatherers. Parts of the initiative industry specialize in signature gathering; indeed, some firms offer money-back guarantees to back up their claims that they will succeed in meeting signature thresholds.[18] In California it now takes more than $1 million to qualify a statewide question using only paid circulators,[19] and groups are willing to pay such sums because they thereby ensure qualification. For a number of reasons—ready availability of paid circulators, virtual assurance of qualification, short circulation period, and large number of signatures required—even some cit-

---

18. See California Commission on Campaign Financing, *Democracy by Initiative: Shaping California's Fourth Branch of Government, Report and Recommendations of the California Commission on Campaign Finance* 157 exhibit 4A (1992) (reproducing an advertisement of Advanced Voter Communication).

19. Charlene Wear Simmons, California's Statewide Initiative Process, 1997 CAL. RES. BUREAU 9. This figure is a conservative estimate. See David S. Broder, The Ballot Battle: Collecting Signatures for a Price, WASH. POST, Apr. 12, 1998, at A1, A28 (estimating that the cost in California is closer to $2 million). See also Jean McMillan, Corporations Spending Big Bucks for Signature Gathering, THE PATRIOT LEDGER, Jan. 24, 2000, at 2 (noting that corporations have spent $2-$4 per signature in petition drives in Massachusetts and that paid gatherers are more frequently used now than before).

izen groups that have traditionally relied on volunteers are now turning to paid circulators and professional firms for help.[20]

As money becomes the only certain route to ballot access, observers of direct democracy worry that the character of the process is determined disproportionately by those with financial resources. Only groups or individuals with access to significant financial resources can afford paid circulators. Thus, the paradox described above holds true in the context of qualification. When success in ballot qualification is determined by the same factors that contribute to influence in the legislature, such as sophisticated direct mail techniques, money, and connections with professional political consultants, then groups with expertise and clout in the traditional legislative arena will also have an advantage with respect to qualifying initiatives and referendums.

Although qualification for the ballot does not ensure that a proposal will become law, qualification carries its own advantages. First, a petition drive and successful qualification effort can catapult an issue to a prominent place on the policy agenda.[21] It can serve as a focusing event and draw the attention of the public and policymakers to the issue, thereby affecting the state and sometimes the national policy agendas. For example, the issue of term limits for state and federal legislators became a prominent issue largely because of direct democracy, and the debate about affirmative action has been fueled by high profile initiatives in California and other states. Second, as noted above, the mere presence of a particular question on the ballot can affect the electoral prospects of candidates running in the same election and thereby influence the composition of a state's legislature or executive branch.

Qualifying an initiative that appears likely to be adopted can also have a different and more complex indirect effect on the traditional legislative process. Proponents can use the possibility that the people will adopt direct legislation as a threat in a bargaining game with the legislature to force representatives to enact legislation on issues that they would rather avoid.[22] In 1998, for example, Silicon Valley entrepreneurs spent $3.5 million to qualify a charter schools ballot question and promised to spend millions more in the campaign. They agreed to pull the question from the ballot only

---

20. See Elizabeth Garrett, supra note 15, at 1852-53.

21. See John W. Kingdon, *Agendas, Alternatives, and Public Policies* 18-19, 208 (1984) (discussing the importance of political processes and entities like political parties in defining the agenda). See also Elizabeth Garrett, supra note 15, at 1855-57 (discussing the role of ballot qualification in setting the statewide and national policy agendas).

22. See Elisabeth R. Gerber, supra note 1, at 51 ("[G]roups may be able to persuade the state legislature to pass a law they support if they can…credibly threaten to pass an initiative the legislature opposes.").

after the state legislature and governor enacted a compromise charter schools law. The credible threat to use direct democracy was necessary to dislodge entrenched interests such as teachers' unions that opposed reform and that exerted influence at several potential bottlenecks in the legislative process.[23]

Although qualifying a measure for the ballot makes a particular issue more salient for lawmakers, the availability of direct democracy may produce indirect effects on representative institutions even in cases where activists do not actually mount a petition drive. Recent empirical work suggests that lawmakers in states permitting initiatives enact a different sort of legislation than laws enacted in states without initiatives. Gerber, for example, concludes that, under certain conditions, legislation on issues that are likely to be the subject of a popular vote will be closer to the preferences of the median voter.[24] The effect is most pronounced in states where access to direct democracy is easiest. Groups can also exert indirect influence by using direct democracy to signal a group's preferences to lawmakers in a costly and credible way. Such a signal can be produced either by supporting a particular ballot question or by opposing one.

Evidence: Money and Election Outcomes

A number of studies have attempted to establish and measure the relationship between campaign spending and election outcomes. Three main results emerge from this body of scholarship. First, it is clear that money does not necessarily determine outcomes. Despite Cronin's assertion that "[m]oney is, other things being equal, the single most important factor determining direct legislation outcomes,"[25] the side that spends the most often fails. Price finds that the side that spent more won in only 55% of the

---

23. See Elizabeth Garrett, supra note 15, at 1859-1861 (discussing the charter schools example in greater detail). See also Steven Rosenfeld, Entrepreneurs Spending Millions in California on Ballot Measures to Have Their Way on Specific Issues, National Public Radio's Morning Edition, Aug. 30, 1999 (discussing this example and others).

24. Elisabeth R. Gerber, Legislative Response to the Threat of Popular Initiatives, 40 Am. J. Pol. Sci. 99 (1996) (finding that legislators in states that allow initiatives pass parental consent laws that more closely resemble states' median voters' preferences than legislators in states without initiatives). See also Elisabeth R. Gerber, supra note 1, at 135 (similar findings with respect to parental consent and death penalty laws).

25. See Thomas E. Cronin, Direct Democracy: The Politics of Initiative, Referendum, and Recall 215 (1989).

29 initiative campaigns he studied.[26] These results are consistent with the large number of studies that analyze the relationship between spending and outcomes, although the studies mask important differences across campaigns, which we discuss below.

A second main result, which emphasizes differences across campaigns, is that money spent to defeat initiatives and referendums is more effective than money spent to pass them. In his important early study, Lowenstein finds that between 1968 and 1980 in California, in elections where spending levels exceeded $250,000 and one side had a two-to-one spending advantage, opposition committees defeated nine of ten measures they opposed and proponent committees won 64 percent of the time.[27] Owens and Wade replicate these results on a larger sample of initiatives, finding that opponents defeated initiatives and referendums through one-sided opposition spending in 91% of the 708 measures they study, although they also find that the one-sidedness emphasized by Lowenstein does not appear to matter to this result.[28] Similarly, Magleby finds that opponents with a substantial spending advantage defeated the measures they opposed 87% of the time.[29] More recent work by Magleby finds that substantial spending increased the likelihood of "no" voting in 24 states with initiatives and popular referendums.[30] These consistent empirical results are buttressed by the findings of several more qualitative studies, revealing a similar relationship between money and the defeat of ballot questions.[31]

---

26. Charles Price, Initiative Campaigns: Afloat on a Sea of Cash, 19 CAL. J. 481, 485 (1988).

27. Daniel H. Lowenstein, Campaign Spending and Ballot Propositions: Recent Experience, Public Choice Theory and the First Amendment, 29 UCLA L. REV. 505, 543-44 (1982).

28. See John R. Owens & Larry L. Wade, Campaign Spending on California Ballot Propositions, Trends and Effects, 1924-1984, 39 WESTERN POL. Q. 675, 684-87 (1986).

29. David B. Magleby, Direct Legislation: Voting on Ballot Propositions in the United States 147 (1984).

30. See David B. Magleby, supra note 2, at 39.

31. See Betty Zisk, Money, Media, and the Grass Roots, State Ballot Issues and the Electoral Process 92-98 (1987); Steven Lydenberg, Business Big Spenders Hit the Referenda Votes, 47 BUS. & SOC. REV. 54-55 (1983); John Shockley, The Initiative Process in Colorado Politics: An Assessment (1980); John Shockley, IRS Administration of Tax Laws Relating to Lobbying (Part I): Hearings Before a Subcommittee of the House Committee on Government Operations, 95th Cong., 2d Sess 239-40 (1978); see also Daniel A. Smith, Campaign Finance of Ballot Initiatives in the American States, in Dangerous Democracy? The Battle over Ballot Initiatives in America, Chapter 4 (L. Sabato et al. 2001) (forthcoming) (discussing studies).

There are several possible explanations for the observed relationship between opposition spending and election outcomes. Perhaps the most compelling is presented by Bowler and Donovan, who consider the relationship between spending and outcomes at the level of the individual voter.[32] Consistent with the aggregate results described above, Bowler and Donovan find that spending to oppose a proposition is associated with a greater probability that an individual votes "no," but that spending in favor of a ballot question does not have the same effect on an individual's probability of voting "yes." They explain this result by linking spending to the information it produces for voters. Many scholars have observed that voters have very little information about ballot questions when they cast their votes; unlike in candidate elections, voters lack the important cues of party affiliation and incumbency.[33] Voters search for alternate cues in direct democracy, and many determine their position on the basis of the identity of the groups supporting and opposing a particular proposition. If a voter knows who is behind an issue and can determine whether her preferences align or diverge from that group, she is more likely to cast the same vote as she would if she had full information.[34] Issue campaigns characterized by heavy expenditures can produce helpful voting cues by revealing the identities of supporters and opponents, by publicizing elite and partisan endorsements, and by placing the campaign within familiar conceptual frameworks. Bowler and Donovan suggest that heavy, one-sided affirmative spending may actually increase negative voting if it reveals that a disfavored group, such as a cigarette manufacturer or an insurance company, is a major backer of the ballot proposal. In addition, although contested campaigns increase voter participation, the noise that the expenditure of so much money produces may actually result in defensive "no" voting as the electorate begins to worry that such a substantial policy change may have unexpected deleterious consequences.[35]

---

32. Shaun Bowler & Todd Donovan, *Demanding Choices: Opinion, Voting, and Direct Democracy* (1998).

33. See Thomas E. Cronin, supra note 25, at 67; David B. Magleby, supra note 29, at 146.

34. See, e.g., Arthur Lupia, Shortcuts versus Encyclopedias: Information and Voting Behavior in California Insurance Reform Elections, 88 Am. Pol. Sci. Rev. 63 (1994); Elisabeth R. Gerber & Arthur Lupia, Campaign Competition and Policy Responsiveness in Direct Legislation Elections, 17 Pol. Behav. 287 (1995).

35. See Bowler & Donovan, supra note 32, at 53-55, suggesting a second effect of money on direct democracy. Campaigns in which large amounts of wealth are deployed are also associated with greater voter participation. This result is not surprising; people are more likely to have formed opinions on issues that have become the subject of visible and contested campaigns, and therefore they are more likely to vote. If one of the benefits of direct democracy is that it increases citizen involvement in governance, decreases feel-

A third main result of the literature on money and election outcomes is that not all campaign money has the same effect. Gerber finds that campaign contributions from citizen groups are associated with greater success in passing initiatives than are contributions from economic groups. Gerber analyzes contributions to 161 ballot measure campaigns in 8 states to assess whether the source of support—from economic interests or from citizen groups—plays a role in its influence on direct legislation outcomes.[36] Economic groups, whose members are representatives of their employers or businesses (if self-employed), tend to deploy substantial monetary resources in initiative campaigns, while citizen groups, whose members are autonomous individuals, rely on their comparative advantage in mobilizing personnel resources. Gerber finds that ballot measures that receive a majority of their support from citizen interests pass at a significantly higher rate than those that receive majority support from economic interests. However, when she employs multivariate statistical analyses to control for other factors that may also affect passage rates, she finds a negative relationship between contributions from economic groups and a measure's vote margin and passage rate and no statistical relationship between contributions from citizen groups and a measure's success.[37] In other words, an additional dollar of contributions from economic groups reduces a measure's vote margin and passage rate, all else constant, while an additional dollar of contributions from citizen groups has no net effect, again all else constant.

There are several possible explanations for this observed negative relationship between contributions from economic interests and a measure's vote margin and passage rate. One possibility is that contributions from and expenditures by economic interests actually reduce voter support for a proposition. As Bowler and Donovan explain, when voters observe large contributions and expenditures being made by groups whose interests are known to be opposed to their own on a particular issue, they may (correctly)

---

ings of alienation, and works to instill civic virtue in people, then expensive campaigns may produce positive outcomes along this dimension. Moreover, if the results of popular elections are legitimate because they reflect the will of the majority of the people, greater voter turnout enhances legitimacy by encouraging more citizens to cast their ballots. Bowler and Donovan's work also suggests that the information provided in such campaigns may increase the likelihood that such ballots are cast competently.

36. See Elisabeth R. Gerber, supra note 1, at 101-120. See also California Commission on Campaign Financing, supra note 18, at 160-61 (1992) (suggesting inverse relationship between dollars spent to qualify a question for the ballot and voter approval); Dennis C. Mueller, Constitutional Democracy 184-85 (1996) (similar results in study of Swiss cantons).

37. These factors include whether the measure is an initiative or referendum, total spending, and other campaign characteristics.

infer that their own interests are better served by a "no" vote. This negative signal often corresponds to the type of groups involved in the campaign. To the extent that many initiatives pit the interests of narrow economic groups against the interests of consumers or broad-based citizen groups, this signaling will produce the observed negative relationship between contributions from economic interests and support. In these cases, campaign activity actually decreases, rather than increases, popular support.

A second possibility is that the difference in passage rates reflects a difference in the substance of the policies advocated by citizen and economics interests. The two types of groups pursue systematically different agendas, and the policies advocated by citizens groups may resonate more broadly with voters than the issues supported by economic interests. To the extent that this is true, we would expect policies advocated by economic interests to receive less public support, independent of any campaign activity. In other words, it may not be the expenditures by economic interests that lead to lower vote shares, per se, but rather the content of the measures these groups advocate. Thus, measures sponsored by economic interests may attract less public support and, all else constant, require higher levels of campaign advertising to achieve comparable levels of support.

To summarize, the empirical literature on money's relationship to direct legislation outcomes confirms that the effects of money are important but limited. Money is sufficient to qualify measures for the ballot. It is necessary but not sufficient to pass new laws by initiative, although it may be used to great effect to defeat ballot proposals. Research on the sources of campaign contributions concludes that resources mobilized by citizen groups are more successful at passing new initiatives, while resources mobilized by economic interests allow them to block new initiatives and preserve the status quo.

Recent Evidence from California, 1992-1998

In the introduction to this chapter, we described how the frequency of initiatives and the amount spent on their campaigns have increased in recent years. We now consider whether these changes have translated into differences in campaign dynamics. Are expenditures to defeat initiatives and referendums still more effective than expenditures to pass them? Does the concentration of resources (i.e., one-sidedness and average contribution size) matter? Do economic interests continue to face greater difficulties in passing new initiatives, despite their advantages in financial resources? To address these questions, we analyze contribution and expenditure data from campaign finance reports filed in California ballot measure campaigns from November 1992 through November 1998. During this period, there were 87 statewide ballot measures, including 43 initiatives and 44 referendums. 24 of these referendums reported no campaign activity for or against the measure and so are omitted from much of the subsequent analysis.

Total Contributions

We begin by describing the amount of money involved in the 63 statewide ballot measures between 1992 and 1998 that reported some campaign activities. Table 1 reports total contributions to all ballot measures, total contributions to initiatives only, average contributions to initiatives, and the standard deviation of contributions to initiatives. We report contributions rather than expenditures because reporting requirements allow us to directly link contributions, but not expenditures, to sources of support.

Over the seven elections covered in this analysis, more than a half billion dollars was spent on the 63 statewide measures. Initiatives accounted for about half of all measures on the ballot and two-thirds of those reporting campaign activity. However, they accounted for the vast majority (nearly 95%) of total contributions. The average contribution to initiatives was $11.5 million, but the standard deviation was over $16 million, indicating a great deal of variability across measures. The minimum

---

Table 1. Contributions to CA Ballot Measures, 1992–1998*

	Contributions
All measures—total	$522,109,052
Initiatives—total	$495,858,624
Initiatives—average	$ 11,531,596
Initiatives—std dev	$ 16,270,388

* Sources: California Secretary of State, "California's Statewide Ballot Measures: 1992 General Election Campaign Financing" August 1993; "California's Special Statewide Election, November 2, 1993, Ballot Measure Campaign Financing," March 1994; "Financing California's Statewide Ballot Measures, 1994 Primary and General Elections," July 1995; "Financing California's Statewide Ballot Measures, 1996 Primary and General Elections," Internet address www.ss.ca.gov/prd/bmc96/coverbm96.htm; "Financing California's Statewide Ballot Measures: Campaign Receipts and Expenditures Through June 30, 1998," Internet address www.ss.ca.gov/prd/bmprimary98_2/98PrimPropsMainPage.htm; "Financing California's Statewide Ballot Measures on the November 3, 1998 General Election Ballot: Campaign Receipts and Expenditures Through December 31, 1998," Internet address www.ss.ca.gov/prd/ bmprimary98_final/bmprimary98_final_mainpage.htm.

Table 2. Supporting and Opposing Contributions,
CA Ballot Measures, 1992–1998

	Total	Supporting	Opposing
All measures—total	$522,109,052	$237,533,788	$284,575,264
Initiatives—total	$495,858,624	$213,818,496	$282,040,128
Initiatives—average	$11,531,596	$4,972,523	$6,559,073
Passed inits—avg	$10,630,772	$6,032,440	$4,598,332
Failed inits—avg	$2,180,189	$4,209,383	$7,970,806

level of contributions to an initiative was $401,648 (Proposition 225, 1998 Primary), while the maximum was $96,301,120 (Proposition 5, 1998 General).

Contributions and Success Rates

We next consider whether money spent to oppose initiatives is more "successful," in terms of leading to a measure's defeat, than money spent to support initiatives, in terms of leading to a measure's passage. Table 2 breaks down contributions according to whether they were made to support or oppose a measure. It also compares these figures for initiatives that ultimately passed and failed.

Approximately 45% of all contributions to initiatives were made to support changes to the status quo, while 55% were made to block new initiatives. Successful initiatives received more supporting contributions than opposing contributions, on average, and received more supporting contributions than did unsuccessful initiatives. Unsuccessful initiatives received, on average, 65% of their contributions from opponents. These patterns are consistent with the findings in the empirical literature that contributions against initiatives are associated with higher rates of failure.

While these aggregate figures are suggestive of a relationship between supporting and opposing contributions and passage rates, they may mask important differences across measures. To reveal some of these differences, we separately analyze initiatives that received more contributions from proponents and those that received more contributions from opponents. This analysis is intended to replicate the work of Lowenstein, Owens and Wade, and Magleby described earlier.

The top row of Table 3 reports that forty-two percent of the 43 initiatives passed. When we limit consideration to those initiatives for which supporting contributions outnumbered opposing contributions by at least

Table 3. Passage Rates of One-Sided Initiatives

	N	% Passed
All Initiatives	43	42
One-Sided Yes	16	75
One-Sided No	16	31
Yes > No	21	57
Yes < No	22	27

two-to-one, the passage rate is substantially higher, at 75%.[38] Measures that were the subject of one-sided opposing campaigns passed at a much lower rate, of 31%. These figures are both higher than those reported by Lowenstein and others. In other words, the passage rate for one-sided supporting campaigns is higher in this recent data, and the passage rate for one-sided opposing campaigns is also higher (i.e., the failure rate is lower).[39]

In the last two rows of Table 3, we compare passage rates of all initiatives for which supporting contributions exceeded opposing contributions, and for which opposing contributions exceeded supporting contributions. These results are roughly similar to those previously reported in Table 3 for one-sided campaigns, although the passage rates for both categories are lower than in the preceding rows, at 57% and 27% respectively.

While the results in Table 3 indicate a clear relationship between campaign spending and passage rates, the results are suspect because they do not account for the possible interactions between campaigns. For example, it is possible that a strong supporting campaign is negated by the presence of a strong opposing campaign or other factors. To control for these possible effects, Table 4 presents the results of several multivariate regression analyses. The dependent variable in each regression is a measure's vote percentage. The independent variables include the level of supporting contributions, opposing contributions, and a dummy variable indicating

---

38. Lowenstein's original analysis considered only "large" campaigns defined as those in which at least $250,000 (nominal data) was spent by one side. Adjusting for inflation, the comparable figure for the current period is between $440,000 and $500,000 (depending on which year is used as the baseline). All but one initiative campaign in the period under study exceeded this amount, so we consider all of the recent campaigns to have been "large." Deflator: California CPI for all urban consumers, California Department of Finance, California Statistical Abstract 1998.

39. Lowenstein and others operationalized "large" campaigns as those for which over $250,000 were spent. It is not clear what would be a comparable figure for the period 1992-1998, so we instead consider those campaigns in which yes or no spending was above the sample average.

Table 4. Regression Analyses

	DV = Vote for All Measures	DV = Vote for All Measures	DV = Vote for All Measures	DV = Vote for Initiatives Only
Contributions for	-.09 (.22)		.33 (.24)	32 (.21)
Contributions against		-.65** (.22)	-.59** (.27)	-.57** (.24)
Initiative			-6.91** (3.45)	
Constant	52.26** (1.74)	54.14** (1.71)	56.49** (2.15)	49.50** (2.45)
Adjusted R²	.00	.08	.12	.08
N	87	87	87	43

whether the measure was an initiative. The final column is restricted to initiatives only. The estimated coefficients tell us the effect of a one-unit increase in the independent variable, holding constant the effects of the other independent variables, on a measure's vote percentage.

The first two columns of Table 3 report the bivariate relationships (plus a constant) between a measure's vote share and contributions to support and oppose the measure, respectively. We estimate this effect to be negative but insignificant for supporting contributions and negative and significant for opposing contributions. When we control for the effect of each type of campaign, plus whether the measure is an initiative, we see that the effect of opposing contributions remains negative and the effect of supporting contributions becomes positive but remains insignificant. In other words, in the multivariate analyses, increasing opposing campaign activity is associated with lower electoral support, while increasing supporting campaign activity is associated with higher (but perhaps random) electoral support. We also find that initiatives receive fewer votes than referendums, controlling for supporting and opposing spending. In the last column, we replicate the preceding analysis for initiatives only and find similar effects of campaign contributions. Together, the results in Table 4 are virtually identical to those reported in Gerber.[40]

To summarize, Tables 3 and 4 indicate that spending in favor of a measure may marginally increase its level of support and chances of passage,

40. Elisabeth R. Gerber, supra note 1, at 107-110.

while spending to oppose a measure substantially decreases its vote share. The large majority of serious efforts to defeat initiatives are successful, with one-sided no campaigns leading to an initiative's defeat between 69 and 73% of the time. While less than the earlier estimates of near 90% failure rates, these figures remain quite impressive from the opponents' perspective. One-sided yes campaigns are associated with passage of an initiative between 50 and 75% of the time. This large range indicates that many more factors play into an initiative's ultimate success. We consider one such factor — the sources of support — below.

Sources of Support and Opposition

One of the major findings reported in the existing literature is that the source of support for and opposition to ballot measures is highly correlated with the measure's success. These findings are based on analysis of the identity of contributors to a large sample of direct legislation campaigns.[41] Unfortunately, comparable analyses are not possible on the more recent data because of changes in reporting requirements. Prior to 1992, the identities of all contributors over $250 were reported and disclosed. Since 1992, the California Secretary of State only requires disclosure of contributors over $10,000. Thus, the identities of the vast majority of individual contributors cannot be known for the post-1992 period.

Still, there is important information in the current disclosure reports. Those interests that contribute over $10,000 are disproportionately economic interest groups and businesses. We can therefore glean some insight into the sources of support for individual measures simply by looking at the share of contributions made in $10,000 increments and above. To the extent that contributors' identities are correlated with the size of their contributions, we would expect measures that receive a greater share of their support from large contributors to receive less voter support, all else constant, and to pass at a lower rate.

Even if the correlation between size of contributions and identity of contributors is imperfect, we might expect the concentration of contributions to be related to a measure's success for other reasons as well. Large contributors that are not businesses or economic interest groups may still share some of those groups' attributes that make their initiatives less popular with large groups of voters. For example, large individual contributors may exhibit outlying preferences and support policies that lack grassroots appeal. At the least, there is no necessary correlation between the interests that wealthy individuals pursue and those of the majority of vot-

---

41. Elisabeth R. Gerber, supra note 1, at 119-120.

ers. More specifically, while there may be broad-based public support for a given issue, the particular solution proposed by groups or individuals with a large concentration of resources may differ from the solution to the same problem that would be proposed by interests with less concentrated resources. As a concrete example, the overwhelming majority of people in California support the general issue of education reform; the specific solution of charter schools described above, however, may be one that appeals uniquely to wealthy Silicon Valley entrepreneurs. To the extent that there is a divergence of interests between those able to fund an initiative campaign, either alone or with a few friends, and the rest of us, we would expect large contributions to be associated with lower voter support and passage rates.

Table 5 reports the share of small (under $10,000) and large ($10,000 and above) contributions to all initiatives, to successful initiatives, and to unsuccessful initiatives. We see that initiatives received a vast majority of both their supporting and opposing contributions from large contributors. Initiatives that ultimately passed received a smaller share of their supporting contributions from large contributors, while initiatives that ultimately failed received a larger share of their supporting contributions from large contributors. This pattern is consistent with the hypothesis that initiatives that are proposed and financed by large, economic interests attract less voter support.

Table 6 reports the passage rates for initiatives that received various levels of large and small supporting and opposing contributions. We see that

Table 5. Share of Small and Large Contributions

	For— % small	For— % large	Against— % small	Against— % large
All Initiatives	.21	.79	.21	.79
Successful	.25	.75	.27	.73
Unsuccessful	.18	.82	.17	.83

Table 6. Passage Rates by Share of Contributions over $10,000

	Large Contributions (For)		Large Contributions (Against)	
	Below Average	Above Average	Below Average	Above Average
% Pass	.50	.36	.69	.30
N	18	25	13	30

of the initiatives that received below average levels of large contributions (i.e., that received relatively more financial support from small contributors), 50% passed. Initiatives that received above average levels of large contributions passed at a much lower rate of 36%. These results are also consistent with the hypothesis that initiatives that receive more of their contributions from smaller contributors are more successful because these small supporters are likely to be citizen interest groups that reflect broad-based interests.

On the opposing side, initiatives that received below average levels of opposing contributions from large contributors actually passed at a higher rate than those with above average levels of large contributions. In other words, opponents who were able to contribute large sums were more successful at defeating initiatives than were small contributors. This suggests that the type of signaling indicated by the analyses of supporting campaigns may not be as important for opposing campaigns. Voters do not seem to respond in the same way to the contributors' identities when funds are being spent to defeat an initiative. However, on the basis of these data alone, we are not able to further isolate the causes of these patterns. It might be the case, for example, that opposing campaigns with high concentrations of large contributions are also characterized by higher overall levels of spending.

To isolate the effects of sources of support and opposition on a measure's success, we again employ a multivariate regression analysis. These analyses allow us to test whether the patterns observed in the passage rates above are affected by factors such as the total size of a campaign, the simultaneous presence of supporting and opposing campaigns, and other factors not considered in Table 6. The first two columns of Table 7 estimate the effects of the share of large contributions on a measure's vote percentage for both initiatives and referendums. The last column estimates these effects for initiatives only.

The only significant effect in Table 7 is for the share of large opposing contributions. We see that in all of the specifications, the greater the share of large opposing contributions, the lower the support a measure receives. This is consistent with the patterns observed in Table 6, where initiatives with above average levels of large contributions pass at a lower rate. The effect of the share of large supporting contributions is also negative but insignificant in all of the regressions. While we can be less confident in this result due to its lack of significance, it is nevertheless consistent with table 6. It indicates that even after we control for the type of opposing campaign and the scale of both the supporting and opposing campaigns, measures that receive a greater share of large supporting contributions are less successful than those that receive relatively more small contributions. Total size of the supporting and opposing campaigns, and whether the measure is an initiative, are insignificant in all specifications.

Table 7. Regression Analyses

	DV = Vote for All Measures	DV = Vote for All Measures	DV = Vote for Initiatives
% Large – For	-5.94	-6.97	-10.56
	(5.17)	(5.22)	(10.82)
% Large – Against	-17.21**	-15.36**	-13.29**
	(6.26)	(6.92)	(6.38)
Total Contributions – For		.37	.35
		(.23)	(.21)
Total Contributions – Against		-.32	-.31
		(.29)	(.26)
Initiative	5.80	5.46	
	(5.72)	(5.73)	
Constant	58.63**	58.70**	65.59**
	(2.53)	(2.53)	(9.43)
Adjusted R^2	.16	.17	.15
N	87	87	43

To summarize, our analyses of sources of support and opposition indicate that the concentration of campaign contributions is clearly associated with a measure's electoral success. Large supporting contributions are associated with lower voter support and passage rates. Large opposing contributions are also associated with lower support and passage rates. These results are important in their own right, as they indicate that where campaign money comes from might be just as important as how much is raised and spent. Since size of contributions is correlated with the identities of the contributors, it also suggests an explanation for these patterns, specifically that voters take cues about the content of a measure from the economic identities and perceived interests of its major supporters and opponents.

Prospects for Reform

The results of this analysis demonstrate the benefits of going beyond the aggregate numbers to the details of the data, here, the sources of the wealth deployed in initiative campaigns. For example, had the data shown that funding for direct democracy campaigns came predominately in the form of many small contributions, it would have cast doubt on claims that the system is biased in favor of the wealthy. Instead, a well-stocked political war chest would have been a signal of broad-based public interest and evidence that direct democracy is functioning as its populist supporters hoped it would. Certainly, critics of direct democracy would remain; many who are skeptical or hostile toward initiatives and referendums worry that majoritarian decisionmaking, unmediated by the filter of representative government, produces oppressive, intolerant, and poorly conceived policies.[42] But these are very different arguments from the egalitarian ones we identified at the outset.

Our data does not suggest that small contributions dominate the direct legislation landscape, however. Instead, Table 5 indicates that the initiative campaigns we studied received a vast majority of their contributions, supporting and opposing, from large contributors. Does this mean that wealthy interests dominate the process? Surely not. Our work and previous research clearly show that the effect of this money is quite limited. Previous studies reveal that spending money for paid petition circulators guarantees ballot access. Thus, to the extent that access itself generates advantages, those who can command substantial financial resources may benefit disproportionately. This paper focuses on electoral outcomes and provides further support for the consistent finding in the literature that large amounts of money can defeat initiatives, but it is much less successful in passing them. Opposition campaigns funded by large contributions, primarily from economic interests but perhaps also from a few wealthy individuals, are likely to be successful in preserving the status quo. In contrast, campaigns funded by large contributions seldom succeed in passing ballot questions and are less successful than campaigns funded by small contributions and which thereby demonstrate significant grassroots involvement.

Those who decry the influence of money in direct democracy outcomes must therefore focus on this enhanced blocking ability or the disproportionate power to protect the status quo from change via popular vote. Presumably, the same economic interests that can relatively easily defeat direct legislation also disproportionately influence outcomes in state legislatures because of the clout that derives from their wealth. Their ability to oppose with great success attempts to circumvent the legislative process and to dislodge entrenched interests undermines the power of initiatives and referendums to force unwilling lawmakers to consider ideas or policies with strong grassroots appeal. In short, this effect of money, while limited, nonetheless could deprive direct democracy from serving as a robust alternative avenue of lawmaking and policy formation.

Perhaps the most compelling conclusion from the data is that our analysis underscores the need for aggressive disclosure of the amount and sources

---

42. See William N. Eskridge, Philip P. Frickey & Elizabeth Garrett, *Legislation and Statutory Interpretation* 24-25, 30-33 (2000) (discussing this critique).

of contributions and expenditures in initiative and referendum campaigns. Consistent with the work of others, this study supports the conclusion that such disclosure provides voters helpful information and equips them to vote more competently in a low information environment. Money is used to communicate with voters, and the communications provide voting cues including the identity of the interests that support and oppose a measure, partisan and other elite endorsements, and the alignment of the issue with the agendas of political parties or other well-known ideological groups.

Reforms that would re-channel financial resources into forms that are harder to discover or are less traceable to particular interest groups, such as limitations on contributions, could be counterproductive.[43] Instead, reformers would do better to focus on enhanced disclosure. Is data disclosed in a timely fashion before an election so it can be used by policy entrepreneurs, the media, and the public? Is disclosure structured so that the real interests are revealed, rather than being obscured through the use of coalition names that mask the identities of major participants? Are state officials making wise and efficient use of modern technology, including the Internet, both in collecting and in disseminating data about funding sources and amounts? Is detailed data being collected about the nature and timing of expenditures?

The relationship between particular kinds of information about contributions and expenditures and the ability of citizens to vote competently also suggests a new judicial strategy for reformers seeking to defend aggressive disclosure statutes from constitutional attack. Far-reaching disclosure statutes will raise constitutional issues; ironically, the more a law succeeds in revealing the identities of supporters and opponents, the more serious the constitutional concern. The Supreme Court has long protected anonymous political speech because without the cloak of anonymity, some disfavored viewpoints would never be heard and political discourse would be less robust.[44] Disclosure certainly chills some kinds of political speech, especially when it links the speaker to disfavored groups or ideas, and some individuals and organizations may be less likely to sponsor ballot questions, or oppose them, if their involvement will be publicized. In addition, the more complex the reporting requirements, the more costly the burden placed on those who must provide information to the state. More-

---

43. Cf. Samuel Issacharoff & Pamela S. Karlan, The Hydraulics of Campaign Finance Reform, 77 Tex. L. Rev. 1705 (1999).

44. See, e.g., McIntyre v. Ohio Elections Commission, 514 U.S. 334 (1995) (holding that the First Amendment protects a person's decision to remain anonymous while distributing campaign literature for issue-based election).

over, such a burden affects grassroots groups with few monetary resources and less access to consultants more severely than it does well-funded groups and sophisticated political players.[45]

The First Amendment inquiry is a balancing test, however. The interest in political speech and the burden imposed by the regulation are weighed against the government's interest in regulation. Our data could support the argument that disclosure serves the interest of a better informed citizenry, certainly a compelling interest in a democratic system that includes initiatives and referendums as part of lawmaking. Interestingly, some state supreme courts have upheld disclosure statutes concerning expenditures in direct democracy and have identified this informational interest as a compelling one. In *Messerli v. Alaska*,[46] the court held:

> The need for an informed electorate applies with full force to ballot issues. Such issues are often complex and difficult to understand. Proper evaluation of the arguments made on either side can often be assisted by knowing who is backing each position.... Similarly, a ballot issue is often of great importance financially to its proponents or opponents, or both, and multi-million dollar advertising campaigns have been waged. In such circumstances the voter may wish to cast his ballot in accordance with his approval, or disapproval, of the sources of financial support.[47]

There are indications in the campaign finance cases of the U.S. Supreme Court that it will be willing to entertain such arguments in the context of disclosure statutes. In a footnote in *First National Bank of Boston v. Bellotti*,[48] the case striking down prohibitions on corporate expenditures in issue campaigns, the Court noted that "[i]dentification of the source of

---

45. See Bradley A. Smith, Faulty Assumptions and Undemocratic Consequences of Campaign Finance Reform, 105 YALE L.J. 1049, 1082-83 (1996) (arguing that any sort of regulation disadvantages grassroots movements relative to the wealthy because "regulation favors those already familiar with the regulatory machinery and those with the money and sophistication to hire the lawyers, accountants, and lobbyists needed to comply with complex filing requirements").

46. 626 P.2d 81 (Ala. 1981).

47. Id. at 87 (footnotes omitted). See also Bemis Pentecostal Church v. Tennessee, 731 S.W.2d 897, 904 (1987) ("The informational purpose of disclosure is no less compelling in referenda. Referenda are the most direct expression of popular will and should be conducted in an open forum for the debate of public policy....[R]eferenda often commit the State or its political subdivisions to what may be, as a practical matter, essentially irreversible and costly courses of action.").

48. 435 U.S. 765 (1978)

advertising may be required as a means of disclosure, so that the people will be able to evaluate the arguments to which they are being subjected."[49] To use the language typically seen in the Court's opinions concerning campaign finance reform, an electoral system that is not designed to produce informed, competent voters may not produce democratically legitimate outcomes and is therefore to some extent "corrupt."

Finally, this data suggests several directions for further research. We focused on the source of contributions; in addition, the timing of expenditures may also be important to electoral outcomes, as well as the use to which the money is put. We have also begun to identify some differences (as well as similarities) between referendums and initiatives. For example, initiatives accounted for half of the number of ballot measures in our study, but they received nearly 95 percent of total contributions, and over half of the referendums reflected no campaign activity at all. In addition, initiatives receive fewer votes than referendums, controlling for supporting and opposing spending. Yet, the influence of large contributions on electoral outcomes seems not to be affected by whether the measure is an initiative or a referendum. This latter result is surprising. A referendum is characterized by a richer information environment because the legislature has already taken a position and the issue is often associated with politicians and perhaps political parties in ways that should provide more helpful voting cues. In an environment of more information, each additional piece of information provided by financial disclosure should have less effect on the outcome.

Further research on the differences, if any, between initiatives and referendums would be valuable for several reasons. First, some cautious supporters of direct democracy advocate a hybrid system where a popular vote alone is not sufficient to enact legal change but must complement the traditional legislative process. To the extent that the dynamics of initiative and referendum campaigns differ, the ultimate character of such a mixed system will be difficult to predict. Second, some countries outside the United States have held or proposed national referendums on prominent issues, such as Quebec's status in Canada, the relationship of a country to the European Union, or the peace accord with Syria in Israel. More information on the particular characteristics of this form of direct democracy could be helpful to policymakers outside the United States.

---

49. Id. at 792 n.32 (noting also the prophylactic effect of disclosure relating to corruption). See also Buckley v. Valeo, 424 U.S. at 67-68 (suggesting that information function of disclosure might be an independent compelling state interest but not clearly separating this interest from the traditional corruption rationale).

Conclusion

More sophisticated empirical research disaggregating the various components of initiative and referendum campaigns should allow reformers to move past imprecise suggestions for change to more targeted responses to problems in the operation of direct democracy. Our study of the sources and size of contributions reveals that large contributions, primarily from economic interests, have different effects on electoral outcomes than do small contributions. The effects are more limited than some claim, but they are significant and suggest directions for meaningful reform and legal arguments to support such reforms if they are challenged on constitutional grounds.

Chapter 6

Silence Isn't Golden: The Legislative Assault on Citizen Initiatives

By Paul Jacob

A war is raging in American politics, a power struggle between the politicians and the people. In this conflict, precipitated by the citizenry's attempt to reassert control over its supposed public servants, the issue of term limits has been the people's main offensive weapon. And the people's most, perhaps only, effective "delivery system" has been the initiative process, whereby entrenched, self-interested politicians are bypassed allowing the people to act directly.

It's not surprising, therefore, that the battle between the people and the politicians has now engulfed the initiative and referendum process itself. In the 23 states that have a viable process (commonly called I&R), legislators are attacking the process through increased regulation designed to silence, not enhance usage.

While citizen activists view the initiative as often the only vehicle for implementing the public will, the politicians view it as a dagger aimed directly at them. Yet, unlike most political battles that citizens can watch on their television sets and read about in the newspapers, this conflict has largely taken place behind the scenes. Perhaps because the battle lacks any ideological or party identity. It's not a left-right or Republican vs. Democrat issue. Large majorities of every demographic group favor the initiative process while legislators, regardless of party affiliation, generally oppose it. Thus, the most vocal political players have not found the issue to be a useful political football. Furthermore, most of the country, lacking a statewide initiative and referendum approach to lawmaking, is not engaged in the struggle.

Still, the outcome will have serious ramifications for the country. Numerous ideas anathema to legislators have been popularized through the initiative. The loss of an accessible process will not only thwart various political reforms in the initiative states, it will also deny the entire nation the new ideas that are tried and tested through the I&R process and then often exported to other governments.

Legislative Motives

Even a cursory look at the actions of legislatures forecloses the possibility that increased regulation comes from a genuine attempt to improve the process. Virtually every bill introduced by state legislators on the subject would make access to I&R more cumbersome and expensive. In the last few years, no legislature has moved to open access or expand the process. The overwhelming evidence shows that legislators have but one purpose in regulating the initiative process: to prevent citizens from effectively using it.

The animosity of legislators to I&R is not new or unexpected. Legislators have always had self-interested reservations. Without a citizen initiative procedure, the legislature would possess a complete monopoly on lawmaking. Just as in the private sector, such a monopoly provides tremendous power to legislators. We've learned that monopolies do not serve the interests of consumers nearly as well as entities that face competition. Political monopolies are no different.

In establishing the citizen initiative, eight states — Arkansas, Massachusetts, Mississippi, Nebraska, Nevada, North Dakota, Ohio and Washington — placed provisions in their constitutions specifically preventing the legislatures from writing laws to govern the process which might actually be intended to undermine it. For instance, Arkansas' Constitution reads, "No legislation shall be enacted to restrict, hamper or impair the rights herein reserved to the people." These constitutional protections haven't always blocked the ingenuity of legislators, but by their very existence these provisions show the fears drafters had about the malice of politicians.

Moreover, in the wake of a decade of citizens reasserting their control of government primarily through initiatives — blocking pay raises, cutting taxes or requiring voter approval, regulating campaign financing, imposing ethical standards, setting term limits — legislators are ferociously and strategically striking back through increased regulation. The new regulations are aimed at gutting a process both naturally at odds with the self-interest of legislators and, at present, imposing policy outcomes particularly unpopular with politicians.

At a recent meeting of legislators from 13 western states, the backlash against I&R was on full display. Pat Murphy of the *Sun Valley Tribune* in Idaho reported: "Lawmakers from 13 Western states were told in no uncertain terms Saturday that the days of carefree legislative politics in state government are changed forever, ended by the twin demons of term limits and lawmaking by citizen initiatives.... [University of California at San Diego professor of political science Elisabeth] Gerber warned lawmakers that trying to drive ballot initiatives out of business by enacting stiff new laws limiting campaign spending, requiring disclosure of backers and geographic distribution of signers would backfire, and probably be unconstitutional."

In the last decade, term limits have swept the country. Term limits laws now affect 18 state legislatures, 38 governors and local officials in eight of the country's 10 largest cities. The advance of term limits would have been impossible without the initiative process. Legislatures, consumed by the self-interest of members, refused to consider such limits. With precious few exceptions, only by putting the issue directly before voters were term limits implemented.

The self-interest problem, rather than intellectual opposition to term limits as policy, is the only explanation for why Congress mustered a two-thirds vote for presidential term limits, while at the same time the Senate voted 80 to 1 against term limits for themselves. The pervasive conflict of interest among legislators and the necessity of I&R are also evidenced by the fact that all but one of the 18 states with legislative limits are initiative states.

Thus term limitation forms a nexus with I&R—term limits required the initiative process and the imposition of term limits galvanized legislators to attack the initiative process as a way to prevent further reforms. In many states, where legislators are attempting to regulate the initiative to death, there is little disagreement on either side of the debate that the enactment of term limits precipitated the legislative assault against I&R.

Regulation of Petition Circulators

One of the most recurrent regulations of the initiative process is restricting who can collect signatures and how or whether they can be paid. In *Meyer v. Grant*, the U.S. Supreme Court overturned a Colorado law that banned payments to signature gatherers. The Court ruled that collecting signatures on petitions was fundamental First Amendment activity that should receive the highest protection from state regulation.

But in open defiance of the U.S. Supreme Court decision in *Meyer v. Grant* (whose logic was again asserted by the High Court in 1999 in *ACLF v. Buckley*), legislators in Maine, Mississippi and Washington State passed new laws forbidding paying signature gatherers on a per signature basis or paying them at all. These facially infirm statutes have been struck down after lawsuits, but not before they denied numerous citizens—those lacking the financial resources or legal knowledge to challenge the statutes— their constitutional rights.

Legislators have a responsibility not to pass any law they know to be unconstitutional. Yet, concerning the initiative process, legislators have routinely passed statutes they knew to be illegal in order to create stumbling blocks for citizens. A North Dakota law outlawing payment on a per signature basis in now being litigated.

There are other restrictions placed on petition circulators, again usually designed to simply make it harder to put a measure on the ballot. In a 1996 Nebraska lawsuit, *Bernbeck v. Moore*, the federal courts struck down a requirement that petitioners be registered voters. The court marveled at the double standard applied to I&R by the Nebraska Legislature. As the Eight Circuit Court of Appeals pointed out, "...in no other situation does Nebraska law prohibit or restrict Nebraskans who advocate or oppose electoral measures from hiring or recruiting non-registered voters to champion their cause, including hiring non-registered lobbyists, non-registered campaign workers or campaign managers, or non-registered persons to run a telephone bank opposing various initiatives."

Campaign Finance Regulation

The idea of campaign finance reform is popular precisely because Americans feel their legislators are easy prey for special interests with campaign contributions. Support erodes somewhat when citizens consider the details of allowing government to regulate the speech of political candidates and other participants. Especially frightening is the dominant role played by incumbent legislators with a large personal stake in the outcome of campaign regulation.

Opponents of the initiative process would like to apply the same restrictive measures to initiatives that are applied to political candidates without regard for the fundamental difference between candidate elections and initiative campaigns. In terms of corruption, the initiative process offers tremendous advantages over the legislative process. Power corrupts men, but an initiative is a piece of paper. It cannot be corrupted. It cannot change after the election. It's written down in black and white. Voters only wish their elected officials were as predictable.

There is a long, ugly history of legislators taking bribes and doing the bidding of special interests. But special interests cannot pay off an entire city or an entire state. As the U.S. Supreme Court wrote in *First National Bank of Boston v. Bellotti*, "The risk of corruption perceived in cases involving candidate elections...simply is not present in a popular Vote on a public issue."

Campaign finance regulations have not only failed when applied to initiatives, but they have been seriously counterproductive, giving significant advantages to the organized interests whose influence they are supposed to curtail while punishing the less organized grassroots interests they are supposedly intended to help.

In California, for instance, just understanding the law and filling out the forms for contributions and expenditures usually requires paid legal representation. Better-financed efforts are obviously better able to afford legal and accounting help. Furthermore, draconian and uneven enforcement—in one case a $800,000 fine imposed on a proponent who failed to file reports—have a chilling effect on the entry of numerous people into the initiative realm, precisely those with less financial clout.

In 1997, the Nebraska Legislature passed new regulations on financing initiative campaigns, with the clear intention of blocking a third attempt at term limits. Some in the legislature referred to the new law as "the U.S. Term Limits law." It stipulated that any group contributing more than $10,000 to an initiative must divulge the names and addresses of all their donors. Term limits groups, fearful of the wrath of powerful politicians strongly opposed to the movement, have long been unwilling to allow public dissemination of their donors. It seems clear that the goal of the Nebraska law is to block funding by intimidating potential donors.

Some initiative critics contend that powerful interests can in effect buy legislation through initiatives. But money has far less influence in the outcome of initiative campaigns than in candidate races. While outspending one's opponents has often been successful in defeating ballot measures, heavy spending to pass an initiative has not been a successful strategy. Historically, when initiative proponents spend twice as much as opponents of a measure, the initiative still has less than an even chance of winning. Compare that to candidate elections where at the congressional level the higher spending candidate wins 96 percent of the time.

Geographical Distribution

Many states require that signatures be collected according to a geographic distribution representing different political subdivisions of the state. Not only is this a foreign concept of "representation" in America, but it is also a costly hoop through which initiative proponents must jump.

In the landmark case, *Baker v. Carr*, the U.S. Supreme Court struck down the method of drawing state senate districts on a geographical rather than population basis. The case established a "one man, one vote" principle. Essentially, the court ruled that to give weight to geography instead of people necessitated a system where some people's votes counted more than others did simply according to where they lived—as if the dirt, rocks and trees that surrounded rural voters deserved representation, too. Should 500 citizens of one county be able to veto the desires of a million people in another county? No, the U.S. Supreme Court ruled.

After *Baker v. Carr*, every representative body in the country—from city councils to state legislatures (except for the U.S. Senate, for which representing a state without regard to population was specifically mandated in the Constitution)—had to apply the "one man, one vote" framework. Yet, most petition requirements regularly violate this principle. And because geographic distribution means additional cost and difficulty for initiative proponents, more legislatures are imposing new burdensome geographic requirements in violation of one of our country's basic democratic tenets.

Idaho's legislature has been fighting a battle against term limits since they were established on local and state officials by initiative in 1994. In 1998, legislators placed an advisory measure before voters with loaded wording urging a repeal of term limits. The measure failed at the polls as voters embraced term limits for the second time. However, key legislators and powerful lobbyists immediately proclaimed they would consider repealing or lengthening the limits in contradiction to the expressed will of the voters.

Still, any repeal by legislators could be blocked by a referendum, so legislators enacted a requirement that initiative petitions must get more signatures statewide and that the signatures include at least 5 percent of the voters in 22 of the 44 counties. The cost of petitioning in some of these rural counties is two to three times the cost of gathering signatures in more populous Boise.

One way around the high cost of rural signature gathering was to collect signatures at the Boise Riverfest that's held each summer. The Riverfest attracts hundreds of thousands of people from all over the state. But the legislators were both smart and malicious; the new legislation moved the petition deadline prior to Riverfest.

No initiative has yet qualified under the new Idaho regulations. Even more important, if legislators repeal the statutory term limits law twice supported by clear majorities of the public, a voter referendum will be exceedingly difficult to mount in time to stave off the legislature's action and put the repeal to a vote. The altered rules for I&R seem to be preparation for the legislature's attack on term limits against the clear desires of the people of Idaho.

Higher Signature Requirements

Much criticism of the initiative process cites the high cost of gathering the necessary petition signatures to qualify a measure and then waging a campaign for or against the measure. In his paper, "Campaign Financing of Ballot Initiatives in the American States," political scientist Daniel Smith states, "Without money, groups backing or opposing ballot measures are almost by definition excluded from the game."

The alleged problem is that while moneyed-interests can utilize the process, so-called grassroots groups have difficulty raising the necessary funding to qualify an initiative. Yet increasing signature requirements hardly seems the answer. The more signatures required, the more expensive the petition drives become, and the more wealthy interests can place initiatives on the ballot while groups without significant funding cannot.

Consider a recent legislative referendum in Oregon to increase the signature requirement by 50 percent. An advocate admitted the proposal had problems and might indeed be counterproductive. Yet, he still supported the increase, saying, "It is not a solution, but it would give us a breather." Oregon voters wisely defeated the measure.

Initiative critics must decide whether they seek to solve the problems they allege or are merely offering excuses for a campaign to disrupt the I&R process.

Single-Subject

The behavior of courts in several states has been nothing short of tyrannical in striking down initiatives on specious grounds. One of the most seemingly reasonable requirements placed on initiatives, that they contain only a single subject, has become a dangerous legal loophole allowing courts to strike down any initiative with which they politically disagree by redefining the meaning of "single-subject" on a case by case basis.

The Montana Supreme Court last year overturned 100 years of precedent to strike down an initiative requiring voter approval of new taxes. The concept is so simple that I just described it in five words, yet the state's highest court has the chutzpah to tell citizens that such a succinct concept is not a single subject.

Similarly, other state supreme courts have struck down initiatives through an ever-changing definition of "single-subject." Though reasonable on its face, I&R activists now consider legislation requiring initiatives to adhere to a single subject to be open invitations to the state courts, routinely more aligned with the legislature than with initiative proponents, to block measures viewed as hostile to the interests of those in power. The state legislatures set judges' salaries and appropriate funds to run the judicial branch— a factor that can provide serious leverage for legislators over the courts, thus compromising the critical independence of our judiciary.

Lawlessness

The hostility of legislators toward I&R is well established. But while legislative opposition, in terms of enacting destructive regulations, is problematic, the most disturbing trend in the assault on initiative rights is the utter lawlessness exhibited by many legislators and state officials.

In 1994, term limits proponents sued to block what they deemed a negatively slanted ballot title written by the state's attorney general for an initiative to limit Oklahoma's congressional delegation. Oklahoma's Supreme Court agreed the ballot title was a thinly veiled opposition argument. The Court authored a new ballot title and ordered election officials to place the judicially approved language on statewide ballots. For the first time in Oklahoma history, the Court's order was ignored and the overturned language was placed on the ballot anyway.

Without explanation, the usual precautions and double-checking of the ballot did not take place for the election on term limits. Perhaps it was all a simple mistake—the term limits initiative still garnered 67 percent of the vote. But the fact remains that initiative proponents were denied their right to a fair and impartial election.

In Alaska, election officials regularly produce a pamphlet for voters with pro and con arguments about initiatives that qualify for the ballot. In 1994, for the first time, the arguments lacked the information as to who had written them. After repeated media inquiries, the head of the election division admitted that he wrote the argument against term limits. In prior elections, no statement was published if a proponent or opponent for a measure failed to come forward, but the election official's personal opposition changed the rules when it came to term limits.

By far the most serious abridgment of law took place in Massachusetts. Through the initiative, Massachusetts's voters presented legislators with a petition for a constitutional amendment for term limits. The state's constitution says the legislature "shall" vote on these measures. But the Legislature of Massachusetts, though under a direct legal obligation to cast a vote on the measure in constitutional convention, refused.

As the Supreme Judicial Court wrote in a later opinion on the subject, "The proponents of term limits...have cause for discouragement. Efforts to obtain term limits by a constitutional amendment foundered in 1992 because of the refusal of the Legislature in joint session to take final action on such a proposal *as the Constitution of the Commonwealth directed.* We concluded in *LIMITS v. President of the Senate, supra,* that this court should not direct the Legislature to exercise *its mandated function.* We did so based on principles of separation of powers." (Emphasis added.)

For the legislators to refuse to abide by the Massachusetts Constitution is the highest form of lawlessness. A proper response to the illegal behavior of the Massachusetts Legislature would be for Congress to declare the Commonwealth of Massachusetts no longer a republican form of government (as stipulated in Article IV, Section 4 of the U.S. Constitution), and to deny Massachusetts' two U.S. Senators their seats in Congress.

Don't hold your breath waiting for Congress to uphold the Constitution, however, especially over the issue of term limits.

Those who attack the initiative process as outside the checks and balances of representative government should pay closer attention to the actions of public officials like those in Massachusetts. Initiatives must and do conform to the constitutional rule of law. It is the opponents of initiatives, in legislatures and other governmental positions, who have attempted to break through the checks and balances of our system. Too often they have succeeded.

Representative Government

While legislative assaults on the initiative process are transparently self-serving, there has been an intellectual defense for these attacks—most notably by *Washington Post* reporter David Broder in his recent book *Democracy Derailed*. Broder argues the initiative process destroys representative government. That sounds pretty ominous. Should we fear letting the public vote directly on issues?

The political elites—the politicians, lobbyists, pundits—oppose voter initiatives as destructive to representative government. But their conception of representative government is skewed. They apparently believe we elect representatives, not as a way to facilitate citizen control of government, but rather as a grand design to block the people from controlling their government. "We the People" established the Constitution. Did we really do so to somehow keep ourselves *out* of decision-making?

Broder forgets that James Madison, the architect of our representative form of government, said, "The people are the only legitimate fountain of power." Alexander Hamilton echoed Madison in *Federalist 78*: "To deny this would be to affirm that the deputy is greater than his principal; that the servant is above the master; that the representatives of the people are superior to the people themselves." This is precisely what Mr. Broder and other modern opponents of the initiative process are arguing. To hear them tell it, one would think the American Revolution was fought against democracy rather than monarchy.

Even Edmund Burke, the famous member of the British Parliament who argued a representative should follow his own conscience in complete disregard for the wishes of his constituents, never argued for a legislature so removed from the people. Burke spoke this truism, "In all forms of government the people is the true legislator."

Of course, much of the opposition to citizen initiatives actually stems from policy disagreements with how the people ultimately vote. Most members of what's been called "the political class" oppose term limits and tax reforms that have captured the public imagination. These reforms have come about almost exclusively through the citizen initiative process.

It is also argued that initiatives escape the checks and balances built into our system. Yet, our Constitution protects us from laws that abridge our rights, whether those laws are passed by voters or imposed by politicians. In fact, in practice citizen initiatives face a much tougher standard—they are regularly struck down by the same courts that quite rarely overturn acts of the legislature. Virtually every controversial initiative must survive two tests: first, at the polls, and second, in court. Not so for the far more numerous but less well-publicized enactments of our legislatures.

Broder presents no defense of legislators, admitting:

> ... most Americans believe their elected officials look out first for themselves, then for their contributors, and put serving the public well down on their list of priorities. To tell American voters today that a politician is better motivated, more civic minded, and a better custodian of the commonweal than the voters themselves might be an insult to their intelligence.

It's instructive that there has been no dramatic action by legislators to address their poor level of public support—except their attempt to close avenues like the initiative process where the people still have a chance to speak.

Conclusion

There are those who don't think very much of the average voter; who see the people dismissively as just millions of Joe Six-Packs, as barbarians to be kept at bay. They say let elected officials, not voters, decide all of our nation's issues. Shirley Spellerberg, the leader of Eagle Forum in Texas, argues against giving Texans the right to initiative. She asks, "Do we want to run the risk that issues such as homosexual marriage, right to life, right to carry [gun] laws, tort reform, home schooling and casino gambling would be decided by a poorly informed and growingly apathetic electorate?"

The people are neither "poorly informed" nor "growingly apathetic" as Spellerberg asserts, but the answer to her question is "Yes." Who else should decide? Our elected officials chosen by those same voters that Ms. Spellerberg disparages as unfit to make decisions? There is no logical reason why the same people would be enlightened when choosing between candidates, but dangerous dolts in deciding issues.

The initiative process is arguably the only avenue for citizens to reassert their control over government. But Americans, already dissatisfied with the unrepresentative nature of legislators, are about to discover that the very career politicians voters seek to rein in are destroying this avenue to reform.

The goal of legislators and critics of the initiative process is clearly not to correct the perceived flaws but to kill the process in its entirety and to restore a legislative monopoly for the politicians who have fallen into such ill repute among the people. The war between the people and the politicians may well be decided by whether the initiative process survives the current legislative assault.

To contradict the cliché: silence is not golden. For representative government to work requires that the people be able to check the entrenched power of legislatures and hold ultimate sovereignty. Regulation of the I&R process appears to be one more area of legislating that the people must take into their own hands.

Chapter 7

The Animal Protection Movement: A Modern-Day Model Use of the Initiative Process

By Wayne Pacelle

In 1963, Judge Kirksey Nix of the Oklahoma Court of Criminal Appeals overturned a lower court's convictions of several individuals charged with illegal animal fighting. Judge Nix did not find for the defendants for a lack of evidence of cockfighting, but instead declared that chickens are not animals and therefore are not protected under the state's anti-animal fighting law. Though the judge seems to have arbitrarily reshuffled the taxonomic deck, his ruling was the final judicial word on the subject: cockfighting was legal in Oklahoma.

Believing that the vast majority of citizens in Oklahoma opposed cockfighting, humane advocates turned to the legislature to correct the court's bizarre ruling and restore the state ban on cockfighting. But rural legislators sympathetic to cockfighters stymied these efforts, preventing any bill from being considered by the full House or Senate. Perhaps the most passionate opponent of cockfighting in the capitol was former State Representative John Monks who thundered on the floor of the House, "[t]he first thing the communists do when they take over is ban cockfighting."

Failing time and again to win support for a ban on cockfighting in the legislature, opponents of cockfighting turned directly to the citizens in 1999. Oklahoma is one of 24 states to provide for the initiative process in the state constitution, though its requirements for qualification of a proposed statute or constitutional amendment are among the most stringent in the country.

To qualify a statutory measure for the ballot, petitioners must amass nearly 70,000 valid signatures of registered voters in just 90 days. As a practical matter, they must gather approximately 100,000 signatures to account for invalid signatures. That's more than 1,000 signatures per day for the duration of the petition drive.

Petitioners, mainly volunteers, faced not only a narrow time frame in which to amass the necessary signatures, but also a concerted campaign of harassment from cockfighters. Cockfighting enthusiasts filed a series of lawsuits against petition organizers, charging them with defamation for stating that cockfighting is associated with drug dealing, illegal gambling, and violence. The lawsuits, though doomed to fail on their merits, had a purpose other than securing a defamation judgment: to drain the time, money, and enthusiasm of petition organizers during the crucial three-month signature gathering period. Cockfighters also targeted the chairperson of the anti-cockfighting campaign, Janet Halliburton, a 20-year veteran of the Oklahoma State Bureau of Investigations and its general counsel. They orchestrated a phone calling campaign to Halliburton's superior, falsely charging that Halliburton had campaigned against cockfighting on her state time. *The Daily Oklahoman*, the state's largest newspaper, called for Halliburton's resignation. Though *The Daily Oklahoman* made no charge that Halliburton had used her office or state resources to advance the initiative campaign, the newspaper's editorial page argued that her advocacy presented the appearance of a conflict of interest.

To decrease public confidence in the initiative petition, cockfighters also placed ads in newspapers throughout the state claiming that the plainly worded measure to ban cockfighting was the first step towards the elimination of hunting, fishing, rodeo, and other long-pursued pastimes in Oklahoma. "Beware Hunters," blared the headline of one of the cockfighters' ads. "Animal rights activists want to ban all hunting and fishing." And perhaps most significant, cockfighters traveled in clans around the state to disrupt petition gatherers, surrounding petitioners and intimidating them. They also accosted prospective petition signers, warning them that the plainly worded measure was the first step toward a ban on all hunting. Most ominously, cockfighters made death threats against petition organizers.

In spite of the stringent requirements for qualification of a measure, which were compounded by the cockfighters' campaign of harassment aimed at petitioners, the Oklahoma Coalition Against Cockfighting turned in 105,000 signatures to the Secretary of State in December 1999 - more than the 70,000 signatures needed for qualification for the November 2000 ballot. Reputable polls conducted by *The Daily Oklahoman* and *The Tulsa World* — the state's two largest newspapers — reveal overwhelming support for the measure.

In short, when judges subverted the law and when legislators failed to heed the wishes of the mainstream Oklahomans, answering instead to a vocal minority interest bent on perpetuating a cruel practice, citizens had recourse. The course, in the case of the anti-cockfighting effort, was laden with a variety of challenges and obstacles for citizens dedicated to effecting social change. The initiative, a tool designed for citizens as a means of effecting needed change, served as a critical safety valve for policy making in Oklahoma.

Marking the Evolution of Thought Through the Initiative Process

The animal protection movement had a poor record of qualifying and passing ballot initiatives during much of the 20th century. The first animal protection ballot measure were advanced in the 1920s and 1930s on subjects ranging from banning vivisection to restricting rodeos and trapping. The results were consistently poor. From 1940 to 1990, voters passed just one animal protection ballot initiative—a measure in South Dakota, in 1972, to ban dove hunting. Voters rejected a series of initiatives restricting the killing of wildlife and rearing of farm animals in confinement. In fact, just eight years after approving the dove hunting ban, South Dakota voters revisited the topic and renewed a hunting season, invalidating the single victory achieved in a 50-year period.

It was a period of hegemony for industries using and exploiting animals. The values of the animal protection movement had not taken root in communities throughout the country. What's more, when animal advocates did launch ballot measures, they did not have either the resources or the campaign savvy to best their opponents and alter the status quo.

But with the increased scientific understanding about the similarities between people and animals, a recognition that animals do suffer, and the emergence of a body of literature that argued for a new ethic in the treatment of animals, the humane movement grew considerably in strength in the latter part of the century. By 1990, The Humane Society of the United States—just one of more than 3,000 organizations in the field—claimed more than one million members.

But policy makers are often among the last to recognize the currents of change in culture. It was not surprising then that state legislators and executive agencies remained stubborn in their opposition to even modest reforms. Take the case of Colorado. There, the state Division of Wildlife authorized two major public attitude surveys about bear hunting practices targeted by animal activists. One poll revealed that 90 percent of citizens opposed hunting black bears during spring, when females nursed dependent young. If a hunter shoots a lactating female—a likely consequence of spring hunting because it's impossible to determine the sex of a bear by spotting the animal—the entire family group will be lost. Public attitude surveys also revealed that three-quarters of citizens opposed the hunting of bears with packs of hounds or with bait, in which hunters lure bears with mounds of food, hide in a tree stand, and then shoot the feeding animal. Voters considered all three hunting practices inhumane and unsporting.

The Colorado Wildlife Commission was forced to examine these policies and accept public comment. Buttressing the attitudinal surveys, public comment calling for an end to spring, bait, and hound hunting ran 15 to 1 in favor of the hunting restrictions. But the Commission thumbed its nose at the data and the public comment. The Commission—dominated by rigidly ideological hunters—actually voted to extend the length of the spring bear hunting season, inviting a ballot initiative targeting these practices. The result should not have surprised any observer; voters approved Amendment 10 in November 1992—banning spring bear hunting and baiting and hounding—by a landslide vote of 70 percent to 30 percent.

The Amendment 10 campaign was a sign of the changing times during the 1990s. During the last decade of the century, voters sided with animal advocates in a more than a dozen campaigns—sharply reversing the course that had been established in the prior decades. Like the voter revolt over taxation, the revolt on animal issues started in California. There, in 1990, voters approved Proposition 117 to ban the trophy hunting of mountain lions. In 1992, Colorado voters approved the above-mentioned Amendment 10. In 1994, voters approved two measures—a ban in Arizona on the use of body-gripping traps on public lands (just two years after voters had rejected a similar measure) and a measure in Oregon to restrict bear baiting and the hound hunting of black bears and cougars.

There was a major surge in ballot initiative activity in 1996, with eight measures on the primary and general election ballots. Voters handily rejected measures backed by hunting interests to repeal the recently approved initiatives in California and Oregon restricting lion and bear hunting. And during the same year, voters approved measures to restrict trapping in Colorado and Massachusetts, to ban bear baiting and the hound hunting of bears, cougars, and bobcats in Washington, and to ban airborne shooting of wolves and wolverines in Alaska. With hunting groups investing huge resources in campaigns to defeat bear hunting initiatives in Idaho and Michigan, voters sided with animal advocates in six of eight races. In 1998, voters approved several more animal protection initiatives, banning cockfighting in Arizona and Missouri and two measures in California—one to ban trapping and poisoning and the other to ban the commercial shipment of horses for slaughter. They did reject a measure to ban dove hunting in Ohio, where hunters spent $2.5 million against the hunting ban. In November 2000, voters adopted three more animal protection initiatives—banning trapping in Washington, restoring a ban on airborne hunting of wolves in Alaska, and halting the shooting of captive wildlife on game farms in Montana.

While animal advocates sustained occasional setbacks—each one produced by enormous investments of dollars by hunting groups—the animal protection movement carefully used the initiative process to codify basic protections for animals, demonstrating its values were in sync with the public's and signaling to policy makers that they could not dismiss the reformers' demands. The initiatives provided a measure of confidence to animal advocates in the political sphere, prompting additional investment not only in initiative campaigns, but also in more traditional legislative campaigns.

Hunting groups did not, however, accept the voters' judgments in any state where their campaigns failed. They launched counterattacks on the initiatives in state legislatures and in the courts, seeking to overturn the initiative results. In Oregon, for instance, after the passage of Measure 18 in 1994 — banning bear baiting and the hound hunting of bears and cougars — legislators allied with hunting groups introduced 15 bills to repeal, damage, or delay implementation of the initiative. Ultimately, not a single bill passed. But in other states, including Massachusetts and Washington, hunting groups did weaken components of the initiatives that restricted trapping and hound hunting.

While the initiatives provided an important means of effecting change, they were not the final word on any subject. The initiatives are tangible indicators of progress in the policy making sphere, but they do not prevent additional rancor over controversial subjects.

Grassroots Citizens and the Initiative Process

Some critics of the initiative process argue that the process has been hijacked by special interests or very wealthy individuals capable of raising and spending enormous sums of money to hire paid petition firms, to draft experts to advocate for the initiatives, and to blitz the electorate with compelling advertising to force consideration of an issue. They provide many case examples to support that thesis.

While there is no question that money plays a major role in the outcome of many ballot measures and candidate campaigns, including animal protection initiatives, the character and conduct of these campaigns meets the ideal that motivated early century reformers to devise the process.

Animal advocates have resorted to the initiative process after policy makers stonewalled popular reforms. For them, the initiative process has served as a safety valve, allowing popular sentiment to prevail over lawmakers bent on perpetuating the status quo.

Humane advocates have not leveraged huge financial advantages to secure initiative victories. On the contrary, in some cases, including the 1994 measure in Oregon to ban bear baiting and hound hunting, they have overcome lopsided financial advantages of hunting groups. At the same time, hunting groups have prevailed only in cases when they amassed huge war chests that allowed them to blitz voters with their message and erode public support for animal protection initiatives. Hunting groups spent $1.8 million against an anti-trapping initiative in Arizona in 1992, $2.5 million in Michigan and $750,000 in Idaho against the bear hunting initiatives, and $2.5 million against the dove hunting ban in Ohio; hunting groups outspent animal advocates by margins from four to one to ten to one in these campaigns.

While animal advocates have not used large cash reserves to influence voters, they also have not used cash to qualify measures for ballots. Generally, they have deployed volunteer petitioners to qualify measures for ballots. Animal protection groups have used volunteer petition drives more consistently than any other interest groups.

It is now viewed as axiomatic, for instance, that initiative qualification in California requires a minimum of $1 million. But animal advocates have bucked this axiom two times. In 1990, Proposition 117, the mountain lion initiative, qualified for the ballot by relying exclusively on volunteer petitioners, though there were paid staff that organized petitioners. In sum, the measure qualified for less than $500,000. In 1998, Protect Pets and Wildlife, a coalition of humane organizations dedicated to banning the use of steel-jawed leghold traps, spent about $350,000 on amassing more than 700,000 signatures, relying largely on 7,000 volunteer petitioners.

In Massachusetts in 1995-96, animal advocates spent a paltry $25,000 to amass nearly 200,000 signatures to qualify a measure to restrict trapping on the November ballot. That year, there were 24 petitions in circulation in the Commonwealth; the trapping measure was the only one to qualify, and, again, it relied exclusively on volunteer petitioners. In 1999, an initiative campaign in Massachusetts to ban greyhound racing spent the astonishingly small sum of $3,500 during the first phase of signature gathering. In the four initiative campaigns in Colorado, Oregon, and Washington, the same standard was observed: volunteer petitioners qualified the ballot measures.

Animal advocates also spent sparingly on polling, attorneys, and campaign consultants. In some respects, this thrift was a consequence of limited resources, not a commitment to using the initiative process as designed. But regardless of its motivation, animal advocates have used the process in a manner that makes a compelling case for the need for direct voting.

Backlash Against Animal Protection and the Initiative Process

Stung by the successes of the animal protection movement through the use of the initiative process during the 1990s, animal use industries are playing a part, sometimes a leading role, in tampering with the integrity of the initiative process and significantly enhancing the degree of difficulty in undertaking an initiative campaign. Their effort is two-pronged: increasing standard for both qualification and voter approval of measures.

In 1996, Idaho hunting groups soundly defeated a measure, Proposition 2, to ban spring bear hunting and the use of dogs or bait to hunt bears. Their formula for success was a campaign targeting "out-of-state animal rights extremists" who, they charged, wanted to do away with "Idaho freedoms." They spent nearly $800,000 to defeat the measure, while proponents spent just a fraction of that amount in favor of the measure.

Hunting groups did not rest and bask in the glow of their successful campaign. In Idaho, they immediately mounted a charge in the legislative session following the November election to increase qualification requirements for initiatives, so they would not have to fight a clone of Proposition 2 in the future. They succeeded in passing sweeping reforms of the process, drastically reducing the time allowed for petitioning and requiring that petitioners collect signatures dispersed throughout the state. The requirement was that petitioners had to amass 6 percent of registered voters in each of 22 of the state's 44 counties; prior to that stipulation, petitioners did not have to reach any geographic distribution requirements.

Idaho hunters patterned their efforts to raise the bar for signature gathering after a successful move by hunting groups in Utah, who succeeded in shortening the signature gathering period and imposed geographic quotas on petitioners. Utah legislators saw fit to pass these additional restrictions on petitioning even though voters had approved only one initiative in state history. Utah had hardly experienced an abuse of the initiative process; in fact, the citizens had barely made any use of the process at all. But legislators, goaded by the hunting lobby, made a rarely used and difficult process even more cumbersome and inaccessible.

In Washington, legislators loyal to hunting groups also pushed for geographic sub quotas to increase the burden on petitioners. But their efforts have not yet met with success.

These measures are designed for the singular purpose of making ballot access more difficult. Rural counties are inherently more difficult venues for signature gathering because citizens are dispersed. There are few places where pedestrian traffic is sufficient to justify the time investment of a volunteer or paid petitioner.

Ironically, the effect of passing these measures, and others with a similar intent, is to make it all but impossible for volunteer, grassroots petition drives to succeed. It is difficult enough to ask citizens to take time from their work and families in order to meet signature gathering totals and quotas that are already difficult. Only well financed measures, pushed by interest groups with major money or wealthy individuals, can hire enough paid operatives to meet guidelines revised to make petition qualification more difficult.

Hunting groups have also started down a second dangerous course in attempting to prevent animal advocates from using the initiative process and effecting moderate reforms. In Utah, it wasn't enough to increase signature requirements. They also worked with their allies in the Legislature—the most devout are known as the "Cowboy Caucus"—to place a constitutional amendment on the November 1998 ballot to require a two-thirds majority of voters to approve any wildlife protection initiative.

Backers of the measure, Proposition 5,—including the NRA, the Safari Club International, Rocky Mountain Elk Foundation, Archery Manufacturers Association, and others industry groups—spent $750,000 in favor of the measure. They also lined up support from the Republican establishment dominant in Utah, including Governor Mike Leavitt and U.S. Senators Orrin Hatch and Robert Bennett. Opponents spent just $50,000, but did have the benefit of most opinion-makers. Almost all major newspapers in Utah denounced the measure as unjustified and unfair. "It doesn't make sense to make an exception for wildlife issues, opined *The Deseret News*. "No other initiative would require two-thirds voter approval, and raising the requirement for wildlife-related matters impedes citizens' right to participate in the democratic process." *The Ogden Standard* weighed in, "The voters of Utah can be trusted to vote on wildlife issue, or any other issue put before them. Proposition 5 should be defeated."

Outspending opponents by a ratio of 15 to 1, Proposition 5 backers spent a substantial portion of their money on television advertisements, communicating that the measure would protect the outdoors and the Utah tradition of fishing. The advertisements said not a word about the supermajority requirement. Instead, the ads asked the question, "Will your children and grandchildren have stories to tell about wildlife and wild areas? Only if you vote for Proposition 5 on November 3."

Voters approved the measure by a margin of 56 percent to 44 percent. Ironically, the measure would not have succeeded if the two-thirds approval requirement it established for one category of ballot measures had been observed in its case. Its practical effect is the imposition of a de facto ban on wildlife protection initiatives. During the 1990s, only one animal protection initiative secured more than a two-thirds majority—the 1992 Colorado black bear initiative, Amendment 10, which garnered a 70 percent yes vote. Viewed as a landslide victory by any electoral standard, Amendment 10 would have been a squeaker if the supermajority requirement had been in effect in Colorado.

A clone of Proposition 5 was narrowly approved in the Arizona legislature in 2000—by a single vote in each chamber—and appeared on the November 2000 ballot as Prop. 102. A principal backer of the measure, Representative Barbara Blewster, argued on the House floor, "We live in a republic, and not in a democracy. We have to really watch too much democracy because it is mob rule." Meanwhile, in Alaska, the legislature is poised to place a measure on the November 2000 ballot that would stipulate that no wildlife protection matter could be decided by voters. Determining whether it's acceptable for people to shoot wolves from helicopters or gun down grizzly bears on wildlife refuges is apparently too complex a topic for voters to understand and decide.

Fortunately, voters soundly rejected both measures in November 2000. Even though hunting groups spent $1.5 million in favor of Prop. 102 and opponents raised only $200,000, voters rejected it soundly 37 percent to 63 percent. Similarly, the Alaska measure, Proposition 1, was defeated 36 percent to 64 percent. These lopsided votes may signal the end of the movement to deny citizens the right to advance future wildlife protection initiatives.

Conclusion

There is no guarantee that the process of representative law making will be free from the influences of money and special interests. The same is true of the initiative process. But while legislators may sometimes be in the vanguard of beneficial social change, so can citizens, through the initiative process. Voters utilizing the initiative process have enacted major reforms such as the direct election of Senators, women's suffrage, and the eight-hour workday. In the modern era, campaign finance reform and animal protection, for example, are two areas of reform made possible by the initiative process.

Unfortunately, the people's ability to utilize this important process is under siege. Legislators, cooperating with individuals and industries stung by initiative reforms supported by the public, are working to complicate and even eliminate the process. The animal protection movement has been successful because it is supported by the people. But individuals whose views conflict with animal protection values still exert significant control over legislators and they are using that power to make qualifying and passing initiatives all but impossible for animal advocates.

Voters need to guard against abuse of the initiative process by special interests. But they also need to guard against the blatant attempts by their elected officials to destroy the tool that has helped advance the cause of animal protection. Blocking the collection of signatures on postal property, increasing signature requirements, increasing distribution requirements, and requiring super-majority votes for the passage of any initiative will make the initiative process accessible only to individuals and organizations with access to large amounts of money. The initiative process, if it survives at all, will then become the tool only of special interests capable of buying ballot placement. Average citizens and legitimate grassroots organizations will then be excluded from using the very political process originally designed for their use and benefit.

Citizen Sponsored Ballot Measures on Animal Protection

				Yes	No
1930	MA	prohibit use of trapping devices	Question 3	69%	31%
1972	SD	prohibit mourning dove hunting	Measure 1	67%	33%
1977	OH	prohibit use of trapping devices	Measure 2	37%	63%
1980	OR	prohibit use, sale of snares, leghold traps	Measure 5	37%	63%
1980	SD	repeal of mourning dove hunting ban	Measure 1	42%	58%
1983	ME	repeal moose hunting season	Measure 1	39%	61%
1990	CA	prohibit sport hunting of mountain lions	Proposition 117	52%	48%
1992	AZ	prohibit use of leghold, snare traps on public lands	Proposition 200	38%	62%
1992	CO	prohibit sport hunting of bears in spring and with bait and hounds	Amendment 10	70%	30%
1994	AZ	prohibit use of leghold, snare traps on public lands	Proposition 201	58%	42%
1994	OR	prohibit sport hunting of bears and mountain lions with hounds	Measure 18	52%	48%
1996	AK	ban same-day airborne hunting of wolves foxes, lynx, and wolverines	Measure 3	58%	42%
1996	CA	allow the trophy hunting of mountain lions	Proposition 197	42%	58%
1996	CO	ban leghold traps, other body-gripping traps	Amendment 14	52%	48%
1996	ID	prohibit the hunting of black bears during spring and ban baiting or hounding of black bears	Proposition 2	40%	60%
1996	MA	ban the use of body-gripping taps, outlaw hounding of bears or bobcats; reform Fisheries and Wildlife Board	Question 1	64%	36%
1996	MI	ban the hunting of black bears with bait or hounds or during the spring	Proposal D	40%	60%
1996	OR	repeal the ban on bear baiting and the hound, hunting of bears and mountain lions	Measure 34	42%	58%

1996	WA	ban bear baiting and the use of hounds to hunt bears, cougars, bobcats, and lynx	Initiative 655	63%	37%
1998	AK	prohibit wolf snaring conducted pricipally for predator control and fur sales	Proposition 9	36%	64%
1998	AZ	prohibit cockfighting	Proposition 201	68%	32%
1998	CA	ban the use of cruel and indiscriminate traps	Proposition 4	57%	43%
1998	CA	prohibit slaughter of horses and sale of horsemeat for human consumption	Proposition 6	59%	41%
1998	CO	uniform regulations of livestock	Amendment 13	39%	61%
1998	CO	regulation of commercial hog facilities	Amendment 14	62%	38%
1998	MN	identify hunting as a "valued part" of the state heritage	Amendment 2	77%	23%
1998	MO	prohibit cockfighting	Proposition A	63%	37%
1998	OH	prohibit mourning dove hunting	Issue 1	40%	60%
1998	UT	require a two-thirds majority of voters for approval of any wildlife protection initiative	Proposition 5	56%	44%
2000	AK	bar any wildlife protection initiatives	Measure 1	36%	64%
2000	AK	ban land-and-shoot wolf hunting	Measure 6	53%	47%
2000	AZ	require two-thirds vote to pass wildlife protection initiatives	Prop. 102	37%	63%
2000	MA	ban greyhound racing	Question 3	49%	51%
2000	MT	ban "canned hunting" and new game farms	I-143	52%	48%
2000	ND	hunting shall be forever preserved	Question 1	77%	23%
2000	OR	ban steel jawed leghold traps, certain poisons	Measure 97	41%	59%
2000	VA	hunting shall be forever preserved	Question 2	60%	40%
2000	WA	ban steel jawed leghold traps, certain poisons	I-713	55%	45%

Chapter 8

The Barriers to Participation:
The Consequences of Regulation

By Angelo Paparella

What keeps a government, any government, from gaining too much power over its citizens? Checks and balances. Unfortunately, our system of representative government has some serious shortcomings in this area. For example, supporters of campaign finance reform believe it will eliminate some of the profit-motivation that undermines the defining principles of democracy. Nice idea on paper, but are we to trust that those who benefit from the present policy would be willing to change it, thereby eliminating their own benefits? And can we blame *them* if we, the people, do not demand and support our own system of checks and balances?

Such a system does exist in many states, counties and cities: initiative and referendum. Referred to as I&R, it gives us the opportunity to actively participate in self-governance, the core principle upon which this country was founded. When our elected representatives stray off course and lose site of those whom they represent, our safety valve is a "peoples' vote." When citizens are dissatisfied with their legislature's actions or, more often, inaction, they can petition the government for a direct vote on a new proposal, or to repeal or reform a legislative act.

At first glance, this seems to be a fairly simple solution. Unfortunately, recent regulations have severely impeded the natural flow of this process, causing it to become very complex and, for many, cost prohibitive. Although those who seek to impose more restrictive regulations claim to be protecting unwary citizens from manipulation by wealthy power brokers, such regulations actually achieve the opposite effect by making the process costly and intricate. As critics in the media rail against the emergence of professional initiative campaign organizers and petition circulators, they fail to recognize that many of the legislative and administrative changes being promulgated only stifle grassroots volunteer efforts.

To fully understand the paradox of the problem, we must look at the practical aspects of the process itself. The first step toward a people's vote is to draft the precise language of the question to be placed on the ballot. This typically requires the specialized services of attorneys. The exact petition document to be circulated must then be approved by the state's designated department. Once it is approved, a petition drive is organized and circulators are recruited to gather tens (and sometimes hundreds) of thousands of signatures from registered voters who live in the state.

Signature requirements are high. For example, in California almost 420,000 valid signatures are required to qualify a statutory measure, and over 670,000 signatures are needed to qualify a Constitutional measure. Nebraska requires ten percent of all registered voters in the state to sign the petition. In addition, many states have detailed geographic distribution requirements, further increasing the burden and cost for initiative proponents attempting to qualify a measure.

Complying with stringent deadlines, all signatures must be submitted to the state's designated government agency, typically town or county clerks or Secretaries of State, who then check for validity: Is the signor registered to vote at the address listed? Did they sign the correct petition for that town or county? In all states, it is crucial to plan on collecting 30-40% more than the required number of signatures, since many will not be validated by the clerks due to illegibility, wrong address, expired voter registration, wrong color ink and other minor details that vary state to state. In addition, many states check for duplicate signatures and apply a complicated and often inaccurate formula to estimate how many valid signatures were submitted.

Administrative or court rulings can make petition drives very costly and burdensome. In a 1999 Massachusetts drive, for example, we were plagued by a court ruling that disqualified all signatures appearing on a petition document that contained any stray marks, such as a faint pen mark in the wrong place, no matter how small or incidental. We were forced to resort to a policy of one signature per petition sheet in order to insure against the loss that a simple errant mark can make. Our solution resulted in more work for the clerks, one of whom threatened to lobby his friends at the election commission for a requirement to fill all signature lines on each petition sheet before submitting them!

After the clerks finish checking every signature and notarizing every document, they are submitted to the Secretary of State for a final tally of validated signatures. If all the state's requirements are met, an announcement is made and any opposing parties have a period of time within which to examine and challenge the validity of signatures.

Even if all the hurdles are cleared and a measure is qualified to appear on the ballot, passing an initiative is a difficult task at best. Voters usually resist change. Unlike many legislators, voters tend to vote "no" when they do not fully understand a proposal. Even educating *philosophically aligned* voters to a sufficient level of understanding so they will feel comfortable voting "yes" is an expensive and formidable task.

Whereas many initiatives are aimed at challenging the goals of one, or more, of many powerful special interest groups, it is easy to understand why more initiatives are defeated than passed. Further, opponents enjoy a distinct advantage since it takes far less money to defeat a measure than to pass it. Failure is too often the result, particularly when the opposition is entrenched in government and/or large special interest groups ready to fund promotion of the opposing view.

In June 2000, Utah lawmakers, lawyers and law enforcement agents gathered to develop strategies to kill a recently qualified initiative aimed at reforming unconstitutional asset forfeiture laws. One provision in the Utah Property Protection Act would divert proceeds from sales of seized assets to the education budget. As in most states, those proceeds now go to the agents and agencies that seize property and they are not required to account for the money. When proponents of the measure turned in 140,000 signatures (only 67,000 were required), opponents wasted no time in dispersing rumors that this initiative would let drug dealers get off easy.

Rather than viewing the initiative and referendum process as a complement to what they do, most legislators view it as an affront to their own power base. Frustrated by their lack of control over the initiative process and resulting laws, many state legislators have been trying to regulate them out of existence. Some have even convinced their most loyal constituents that only legislators are qualified to make such important decisions.

Legislators fight back using a variety of means. In 1998, for example, Missouri passed a law shortening the circulation period; Mississippi passed a law requiring circulators to be residents; and Idaho passed a law increasing the distribution requirement for signatures. In Oregon, the legislature put a proposal on the March 2000 primary ballot to increase the signature requirement for constitutional measures. It was summarily rejected by the voters, but will probably be attempted again. At about the same time, Utah legislators came disturbingly close to passing a Bill that would increase the per-county signature requirements from 66% to 100% of all counties.

Of course, to those with a limited understanding of the hazards of qualifying an initiative, Utah's initiative reform bill might have seemed harmless enough. Yet requiring signatures from 5% of active voters in every Utah county would devastate the initiative process. Sparsely populated rural areas could easily be disqualified with a few simple phone calls from proposal opponents asking petition signers to recant their signatures. It would not take much to disqualify a county in which only 49 signatures are required, and the entire initiative would thereby be disqualified.

What's worse, a varied group of special interests have joined in waging a multi-pronged attack aimed at thwarting the efforts of citizens to qualify initiatives. With and without the assistance of sympathetic legislators, they have done so by directly and profoundly hindering these two major factors: access to petitioners and access to citizens.

Access to Petition Circulators

Until recently, most states required circulators to be registered voters in the state in which the petition was being offered. But in *ACLF v. Buckley*, the U.S. Supreme Court looked at this issue and found it to be an unconstitutional regulation. Not surprisingly, legislators struck back and passed requirements that circulators be residents of the state. This may seem like a sensible regulation until compared with the lack of similar requirements for any other political or lawmaking activity. Neither lobbyists, campaign managers, political consultants nor drafters of legislation are required to be residents of the state in which they seek political change. So why require this of petitioners? Unlike the aforementioned occupations, the petition circulator is not materially participating in the creation of a law, but merely offering it to voters for their consideration.

In some ways, residency is even more difficult for initiative proponents to monitor than voter registration. How can we insure that a person is a legal resident? States have various residency requirements, and the administrative burden of tracking how long a person has actually lived in the state is unwarranted because it serves no valid purpose.

Many states, such as Oregon, Nebraska and Idaho, require that petitions notify voters if circulators are being paid. Further, the intent of the measure must be clearly stated: "Measure to be submitted directly to the voters," for example. With a clear summary printed, the intent of the petition posted, and the exact language of the proposal available to the signer, of what relevance is the petitioner's compensation or residency status? They are simply acting as vehicles to get the petition into the hands of voters.

These requirements are always justified with the same argument: they claim it is needed for tracking down circulators who commit fraud. The same argument was used in attempts to outlaw payment of circulators, demand registered voter status, and now residency requirements. Most of these attempts were eventually struck down by the courts, though not without great cost to citizens.

The problem with the fraud argument is two-fold: (1) there is no evidence of widespread fraud—very few cases exist, and (2) these requirements offer little assistance in preventing or prosecuting fraud. All that is necessary to "track down" forgers is identification and an address. Simply requiring some type of identification on petitions, showing who the circulators are, eliminates the obvious concern as well as the more delicate question of what happens to a signature if the person who collected it is not a bona fide resident of the state. Should the fact that a non-resident collected a signature invalidate it? And, if so, is such a policy respectful of the voter's rights? Apply the same concept to the process of voting: Should a vote be declared invalid if the person who set up the polling booth is found to be a non-resident?

Full cooperation between proponents, their petition drive organizers, and the government agencies involved is key in preventing and detecting fraud. A more effective method for insuring against forgeries is the use of systematic validity checks, beginning early in the signature-gathering phase. In fact, this practice is mandatory for professional petition drive coordinators, as they cannot afford to continue paying circulators who produce unacceptable validity rates. As with any profession, petition drive coordinators who are well paid are compelled to tend to these important issues in order to develop and maintain loyal, satisfied clients.

In criticizing the practice of paying circulators to gather signatures on petitions, opponents play upon a cord of idealism that mourns the days of yore—a time when volunteer success was realistic. Those were also the days when one full-time income could sustain a typical family, however, and at-home mothers could afford to safely walk their neighborhoods with strollers in tow. Today's neighborhoods are much less friendly and the average citizen is struggling to keep pace with the ever-increasing demands of modern life. Given the constant grind for time, even a few hours a week dedicated to circulating a petition is a hardship few can sustain.

The hard reality is that successful volunteer petition drives are wishful thinking. It is difficult to find people willing to circulate petitions—even when offered good pay. Relying upon volunteers is virtually impossible except in very rare cases. Even those who are passionate about a proposed measure find it difficult to gather 100 signatures from friends, family and neighbors.

Gathering signatures from passersby in a public location is a numbers game not recommended for the faint of heart. Responses to the question "Are you registered to vote?" can range from a grateful "yes" to a blank stare to "why are you bothering me?" And the next question, "would you help us get a question on the ballot..." is more volatile still. While a good percentage of Americans appreciate the opportunity to help make a difference with a mere swipe of a pen and the pull of a lever, rejection is a fact of life when petitioning.

The most successful circulators are those with "thick skins" who are being paid and who can maintain a polite demeanor in the face of rejection. Suffice it to say that petition circulators must be highly motivated in order to get the job done. Paid circulators are doing a job in much the same way as the lawyers, political consultants, and politicians—except they don't get paid as much. However, it is encouraging to note that (in my company's experience) most people will not circulate a petition to which they are opposed, regardless of financial remuneration. And for those who attempt it, success is rare.

In *Meyer v. Grant*, the U.S. Supreme Court ruled that prohibiting payment of petition circulators is unconstitutional:

The State has failed to demonstrate that it is necessary to burden [pro-
ponents'] ability to communicate their message in order to meet its concerns. The Attorney General has argued that the petition circulator has
the duty to verify the authenticity of signatures and that compensation
might tempt the circulator to disregard that duty. No evidence has been
offered to support that speculation, however, and we [the Supreme
Court Justices] are not prepared to assume that a professional circulator — whose qualifications for similar future assignments may well
depend on a reputation for competence and integrity — is any more
likely to accept false signatures than a volunteer who is motivated entirely by an interest in having the proposition placed on the ballot.

Ponder this: Why is it acceptable for legislators to accept thousands of
dollars in exchange for votes that satisfy special interest groups and industries, but unacceptable for individuals to be paid for long hours of hard
work in order to offer the people a vote on the issue?

Unlike special interest contributions to legislators, which are withdrawn
if desired laws are not passed, the so-called "big-money" stakes needed to
fund today's complex initiative process insure only one thing: the majority will have its way at the ballot box. Not so in legislatures, where re-
election relies more on those special interest contributions than on the sat-
isfaction of the electorate.

All petitions are required by law to contain an unbiased, clear and con-
cise summary of the proposed initiative. The full text of the proposal is
usually printed on the petition or at least available to prospective signers
for review if requested. How informed a voter chooses to become before
signing a petition is his or her business, not the politicians', just as they
make their own decisions when voting for initiatives or candidates at the
ballot box. For legislators and others to assume that voters need to be protected in this one-on-one encounter with a circulator is condescending
arrogance at best.

Access to Voters

In addition to the painful effects of rejection, circulators are faced with
hostile store managers who prefer that customers spend a few extra
moments shopping rather than participating in self-government. Regardless of numerous rulings in various states upholding the petition circulators' first amendment rights, large stores in many states are still loathe to
allow circulators access to customers entering or leaving the stores.

Court precedents dating back to the early 1970s have allowed petitioners
some access to circulate in front of large retail stores in California, Oregon
and Washington. In 1979, the California Supreme Court's decision in *Robins*

v. Pruneyard Shopping Center established the rights of petitioners to circulate on sidewalks at shopping centers. Now commonly referred to as "Pruneyard rights," the basic philosophy dates back to colonial history when the public often assembled on the sidewalks and courtyards of town squares, where people like Thomas Paine distributed political literature and expressed ideas.

Particularly with the explosion of the use of automobiles after World War II, retail merchandising in the United States has led to larger and larger retail sites which have supplanted those formerly frequented public places where non-commercial expressive activity could occur. Prior to World War II, entrances to most retail shops abutted public sidewalks allowing petition circulators, and others engaged in "core political speech," to reach the pedestrian traffic flow of shoppers without going onto private property.

Today, in states where the issue has been litigated, courts have recognized that in modern society the shopping malls, grocery stores, and so-called "big-box" warehouse stores such as Home Depots, Costco and Wal-Mart, represent the modern equivalent of "Main Streets" from days gone by. Whether a stand-alone store or part of a shopping center, such locations are part of an accelerating economic trend that privatizes once-public spaces such as sidewalks and parking lots.

These rights of access have been critical to petitioning success. The cost to proponents or candidates to qualify for the ballot bears a direct relationship to the number and quality of sites where signature gathering can take place. Without such access, the large signature numbers required in California and Washington would be impossible to achieve without a major increase in costs. A state like Oregon, with fewer signatures required but fewer high-traffic locations, would become just as difficult and expensive. Volunteers, who can usually only work on the weekends, would be denied access to store locations they work in now.

In smaller states, outside these critical Western states, petitioners are often allowed access to store fronts despite the lack of court precedents. Some reasonable store managers simply recognize that petitioners do not interfere with their business, and the vast majority of citizens acknowledge petitioning as an opportunity to participate in direct democracy.

After all, it must be recognized that these stores are places of business. Access to voters at these stores should be subject to some basic common sense rules. Petitioners should not interfere with the business, so things like blocking entrances should be strictly prohibited. Some stores due impose reasonable rules and regulations and those rules *should* be enforced so businesses are protected. By the same token, unreasonable rules designed simply to thwart the process, a practice too often in place by many establishments, should be exposed as simple dishonest attempts to prohibit political activity.

Unfortunately, a number of stores in each of these three Western states believe that a scaling back or elimination of these petitioning rights is achievable, and over the past three years they have launched an aggressive campaign toward that goal.

The largest retail chain in the world, for example, Wal-Mart has one of the worst records of hostility toward the exercise of Pruneyard rights. In California Supreme Court litigation (*Children's Rights 2000 v. Wal-Mart Stores, Inc.*) the non-profit plaintiff exposed a host of restrictions imposed upon petitioners as a veritable smoke screen to deny Pruneyard rights. With the help of pro-bono counsel they were able to seek redress.

Apparently, a corporate Wal-Mart attorney arbitrarily established a set of rules after he got wind of two previous court rulings. The outcome of *H-CHH Associates v. Citizens for Representative Government* allowed reasonable store policies if they were *written,* and the ruling in *Union of Needletrades Industrial and Textile Employees, AFL-CIO v. Superior Court* allowed a ban on Pruneyard activity during holiday blackout days.

Although the Wal-Mart attorney admittedly had little evidence supporting the need for such restrictions at Wal-Mart stores, he proceeded to adopt whatever rules the courts had approved in the *Needletrades* case. In addition to the holiday blackout period, the new Wal-Mart rules required: (1) an application with a 5-day waiting period, (2) a prohibition on more than 3-consecutive days, (3) a maximum of 14 days per year by the same applicant and, (4) identification (on the application) of all petitioners who could be expected at the store. The rules also allowed managers sole discretion to enforce the rules and to designate an area outside the store where the circulator could stand.

Based on these rules, which are devastating to the petitioner's goals, some Wal-Mart store managers made numerous citizens arrests during the 1998 petition cycle. Others did not enforce the rules whatsoever, repeatedly testifying in court that it has never seemed necessary. Some managers went so far as to designate areas more than 20 feet away from the door while Salvation Army activity was allowed adjacent to doors.

During testimony, the Wal-Mart attorney admitted that he devised the rules with no supporting empirical evidence to justify any of the rules. He also reported no knowledge of problems incurred accommodating Pruneyard activity, and no knowledge as to whether the Salvation Army's Pruneyard activities had ever caused any congestion or other problems.

Video footage of eight California stores, supported by expert testimony regarding pedestrian traffic hazard levels, clearly debunked Wal-Mart's claims that Pruneyard activity caused congestion-related safety hazards. Meanwhile, these unnecessary rules imposed by Wal-Mart made a devastating impact on the costs incurred by *Children's Rights 2000,* the proponent group that was working against tight timelines on a statewide initiative.

Perhaps more disturbing, access to other key locations such as municipal buildings, post offices, and publicly accessible special events, has also been diminished in many states. Even on public property, circulators are often treated as if engaged in illegal activity!

On June 1, 2000, a coalition of citizens groups and individuals from across the political spectrum filed a legal complaint against the United Stated Postal Service. In June 1998 the USPS established a regulation to prohibit petition circulation, an activity that was *expressly* recognized by the postal service as a First Amendment right as recently as 1992. Unsupported by any evidence that any behavior had precipitated the dramatic change in policy, the current regulation goes so far as to criminalize the activity.

This suit comes after six months of ardent effort by the Initiative & Referendum Institute to negotiate a resolution with the USPS. But the postal service failed to even offer a compromise. Instead they will waste valuable tax dollars to defend their position against a system designed to protect the very people who provide those tax-dollars!

Twenty-four states and thousands of cities and counties allow ballot-initiatives and referendums. If we can't reach the public through these venues, then very expensive and time consuming door-to-door efforts will be necessary. These problems only serve to eliminate the very essence of the peoples' initiative: to bring the ultimate power of government back to the people. Large special interests, with plentiful budgets, will have no problem paying for mass mailings and door-to-door campaigns. Grassroots and low budget operations will pay the price.

Oregon's Supreme Court has already limited access. In Washington state, the Supreme Court recently ruled that petitioning activity is only allowed at large malls and not in front of retail stores.

Several lawsuits have been litigated over the specific issue of what types of stores should be required to allow petitioning activity. So far the decisions have been a mixed bag sometimes in favor of petitioners and other times in favor of retail establishments. Undoubtedly, the California Supreme Court will eventually have to decide the issue again, as they did in Pruneyard. How they rule will be critical to the future viability of the initiative process in California.

My question is, "Why should any publicly accessible areas be off limits to circulators?" Areas that are open access to the public, in general, without the need for an invitation, admission fee, or permission, should be accessible to petition circulators unless they are disrupting the activity for which people have arrived. After all, the first amendment protects our right to freedom of expression. According to the U.S. Supreme Court ruling in *Meyer v. Grant*, ballot-initiative petition circulation is "core political speech" for which First Amendment protection is "at its zenith." Yet we have experienced strong opposition from bureaucrats at municipal buildings such as DMVs, Courthouses, Town Halls, State offices, libraries and even public parks and dumps!

Considering the fact that freedom of speech is the core foundation upon which our country was built, how can we allow store managers and bureaucrats to deny circulators reasonable access to any area that allows general public pedestrian traffic? If two people stood discussing politics in front of a Wal-Mart store, or waiting in the Department of Motor Vehicles lobby, could they be kicked out? Would they be arrested if they declined to leave or stop talking politics? Not without a huge lawsuit. Does the fact that a petition is in hand transform their discussion into an illegal offense?

Summary

Like any other democratic process, the initiative process is not without its problems. Many reforms can and should be considered and implemented, like clearer summary language on petitions, in order to ensure petition signers are clear about what they are supporting. But limiting proponents in the number of circulators they can recruit, or restricting access to citizens who should have the option of deciding whether they want to see a measure on the ballot, are not reforms. They are simply thinly veiled attempts to slowly kill I&R.

If stated objectives of initiative and referendum reformers are sincere, protecting the integrity of the process can truly be accomplished by reducing signature quantity requirements so volunteer efforts would have a realistic chance. Legislation codifying all publicly accessible areas as open to petitioners — subject only to reasonable and justifiable rules — is also critical. Eliminating residency requirements would also help make it possible for any committed grassroots effort to succeed at qualifying for the ballot.

The ultimate objective of the initiative process is to preserve, and perhaps restore, our rights to self-governance. But don't hold your breath waiting for any legislature to carry this mantle. Like the city clerk in Massachusetts, who threatened potentially devastating restrictions simply to avoid a few hours of labor caused by an existing *absurd* regulation, powerful forces often focus on short-term gain, with little thought given to how it may affect our nation's stated long-term goals.

NOTE: *Subsequent to this chapter being written, the Court of Appeal of the State of California, Second Appellate District, ruled in a split decision in favor of Wal-Mart. Two justices found Wal-Mart's rules constitutional and one justice found the rules unconstitutional. An appeal to the California Supreme Court is under consideration.*

Chapter 9

In the Eye of the Beholder: The Single Subject Rule for Ballot Initiatives

By Anne G. Campbell

In his concurrence with the court's decision in the 1999 *Ray v. Mortham* case, Florida Supreme Court Justice Lewis made the following comment about the Florida constitution's requirement that any revision or amendment to the constitution that is initiated by the people "shall embrace but one subject and matter directly connected therewith:"[1]

> As the majority correctly notes, we traditionally have stated that this constitutional provision requires an initiative to contain a logical and natural "oneness of purpose." ... However, the erratic nature of our own case law construing article XI, section 3 shows just how vague and malleable this "oneness" standard is. What may be "oneness" to one person might seem a crazy quilt of disparate topics to another. "Oneness," like beauty, is in the eye of the beholder; and our conception of "oneness" thus has changed every time new members have come onto this Court.[2]

In fact, Justice Lewis' concern is echoed by many participants in the initiative process. Proponents and opponents of initiatives, state governmental officials, and judges have commented on the unpredictability of the application of the single subject-type rules to initiated ballot measures. This essay examines these "single subject," "one subject," and "one amendment" requirements in the 18 states that restrict the scope of initiatives

---

1. Florida Constitution, Article XI, section 3. This section was amended in 1994 to exempt measures "limiting the power of the government to raise revenue" from the one subject limitation.

2. Justice Lewis concurring in result only in Ray v. Mortham (1999), 24 Fla. Law W. S 412 at 34-35.

for statutes and/or constitutional amendments.[3] It reviews the theory and intentions behind single subject requirements, the differences between single subject requirements for measures proposed by the legislature and measures proposed by initiative, the different single subject "rules" established by the courts, and how the rules are applied by the courts. These questions are analyzed primarily through an examination of the single subject rule decisions made by the courts in the initiative states.

The general conclusion that can be drawn from this review of the different requirements and the different applications of similar requirements in the initiative states, is that single subject restrictions have resulted in the judicial branch assuming a key, sometimes determinative, role in the initiative process. The states' constitutional provisions for the separation of the legislative and judicial powers are often overlooked when the legislative function of lawmaking is exercised by the citizenry. Furthermore, the nature of judicial involvement varies widely across states, as well as over time within some states. In most of the constitutions the initiative is identified as a legislative power "reserved by the people." However, the reality is that for those who would use this legislative power, the key determinant of the scope of that power is oftentimes the state supreme court.

There is a long tradition of state use of single subject rules. Part 1 discusses the legislative and judicial interpretations of the purposes served by the single subject-type provisions. On this issue there is a great deal of consensus. Part 2 reviews the single subject and single amendment-type requirements that apply for legislative and initiated laws and amendments in the 24 initiative states. Particular attention is paid to variations in single subject rules between the two sources of measures, including how and when measures can be challenged and the repercussions of these differences. Part 3 examines the standards of review applied by the different states' supreme courts in adjudicating the single subject and single amendment provisions. It notes how those standards vary over time and amongst states, and compares the standards of review for statutes and amendments originating with the legislature with those originating with the citizenry. Finally, this essay concludes with a summary of the strengths and weaknesses of the single subject rule, with special emphasis on how single subject rules give the states' courts a great deal of influence over the initiative process.

---

3. For brevity's sake, the various types of provisions restricting the scope of legislative and initiatives statutes and amendments — "one subject," "one amendment," or "single subject" — will be collectively referred to as single subject rules.

Part 1: The Purpose of Single Subject Requirements

As Part 3 of this essay will discuss, there is a significant degree of variation in the state courts' interpretations of the proper *application* of the "single subject" or "one amendment" requirements for initiative measures and legislative measures. However, when it comes to the courts' views of the *purposes* that these restrictions are intended to serve, there is widespread consensus. A brief survey of several states' judicial opinions relating to this topic will demonstrate this fact. Indeed, the different state courts often cite each other's opinions on this topic.

An 1893 Colorado case reviewed the history of the single subject provision, noting how the prefixing of a title to an act was relegated to the clerk of the house in the British parliament because it was deemed of so little importance. [4] However, that has not been the rule in the United States where both houses of the legislature aid in framing the title. The court noted that in the United States the title has been made a matter of primary importance in order to protect the legislative process from two separate "evils."

> The practice of putting together in one bill subjects having no necessary or proper connection, for the purpose of enlisting in support of such bill the advocates of each measure, and thus securing the enactment of measures that could not be carried upon their merits, was undoubtedly one of the evils sought to be eradicated. Another object is to prevent surprise and fraud from being practiced upon legislators, and to apprise the people of the subjects of legislation by the titles of bills, so that they might have an opportunity to be heard by petition or otherwise. But few are able, or care to take the time necessary to keep informed of all the legislation proposed at a single session, where it is necessary to examine in detail every bill in order to obtain this information. When, however, each proposed act is confined to a single subject and that subject is clearly expressed in the title, those interested are put upon inquiry when legislation is proposed affecting such subject, without its being necessary for them to examine every bill for the purpose of seeing that nothing objectionable is coiled up within the folds of the measure. [5]

In other words, single subject rules seek to prevent what is today commonly referred to as "logrolling" and to make it easier for both legislators and voters to inform themselves about policy changes being proposed.

---

4. Catron v Board of City Commissioners (1893), 18 Colo. 553, 33P. at 557.
5. Catron at 557-558.

The courts have noted the same logic and arguments apply to the initiative process that was first employed in the states at the beginning of the 20th century. These arguments are found in more recent state supreme court decisions in the initiative states that employ such restrictions. For example, the Massachusetts Supreme Court recounts how that state adopted its prohibition against the inclusion of "unrelated subjects" in initiatives after one of the delegates to the 1917 state constitutional conventions expressed concern over "log-rolling."[6] Indeed, logrolling is the most often-expressed concern, although the informational purposes of single subject rules are also widely cited. Several states' court opinions are illustrative:

In Arkansas: "It is generally agreed that the primary aim of 'one-subject' provisions in state constitutions is the restraint of logrolling in the legislative process."[7]

In Arizona: "...there is no doubt the [one amendment] constitutional provision above quoted was intended to prevent the pernicious practice of 'logrolling' in the submission of a constitutional amendment."[8]

In Florida: "The purpose of the single subject requirement is to allow the citizens to vote on singular changes in our government that are identified in the proposal and to avoid voters having to accept part of a proposal which they oppose in order to obtain a change which they support."[9]

In Washington: "The requirement that all legislative proposals include no more than one subject is consistent with basic democratic principles. The requirement is designed to present clear legislative proposals to the legislature or the public and forestall the combining of issues so that ones with minimal public support are not adopted merely because they are attached to popular proposals."[10]

In Oklahoma: "The purpose of the one-general-subject criterion is to guard against deceit or against the presentation of a misleading proposal as well as to prevent log rolling — the combining of unrelated proposals.[11]

---

6. Massachusetts Teachers Assn. v. Secretary of the Commonwealth (1981), 384 Mass. 209 at 219.

7. Gellert v. State (1974), AK 522 P.2d 1120 at 1122.

8. Kerby v. Luhrs (1934), 44 Ariz. 208, 36 P.2d at 554-555.

9. Fine v. Firestone (1984) 448 So.2d, Fla. at 993.

10. State of Washington v. Waggoner, (1971), 80 Wash. 2d 7, 9, 490 P.2d 1308.

11. In re Petition No. 363 (1996) OK 122; 927 P.2d at 566.

Similar statements can be found for each of the states' courts' decisions on single subject questions. In Colorado, where the single subject provision restrictions were added in 1994 as the result of a Colorado General Assembly referendum, it is clear that this philosophy is still current. In order to explain the purpose of the new section of the constitution, the legislators enacted a law that declared their rationale and their intentions for the single subject amendment. They indicated that the practices they intended to inhibit were logrolling and "to prevent surreptitious measures and apprise the people of the subject of each measure by the title, that is, to prevent surprise and fraud from being practiced upon voters."[12]

In addition to the universally-expressed goals of preventing logrolling and the perpetration of fraud and deceit on legislators or voters, the courts in Florida have added another current of thought to explain their vigilance when it comes to single subject provisions, especially for initiatives. In numerous decisions the court explains that "[t]he single-subject provision is a rule of restraint designed to insulate Florida's organic law from precipitous and cataclysmic change."[13] The Court seeks to protect the constitution from "helter skelter amendments."[14] The Missouri Supreme Court envisions a similar but more constrained role for itself in protecting the state constitution. They recognize a "task of weighing and balancing two contradictory and competing concepts — the need for a stable, permanent organic law versus the inherent right of the people to alter or change that organic law."[15]

The constitutional provisions for limiting the scope of proposed statutes and constitutional amendments bring the state courts into the lawmaking process. In order to achieve protection against logrolling and to maximize the information of citizens, the courts have been drawn into the law-making process. However, the extent of court involvement varies greatly from state to state, as well as over time within states. The next part of this paper discusses the significant variations in the extent and form of the single subject and one-amendment type provisions amongst the states, as well as over time within some of the states. It also examines how the specific procedures put into place to regulate the petition process explicitly or implicitly invite the state courts' intervention in the initiative process. The different forms of single subject provisions, as well as the different views of the courts about their proper role in upholding single subject provisions, leads

---

12. Colorado Revised Statutes 1-40-106.5 (1994 Supp) cited in In re Title, 900 P.2d 104; 1995 Colo. At 107.

13. In re Advisory Opinion to the Attorney General (1994), 636 So. 2d 1336; 1994 Fla. at 1339. See also Ray v. Mortham (1999), 24 Fla. Law W. S 412, 1999 at 15 and Term Limits Pledge, 718 So. 2d at 801.

14. Adams v Gunter (1970), 238 Xo.2d 824, Fla. at 832.

15. Buchanan v. Kirkpatrick (1981), 615 S.W.2d 6 at 11.

to significant variations in the degree of judicial influence over the citizens' law-making powers.

Part 2: "Single Subject" Requirements

An examination of the legal provisions in the 24 states that allow for citizen-initiated changes to the state constitution or statutes reveals that in the vast majority of these states both legislature- and citizen-initiated changes are subject to "single subject" or "one amendment" restrictions. In a few states the single subject requirements apply to only one or the other source of proposed laws or amendments. In addition, there are notable differences in how and when single subject challenges to measures proposed by initiative and to measures proposed by the legislature can be made, which affects the frequency of challenges in the courts on single subject grounds. Finally, there are significant differences in the repercussions for single subject legal challenges for legislative and initiated ballot measures.

Single Subject Requirements for Legislative Acts and Initiated Measures

Table 1 summarizes the different states' legal provisions for single subject-type requirements. In four states — California, Florida, Nebraska, Oregon — there are specific single subject requirements for initiated amendments where there are no such limitations for constitutional amendments proposed by the legislature.[16] In California, Florida, and Oregon the legislative assemblies are even empowered to propose wholesale *revisions* of their state constitutions, while initiated constitutional amendments are specifically limited to one subject.[17] However, in Nebraska, as in most states, the people have reserved the right of major constitutional *revision* to duly appointed constitutional conventions. In either case all revisions are subject to voter approval.[18]

---

16. Even in states that do not specifically limit constitutional amendments to one subject or require a "separate vote on each amendment," the courts have generally recognized that there is a limitation to the extent of changes that can be made as an "amendment" before a measure becomes a "revision" of the constitution. See, for example, Livermore v. Waite, 102 Cal. 113, 36 P. 424 (1894) and McFadden v. Jordan, 32 Cal. 2d 330, 196 P. 787 (1948) discussed in 31 Loy. L.A. L. Rev. 1305 (June 1998).

17. California Constitution, Article 18, Section 1. Florida Constitution, Article 11, Section 1. Oregon Constitution, Article XVII, Section 2.

18. Nebraska's constitution does require separate votes for each amendment if the legislature submits more than one amendment at an election. Article IVI, Section 1.

Table 1. "One Subject" Restrictions for Legislative
and Initiated Statutes and Amendments

State	Statutes Legislature	Statutes Initiatives	Constitution Legislature	Constitution Initiatives
Alaska	Yes	Yes		N/A
Arizona	Yes	Yes	SV	SV
Arkansas	No	No	No	No
California	Yes	Yes	No	1S
Colorado	Yes	Yes	SV + 1S	SV + 1S
Florida		N/A	No	1S
Idaho	Yes	Probably [a]		N/A
Illinois		N/A	1S	1S [b]
Maine	No	No [c]		N/A
Massachusetts	No	Yes [d]	No	1S
Michigan	Yes	Yes	No	No
Mississippi		N/A	SV + 1S	No
Missouri	Yes	Yes	1S	1S
Montana	Yes	Yes [e]	SV + 1S	SV + 1S
Nebraska	Yes	Yes	No	1S
Nevada	Yes	Probably [f]	No	No
North Dakota	Yes	No	No	No
Ohio	Yes	Yes	SV	SV
Oklahoma	Yes	Yes [g]	1S	1S

a. Idaho Attorney General Opinion issued July 7, 1997.

b. Constitution Art. III, Sec. 3 requires legislative Acts and amendments to accomplish a "single objective;" initiatives also per Coalition for Political Honesty v. State Board of Elections (1980), 83 Ill.2d. 236 at 253.

c. Maine Secretary of State "shall advise petitioners that the proper suggested format for an initiative question is a separate question for each issue" per Title 21-A, Chapter 11, Section 906 (A). That provision is only advisory per Suzanne Gresser of the Revisor of Statutes office on November 4, 1999.

d. Mass. Constitution Art 48, Part 2, Sec 3 requires "related subject" for initiated laws and amendments — not as restrictive as "single subject" requirement per Opinion (1992) 413 Mass. 1201; 595 N.E.2d, 292 at 1215.

e. Implied by court in State ex rel. Steen v. Murray (1964), 144 Mont. 61, 394 P.2d 761 cited in Montana Citizens v. Jim Waltermire, 224 Mont. 273; 729 P.2d 1283 at 292.

f. Per Nevada Attorney General Opinion 153 issued in 1934, initiated statutes have same restrictions as statutes originating in the legislature.

g. Implied by court in Initiative Petition #314, 1980 OK 174; 625 P.2d 595.

Table 1. (cont.)

State	Statutes Legislature	Statutes Initiatives	Constitution Legislature	Constitution Initiatives
Oregon	Yes	Yes	SV	SV + 1S
South Dakota	Yes	Yes	No	No
Utah	Yes	No		N/A
Washington	Yes	Yes[h]		N/A
Wyoming	Yes	Yes		N/A

h. Implied by courts since 1974. See WA Federation of State Employees v. State (1995), 127 Wash. 2d 544; 901 P.2d 1028 at 551-552.

Footnotes indicate the source of single subject restrictions when the restrictions are not explicitly based on the state's constitution or statutes.

"Yes"   for Statutes denotes a "one subject" requirement, unless other language indicated.

"SV"   denotes that the constitution requires a separate vote for each amendment to a constitution.

"1S"   denotes the constitution limits constitutional amendments

The vast majority of states also specify that all legislative bills must pertain to one subject. Of the 24 initiative states, only Arkansas, Maine, and Massachusetts do not restrict their legislatures in this respect. Of these three states, Massachusetts is the only one that still limits the scope of initiated statutes, requiring that each initiated measure contain only subjects "which are related or which are mutually dependent."[19] On the other hand, Utah and North Dakota levy the single subject requirement for statutes on their legislators but not on initiative proponents.

In six states — Idaho, Illinois, Montana, Nevada, Oklahoma, and Washington — the applicability of a single subject requirement to initiatives is not explicitly provided for in the state constitution, but is implied nevertheless. In Idaho a 1997 Attorney General Opinion stated that the limitation on legislative bills "most likely" applies to initiated legislation.[20] A similar Attorney General Opinion was issued in Nevada in 1934 — but has yet to be tested in court.[21] In Montana the Supreme Court decided that "the people exercising the initiative are subject to the same rules as the Legislature," finding an initiated statute to be unconstitutional "because

19. Massachusetts Constitution, Art. 48, Pt. 2. Sec 3 [153].

20. Idaho Attorney General Opinion, July 7, 1997 written by Deputy Attorney General Matthew McKoewn.

21. Montana Attorney General Opinion 153 (1934).

it would contain more than one subject."[22] This single subject limitation was imputed to Montana initiatives despite the fact that the constitutional provision regarding single subjects for bills is located in Article V of the Montana Constitution, while the people's right to enact laws by initiatives is located in Article III of the constitution. Similarly, in Oklahoma the Supreme Court has ruled that the "one general subject" rule for constitutional amendments applies to initiatives.[23] They consider that this Article XXIV-1 requirement; which is entitled "Amendments proposed by Legislature — Submission to vote," applies to the initiative power which is discussed in Article V "as a matter of general law." In the state of Washington the court has also ruled that the requirement for single subjects on all *bills* in practice applies to *laws* initiated by the people.[24]

Finally, in the state of Illinois, Article XIV, Section 3 of the constitution limits initiated amendments to "structural and procedural subjects" relating to the legislative article. However, the state supreme court has construed Article III, Section 3's provision that "All elections shall be free and equal" to require separate propositions for "separate and unrelated questions."[25] However, in Illinois the court has also applied this requirement to measures proposed by the legislature.

It appears the tendency is for state courts and government agencies to assume the initiative was not intended to be given more leeway than legislative acts, even when the constitutions do not explicitly establish single subject requirements for initiatives. In Illinois the courts have found that general language about "free and equal" elections implies a single subject restriction exists for both the legislature and initiative proponents where none is explicitly set forth in the constitution for either. However, the discussion in Part 3 of this paper demonstrates that when specific single subject provisions are incorporated for initiatives, some courts can be very attentive to the "letter of the law." In some states the courts determine *whether* a single subject requirement exists for initiatives, as well as *what* exactly that requirement entails.

When Single Subject Challenges Can Be Made

There are significant differences in the courts' determinations of when single subject challenges are allowed for ballot measures proposed by the

22. Steen v. Murray (1964), 144 Mont. 61; 394 P.2d 761.

23. Initiative Petition No. 314 (1980), OK 174; 625 P.2d 595 at 601.

24. Washington Federation of State Employees v. State of Washington (1995), 127 Wash. 2d.544; 901 P.2d at 1028.

25. Coalition for Political Honesty v. State Board of Elections (1980), 83 Ill. 2d 236 at 254.

legislatures and when they are allowed for measures proposed by initiative. It would appear that this also affects how frequently challenges occur. Here the initiative process is at a distinct disadvantage. The ease of access to the courts for those who would challenge initiatives on single subject grounds no doubt plays a large role in the greater percentage of initiated ballot measures that are challenged. In addition, in some states there are formal constitutional or statutory provisions that direct court involvement in single subject determinations, generally in conjunction with their review of ballot titles. For legislative referenda there are rarely such provisions.

In most if not all states, single subject challenges to initiatives may occur early in the process. In an attempt to ensure that the electorate is fairly informed about the subject matter contained in a given petition, the states regulate the form of the petitions circulated for an initiative. The route to court appeals is also intended to protect the rights of an initiative's proponents and opponents to get a fair title set for a measure. In general, the process works in the following manner. Either the Secretary of State's office or the Lieutenant Governor's office approves the petition form before it is circulated, with one element of that form being the ballot title or ballot question. The ballot title or question is the same one that will appear on the actual ballot on election day; it is generally set by the attorney general. It is, of course, paramount that these formal statements of the ballot subject matter be clear and correct as to the major provisions of a proposed measure; this is what the electorate will vote on and this is what indicates the content of the petition that will be circulated. It is at this early stage of the process, in most cases before any petition can be circulated, that challenges based on the single subject rule are normally allowed under provisions for appeal of ballot titles. The administrative decisions of the title setting authority, regarding single subject compliance or the specific language of the title, may be challenged by any citizen, usually in the state's supreme court.[26]

On the other hand, the titles for legislative referenda are generally set, as are the titles for hundreds of legislative bills, by the legislators and legislative staff who draft proposed bills.[27] Undoubtedly due to the routine nature of the legislative title setting process, as well as to the subsequent opportunities for revisions to titles after a measure has been introduced, the states have not developed specific constitutional provisions for appeal of the title of a legislative referendum prior to its being placed on the bal-

---

26. When the single subject requirement is a constitutional requirement, single subject rulings by inferior courts are appealable to the state supreme courts.

27. There are exceptions. For example, in Ohio a "ballot board" prescribes the ballot language for constitutional amendments proposed by the legislature. Ohio Constitution, Section 16.01.

lot. The ballot title, like the substance of the referendum itself, is subject to revision in the legislative chambers. The citizen's chance to affect the title and/or substance of a legislative referendum is while it is being considered by the legislature. While there are no explicit provisions in the state constitutions *prohibiting* single subject challenges in the courts, the courts are usually reluctant to "intervene in the legislative process" when it is the legislature proposing the laws. Hence, most single subject challenges to legislative referenda occur *after* a measure has been voted on by the electorate.

There is a significant amount of disagreement amongst states and amongst judges within states regarding when a single subject question is "ripe" for review. Oklahoma provides an example of where the courts have been reluctant to review either legislative referenda or initiatives for single subject compliance and fair ballot titles prior to a vote. That Court has declared several legislative bills to be unconstitutional because they violated the single subject rule, but the challenges occurred *after* bills had been enacted.[28] However, in contrast to Colorado and Montana, the Oklahoma Supreme Court has exhibited the *same* reluctance to disqualify *initiated* ballot measures for single subject violations, and has done so consistently over time:

> The doctrine of separation of powers prevents judicial interference with the initiative law-making process with the same force that it prevents legislative restriction upon this court's inherent powers... we have consistently confined our pre-election review of initiative petitions under [statutes] to clear or manifest facial constitutional infirmities.[29]

Florida provides a somewhat unique case, in that all initiatives are *required* by the constitution to be sent by the attorney general for a supreme court opinion with respect to the single subject and ballot title requirements.[30] There is no such requirement for ballot titles for legislative referenda. In fact, the constitution gives the legislature the power to propose constitutional amendments that amend the *whole* of the constitution. Legislative acts are similarly favored in Ohio where the constitution specifies that no bill shall contain more than one subject, but it is up to the presiding officer of each house of the legislature to determine that this requirement is met.[31] For initiatives, on the other hand, the constitution specifies that "All decisions of the secretary of state in the petition process are subject to review by the supreme court in the exercise of original jurisdiction."[32]

---

28. See for example, Campbell v. White, 1993 OK 89; 856 P.2d 255, 1993 Okla.
29. In re Initiative Petition No. 358, 1994 OK 27; 870 P.2d 782.
30. Florida Constitution, Article IV, Section 10.
31. Ohio Constitution, Article 2, Section 15 (D) and 15(E).
32. Ohio Constitution, Article 3, Section 7.

A Missouri Supreme Court Justice quoted a law review article that opined that it was improper for courts to adjudicate pre-election challenges to a measure's substantive validity. Justice Rendlin judged pre-election reviews of initiatives to be particularly problematic because:

> A lawsuit to strike an initiative or referendum from a ballot is one of the deadliest weapons in the arsenal of the measure's political opponents. With increasing frequency, opponents of ballot proposals are finding the weapon irresistible and are suing to stop elections.[33]

Rendlin argued that Missouri's legal precedent for *post*-election review for single subject compliance was set in previous cases such as *Buchanan v. Kirkpatrick* (1981). However, he was in the minority on the Missouri Supreme Court that held in 1990 that a pre-election single subject challenge to an initiative was ripe for judicial determination once the Secretary of State made a determination on whether a petition complies with the Constitution of Missouri.[34] Challenges to legislative acts compliance with single subject rules have only appeared after bills were passed, so no comparison between legislative and initiated measures can be made for Missouri. However, the next section of the paper will discuss the significance of the court's decision to hear pre-election reviews of initiatives.

Colorado provides a clear example of a state court's view that legislative referenda should be treated differently than initiatives when it comes to the timing of single subject challenges. The Colorado Supreme Court decided in a 1996 case that "neither the single-subject requirement itself nor any statute confers jurisdiction on the courts to review a legislative referendum *before it has been adopted* [emphasis added]"; and it also stated that "Our case law embodies a strong tradition which holds that courts cannot interfere with the ongoing legislative process except in extraordinary circumstances."[35] However, the same court has disqualified numerous initiated amendments from being submitted to the people for violating the exact same single subject rule.[36] In a dissenting opinion that was twice as long as the majority opinion, Justice Scott criticized the court for not adhering to the language of the Colorado constitution that expressly prohibits the submission to the electorate of measures that violate the single-subject requirement.

---

33. 64 Notre Dame Law Review 298 (1989) cited in Missourians v. Blunt,.799 S.W.2d 824, 1990, Mo.

34. Missourians v. Blunt (1990), 799 S.W.2d 824, Mo.

35. Polhill v. Buckley (1996), 923 P.2d 119; Colo.

36. For example, see Outcelt v. Buckley (1999), 977 P.2d 856; Colo. and Aisenberg v. Campbell (1998), 960 P.2d 1192; Colo. There are several cases involving tax limitation initiatives and judicial reform initiatives that involve these parties where the court reversed the title setting board's decisions that initiatives did meet the single subject criterium.

I find the plain language of Article XIX sufficient to obligate this court to enforce the constitutionally mandated single-subject requirement equally against legislatively referred measures as well as against citizen initiatives... By waiting until after the November election, the majority subjects the electorate to the very harm the people intended to avoid and requires opponents and proponents alike to assume the risks and unnecessary costs of opposing or supporting a measure that may be constitutionally infirm.[37]

The fact that the "plain language" of the Colorado constitution is the same for legislative amendments to the Constitution as it is for initiative amendments has not deterred the majority from treating the two types of amendments differently.

In Montana both initiated and legislature-proposed constitutional amendments have single subject restrictions. The Montana Supreme Court has yet to hear a case involving a single subject challenge to a legislative constitutional referendum. However, their opinions on initiated amendments indicates that their views on the subject have changed over time. In a 1986 decision the court indicated that they would avoid the *pre-election* review of constitutional changes "unless it appears to be absolutely essential" and with respect to single subject determinations they determined that "this type of multiplicity is not a proper basis for this Court's intervention in the initiative process prior to election.[38] However, 13 years later the Montana Supreme Court invalidated an initiative that sought to reform legislative processes, ruling that it constituted more than one subject because it also made changes that applied to executive branch officials.[39]

In a similar vein, a 1999 California Supreme Court decision demonstrates a reversal of that body's long-term record of denying pre-election review initiatives for compliance with the single subject rule. Up until the 1999 decision in *Senate of the State of California v. Jones,* the Supreme Court had granted pre-election review for single subject compliance on only one other occasion, *Perry v. Jordan* in 1949. As Justice Kennard explained in his dissent in the *Jones* case, the circumstances in that case were very different, as the Supreme Court agreed to hear that case because of the possibility that another court would issue a writ to keep the measure off the ballot.[40] And, in that case, the Supreme Court ruled that the

---

37. Polhill v. Buckley (1996), 923 P.2d 119; Colo. at 11-12.

38. State ex rel. Montana Citizens for the Preservation of Citizens' Rights v. Waltermire, 224 Mont. 273; 729 P.2d 1283.

39. Marshall v. State (1999), MT 33; 975 P.2d 325.

40. Senate of the State of California v. Jones (1999), 21 Cal. 4th 1142; 988 P.2d 1089 at 1170.

initiative did not violate the single subject rule. The new precedent has been set, however. In its significantly expedited *Jones* decision, the Supreme Court concluded that, "the California Constitution compels the court to preclude the submission of a multi-subject measure to the electorate."[41]

The state courts often cite their wariness at getting involved in the "legislative process." The courts are rarely asked to rule on the legislatures' compliance with single subject provisions, especially when the number of challenges as a percentage of all legislative acts are considered. However, single subject challenges to proposed ballot measures are much more common, particularly considering the relatively small number of initiatives that are proposed or that qualify for the ballot. Of particular importance is the ability for opponents of an initiated measure to challenge a measure *prior* to being put on the ballot. If the recent court rulings in California, Colorado, Missouri, and Montana are any indication, the trend is for the courts to overcome their reluctance to intervene in the "legislative process" when it comes to ruling on single subject provisions for initiatives. Pre-election review of initiatives for single subject compliance by the courts is becoming the rule, rather than exception. The opposite is true for legislative referenda.

Repercussions of Different Provisions and the Timing of Single Subject Challenges

The opportunity to challenge initiated measures' compliance with the single subject rule early in the process, prior to the circulation of any petitions in most cases, is undoubtedly related to the large number of initiatives that are challenged in court. The record of single subject challenges on legislative statutes and amendments is short, particularly considering the dozens of legislative acts promulgated each year. Initiatives, on the other hand are challenged with much greater frequency. This is likely related to the advantages pre-election review provides to an initiative's opponents. Post-election judicial review of ballot measures lends itself to the application of "severability" clauses, with the courts upholding the portions of the measures that are deemed related to the valid single subject expressed in the ballot title. On the other hand, pre-election review of initiated ballot measures leads to the invalidation of any signature-gathering efforts if the court finds that single subject or ballot title provisions have been violated. Secondly, as some court opinions have explicitly noted, it is only natural that the courts would be more deferential to a measure that has been passed by the majority of the voters. The judiciary is likely to exercise more restraint in post-election reviews.

---

41. California v. Jones at 1168.

In their review of the initiative process in California, the Center for Responsive Government notes that "single-subject violations are routinely alleged as a first ground of attack by persons who have opposed the measure during its campaign."[42] The stakes are high. The costs associated with qualifying an initiative on the ballot are high. The costs of running a campaign against a ballot initiative are often even higher. With millions of dollars in the balance, it is clear why both proponents and opponents of a particular initiative look to the courts for justice. As Part 3 of this essay will reveal, it is often difficult to predict how the courts will decide on a particular measure. Standards of review vary greatly amongst the states, and they often vary significantly over time *within* a given state. However, for the *opponents* of a measure, it is an economical means of stalling the petition process, even if the single subject challenge is ultimately shot down. In most states a petition cannot be circulated until the ballot title is set. Even if the courts expedite review, a challenge may effectively keep a measure off of the ballot for at least a year or two. And if a state permits petitions to be circulated pending judicial review of the measure, the petitioners risk the invalidation of every signature collected if the court changes any part of the title.

Clearly individuals or groups that are supporting a ballot measure and that have limited resources are going to be hit the hardest by pre-election delays and court costs. A wealthy group can simply pay more petition circulators to make up for lost time. Volunteer efforts do not have that same luxury. In addition, the costs of defending against a pre-election challenge are borne entirely by the initiative proponents, while post-election challenges are defended by the state. Furthermore, a post-election single subject challenge would generally lead to the court's upholding all of the parts of the initiative that were adequately expressed in the ballot title.[43] For all of these reasons, the opponents of a proposed measure would clearly find it much more advantageous to kill a measure *before* it ever gets onto the ballot. The single subject provision provides an economical means to those ends. As the Arizona Supreme Court recognized, allowing *pre-election* review of initiatives is likely to lead to an increase in the number of appeals that a court will confront. Determining the validity of an initiative before the voters have an opportunity to vote on it would:

> ... be tantamount to claiming the power of life and death over every initiated measure by the people. It would *limit the right of the peo-*

---

42. Democracy by Initiative: Shaping California's 4th Branch of Government, Center for Responsive Government (1992) at 313.

43. For example, see Raven v. Deukmejian (1990), 52 Cal. 3d 336 and Ray v. Mortham (1999), 24 Fla. Law W. 412.

ple to propose only valid laws, whereas the other lawmaking body, the Legislature, would go untrammeled as to the legal soundness of its measures.[44]

Still, the Arizona Supreme Court has ruled that pre-election challenges to initiatives on single subject grounds are permissible.

Finally, it is only natural that the courts would be more reluctant to find a measure to be in violation of a single subject provision after it has been passed by the people. The purpose of the single subject rule is to prohibit logrolling and to avoid the perpetration of surprise and/or fraud on the voters. However, as the California Supreme Court has noted, courts are hesitant to reverse the course of an election, because:

> ...we should not lightly presume that the voters did not know what they were about in approving Proposition 8. Rather, in accordance with our tradition, "we ordinarily should assume that the voters who approved a constitutional amendment...have voted intelligently upon an amendment to their organic law, the whole text of which was supplied each of them prior to the election and which they must be assumed to have duly considered."[45]

The Missouri Supreme Court explicitly stated that "some matters objected to prior to election may be judged by a different standard following the election," and that:

> Since the amendment has already been adopted and the people have demonstrated their will, this Court's duty is not to seek to condemn the amendment, but to seek to uphold it if possible.[46]

To summarize, there are several reasons why pre-election legal challenges to ballot initiatives are common in some states, while they are rare for legislative referenda. First, some courts permit pre-election challenges to the former but not the latter. Second, when pre-election challenges are allowed, it is an economical way for opponents of an initiative to defeat the measure in its entirety. It is cheaper than staging an opposition campaign to convince the public to vote against the measure. Finally, the courts are less likely to find a measure to be unconstitutional because of a single subject defect after it has already been passed by the voters. It is, therefore, a

---

44. State v. Osborn (1914), 16 Ariz. 247, 249-50, cited in Winkle v. City of Tucson (1997), 190 Ariz. 413 at 415-416.

45. Brosnahan v. Brown (1982), 32 Cal. 3d 236; 651 P.2d 274 at 252, citing from Amador v. State Board of Education (1978), 22 Cal.3d 208 at 243-244.

46. Buchanan v. Kirkpatrick (1981), 615 S.W.2d 6 at 12.

very significant matter when the court determines whether or not it will hear *pre-election* single subject challenges to initiatives.

Part 3: Varying Standards of Review

An examination of state supreme courts' decisions regarding single subject challenges to statutes and amendments reveals significant variation in the courts' standards of review. In some states the highest courts have maintained a constant standard of review for "one subject" limitations over several decades; in others the standards applied by the courts have changed over time. In addition, the courts demonstrate diverse views regarding what is the proper level of scrutiny to be applied to measures originating in the legislature versus those originating by petition. Once again, there is a great deal of support for Justice Lewis' assessment that the "oneness" standard for initiatives is "in the eye of the beholder" — and the relevant "beholders" are ultimately the justices that sit on the state supreme court.[47]

Consistency or Variation in a Court's Standard of Review Over Time

This section focuses on the extent to which the courts change the standards or "tests" they apply in order to determine whether an initiative or a referendum violates the "one subject" or "one amendment" restrictions. In general when it comes to jurisprudence courts are reluctant to reverse their earlier decisions, following the doctrine of *stare decisis* ("let the prior decision stand"). As Florida Justice Boyd said in concurring with a majority opinion on a single subject determination in 1978:

> Under the doctrine of *stare decisis*, and in order to permit the public to know what standards are acceptable to this Court, we should adhere in this case to the philosophy expressed in the opinion of Weber v. Smathers....[48]

---

47. The following discussion is based upon state supreme court cases for those states with single subject-type requirements for initiatives, and which also had sufficient relevant case histories on the various aspects of review standards. Cases derived from Lexis searches of each state's supreme court cases.

48. Floridians Against Casino Takeover v. Let's Help Florida (1978), 363 So. 2d 337 at 342.

The rationale for consistency is obvious; as one constitutional scholar notes, *stare decisis* promotes "the certainty, uniformity, and stability of the law."[49]

Consistent Standards of Review

In a few states the courts have maintained a relatively consistent standard for adjudicating single subject challenges. For instance, Arizona's Supreme Court in the 1990s is still applying the standard it established in 1934. Its standard is that a proposed measure constitutes "one amendment" if the Constitution, as amended, "shall constitute a consistent and workable whole on the general topic" and "voters supporting [a measure] would reasonably be expected to support" different parts of the measure.[50] The Supreme Court in Oklahoma specifically indicated its concern for consistency in its application of the "germaneness" standard for determining whether initiatives met the requirement for constitutional amendments to embrace "one general subject" in 1984 and 1996 opinions.[51] In the latter opinion the court noted that the standard it would continue to apply originated in the 1955 *Rupe v. Shaw* case on a legislative amendment and a 1962 initiative amendment case.[52] However, Oregon has demonstrated what is perhaps the longest consistent application of "one subject" standards. In a 1997 opinion denying that an initiative violated Oregon's "one subject" rule, the Court noted the continuity of court cases interpreting that provision over the "last century."[53] Washington's Supreme Court's standard of review also appears very consistent over the years, once the general or restrictive nature of the legislative or ballot title is factored in.[54]

The Alaska Supreme Court has perhaps been the most assiduous in its application of a relatively liberal single subject test for initiatives. Their standard is that the act "should embrace some one general standard...

49. David M. O'Brien. (1997) Constitutional Law and Politics: Struggles for Power and Governmental Accountability, Volume 1, Third Edition. W.W. Norton & Company, New York, p. 116.

50. Kerby v. Luhrs (1934), 44 Ariz. At 221, 36 P.2d at 554, cited in Slayton v. Shumway (1990), 166 Ariz. 87; 800 P.2d 590 at 593.

51. In re Initiative Petition No. 319 (1984), OK., 682 P.2d 222, 224. In re Initiative Petition No. 363, 1996 OK 122; 927 P.2d 558 at 566.

52. Rupe v. Shaw (1955), 286 P.2d 1094 and In re Initiative Petition No. 271 (1962), 373 P.2d 1017.

53. Caleb v. Beesley (1997), 326 Ore. 83; 949 P.2d 724 at 89-90.

54. See Washington State v. Broadaway (1997), 133 Wash. 2d 118.

should fall under some one general idea…germane to, one general subject."[55] The court even noted that despite "reservations" about a their opinions on previous cases, they would not overrule their prior cases for three reasons. First, they doubted there were more workable stricter standards. "Second, the sponsors of the initiative have relied on our precedents in preparing the present proposition and undertaking the considerable expense and time and effort needed to place it on the ballot." Third, the court noted that the "initiative is an act of direct democracy guaranteed by our constitution" and any doubts should be resolved in favor of the proposed measures.[56] This majority view was not, however, unanimous. Two justices dissented, and one, Justice Moore, severely criticized the majority saying that it was because of its "extremely liberal interpretation that the [single subject] rule has become a farce."[57]

California's courts have been similarly constant in their repeated application of the standard for reviewing single subject compliance for initiatives. In its 1949 *Perry v. Jordan* decision the court ruled that in order to be meet the single subject requirement, the provisions of a measure must be "reasonably germane" to each other. [58] In a 1990 case, *Raven v. Deukmejian*, Justice Mosk noted, "*Perry* has been expressly or impliedly followed, without deviation, in the years that followed."[59] However, Justice Mosk in his dissent also noted that there had been a "bare majority of four justices to three" who had rejected a more recent single subject challenge, and he proposed that the California Supreme Court was being too liberal in its construction of what constituted a single subject.[60] In the 1999 *Senate v. Jones* case, the Supreme Court cited the same "reasonably germane" standard. However, while one of the proponent's arguments for single subject compliance was that it was a lot less general than other initiatives previously upheld by the court, the court found that the measure's provisions for taking away the legislature's power of reapportionment and reducing legislative pay were not reasonably germane.[61] While the standard of review may not have changed, it is uncertain that the application of that standard has remained the same.

---

55. Yute Air Alaska, Inc. v. McAlpine (1985), 698 P.2d 1173 at 1180-1181.

56. Yute Air Alaska, Inc. v. McAlpine at 1181.

57. Yute Air Alaska, Inc. v. McAlpine at 1182.

58. Perry v. Jordan, 34 Cal. 2d 87 (1949) at 92. Also see discussion in Democracy by Initiative: Shaping California's 4th Branch of Government, Center for Responsive Government.

59. Raven v. Deukmejian (1990), 52 Cal. 3d 336 at 362.

60. Raven v. Deukmejian at 363-364.

61. Senate of the State of California v. Jones (1999), 21 Cal. 4th 1142.

Changing Standards of Review

In addition to the potential for the courts to change how they *apply* single subject rules in practice, at least a few of the state courts have made more than minor adjustments in the actual *standards* of review they apply to judge single subject compliance. Some of the new standards are due in part to changes in the actual single subject provisions set forth in the constitutions. But even considering the changes in constitutional language, the courts have demonstrated some amazing reversals, and there are indications that other states' courts may follow. One source of information on courts' reversals on single subject reviews comes from the opinions of those judges who differ from the reasoning and/or conclusions of the majority. Florida, Montana, and Illinois justices in dissenting/concurring opinions have questioned the application of new standards for single subject review, often forcefully and sometimes at great length.

The constitution in Florida requires that for initiatives that propose to change the constitution, "any such revision or amendment, except for those limiting the power of government to raise revenue, shall embrace but one subject and matter directly connected therewith."[62] Prior to 1972 the constitution permitted initiatives to amend any "section" of the constitution. However, after the court struck down one initiative calling for a unicameral legislature because it affected more than one section of the constitution, a legislative referendum was passed in 1972 that provided for the revision or amendment of "any portion or portions" of the constitution as long as the proposal embraced a "single subject and matter directly connected therewith."[63] The controlling precedent for single subject determinations after this change was *Floridians Against Casino Takeover v. Let's Help Florida*, a 1978 case. This case established several "principles" which "settled the standard of review by the judiciary when confronted by an assault upon a particular initiative proposal."[64]

First, "the 1972 change was designed to enlarge the right to amend the Constitution by initiative petition." Second, the burden upon the opponent is to establish that the initiative proposal "is clearly and conclusively defective." Third, "the 'one subject' limitation was selected to place a functional, as opposed to locational, restraint on the range of authorized amendments." Last, in applying the foregoing principles to the amendment there under consideration, which arguably

---

62. Florida Constitution, Article IX, Section 3.
63. Floridians Against Casino Takeover v. Let's Help Florida (1978), 363 So. 2d 337 at 339-340.
64. Floridians Against Casino Takeover v. Let's Help Florida at 340.

embraced at least five "subjects" ... one subject limitation should be viewed broadly rather than narrowly.[65]

However, in 1984 the Florida Supreme Court "receded" from its ruling in *Floridians*. In *Fine v. Firestone* the court found that it should require "strict compliance" with the single subject rule for initiated constitutional amendments "because our constitution is the basic document that controls our governmental functions, including the adoption of any laws by the legislature."[66] The majority went on to explain,

> In *Floridians* we also held that the question of whether an initiative proposal conflicted with other articles of sections of the constitution had no place in assessing the legitimacy of an initiative proposal. We recede from that language and find that how an initiative proposal affects other articles and sections of the constitution is an appropriate factor to be considered in determining whether there is more than one subject included in an initiative proposal.[67]

This major shift in the court's standard of review did not transpire without criticism. In Justice Shaw's special concurrence in *Evans v. Firestone* decided later that same year, he criticized the "canonization" of the "function of government test" created in *Fine*, opining that "as a practical matter the function of government test would make the one-subject limitation of the constitution practically insurmountable."[68]

In a major reversal of opinions, the Montana Supreme Court recently shifted its standard of review (at the same time it reversed its position of not considering pre-election challenges on single subject grounds) when it disqualified a tax limitation initiative for violating the "one amendment" requirement. The 1999 decision in *Marshall v. State* abandoned the longstanding test that originated in the 1914 Montana *Hay v. Alderson* case that required proposed constitutional amendments to demonstrate "unity of subject," and concluded that "the unity required by this section is served notwithstanding the existence of many provisions in an Act where such provisions are germane to the general subject matter expressed."[69] In determining the 1999 initiative violated the single amendment rule, the Montana court relied heavily on the logic of the Oregon Supreme Court's 1998 *Armatta v. Kitzhaber* ruling, instead of its own precedents, stating that:

---

65. 363 So. 2d 337 at 340. Quotations indicate passages cited from the 1976 Florida Supreme Court case Weber v. Smathers, 338 So. 2d 819.

66. Fine v. Firestone (1984), 448 So. 2d 984 at 989.

67. Fine v. Firestone at 990.

68. Evans v. Firestone (1984), 457 So. 2d 1351 at 1360.

69. Hay v. Alderson, 49 Mont. 387 at 405, 142 P. at 213.

The unity of subject rule that the Court applied in *Hay* and *Cooney* is so elastic that it could swallow Montana's entire Constitution. We decline to affirm such a rule.[70]

The court overturned its own precedent that it had followed in numerous cases over the years, adopting a neighboring state's standards of review.

Illinois presents another example of a Supreme court reversing its earlier opinions. As discussed previously, there is no explicit provision in the constitution that limits constitutional amendments to a "single subject" or "separate questions" as is the case in many states. However, the courts have interpreted Article III, Section 3's provision that "All elections shall be free and equal," to indicate that separate questions cannot be combined in a single proposition, and that the voter has the right to vote upon each question separately.[71] But their interpretation also changed over time. Considering a request to direct the State Board of Elections to certify a constitutional ballot proposal that was denied based on "separate questions" provisions. The majority noted that:

Some of our early cases considered identical language in article II, section 18, of the 1870 Illinois Constitution and can be read as indicating that separate questions cannot be combined into a single proposition, and that the voter has a right to vote upon each question separately... Our more recent opinions, however, clearly establish that it is only separate and *unrelated* questions which cannot be combined in a single proposition.[72]

The general pattern observed in other states with changing standards follows here also; two strongly worded dissents, including one by the Chief Justice, objected to the change in the court's standards of review.

The record in these states indicates that while the courts' standards of review for compliance with single subject restrictions remains constant in some states, the standards, or the application of those standards, has changed significantly in other states. We see examples of courts reversing or significantly redefining their earlier standards of review, as well as a significant degree of disagreement amongst justices when it comes to determining the proper test for compliance with single subject provisions. What constitutes a "single subject" or "one amendment" has varied within the states over time; and the changes have tended to be in the direction of

---

70. Marshall v. State (1999), 975 P.2d 325 at 331.

71. Coalition for Political Honesty v. State Board of Elections (1980), 83 Ill. 2d 236 at 253.

72. Coalition for Political Honesty v. State Board of Elections, 83 Ill. 2d 236 at 253-254.

more restrictive review of initiatives. Furthermore, these changing standards of review are often accompanied by significant disagreement amongst a state's justices, as demonstrated by some lengthy and strongly worded dissenting opinions. Certainly there is a demonstrable lack of judicial consensus on the single subject standards that their constitutions require for initiatives. Furthermore, the major source of that lack of consensus would appear to be the reluctance of some justices to "interfere" in the legislative process.

Standards of Review for Legislative versus Initiative Acts

There are also large differences in the justices' views on the type of scrutiny they should apply to single subject tests for bills and amendments proposed by the legislature versus measures proposed by initiatives. An examination of the states' supreme court decisions reveals that the different opinions are more the result of the different philosophies of the justices, rather than significant differences in the single subject provisions they are interpreting. And once again, some strongly worded dissents challenge the tests employed by the majority. There is certainly a great deal of variation amongst the states' courts as to whether legislative action by the people deserves more, less, or the same degree of deference than the court applies to legislative action by the people's elected representatives. The underlying principle is, again, the separation of legislative and judicial powers. There is also the oft-unstated question about the capacity of the people to exercise their legislative powers wisely.

Same Standards for Legislative and Initiative Measures

The state supreme court decisions in Alaska, Arizona, California, Ohio, Oklahoma, and Oregon reveal that these states have roughly the same standards of review to determine whether either legislative or initiative measures contain a single subject. In Alaska's *Yute Air* case the dissenting justices note that "This court has ... continued to apply the same extremely deferential standard of review to initiatives that it applies to legislation."[73] The majority explained the reason for their deferential standard:

Justice Moore's contention (discussed at dissent at p. 1184-5) that the single subject requirement should be more strictly applied in the initiative (as opposed to legislative) context not only is adverse to our deferential attitude toward initiatives, it also ignores the explicit constitutional directive to the contrary. Alaska Const. Art. XII, Sec-

---

73. Yute Air Alaska, Inc. v. McAlpine (1985), 698 P.2d 1173 at 1184.

tion 11 provides: "Unless clearly inapplicable, the law-making powers assigned to the legislature may be exercised by the people through the initiative...." A one subject rule for initiatives which is more restrictive than the rule for legislative action is not permitted.[74]

However, two out of the five justices took exception to the Alaska Supreme Court's determination to abide by precedent and apply a constant, relatively liberal standard of review to initiatives over time. The dissenting justices cited the greater dangers of logrolling, one-sided advertising by initiative proponents, and the judges' assessment that many voters never read the full text of the initiative before they vote as the rationale for abandoning the court's precedents.[75] Certainly the likelihood that this standard will endure is reduced by the fact that a significant minority believes that the review of initiatives should be stricter than the review for legislative measures.

California's Supreme Court has maintained a notably constant standard of review for measures originating from the legislature and from the citizenry. In the case of *Perry v. Jordan*, which challenged an initiative with violating the new single subject provision for initiatives, the court considered that:

> The problem of whether more than one subject is embraced within one legislative act is not new in this state. Although section 1c has been newly added *extending the requirement to initiative constitutional amendments*, the Constitution for many years has required that "Every act shall embrace but one subject, which subject shall be expressed in its title."[76]

The court then extended the existing standard of "reasonably germane" to initiated constitutional amendments. In the ensuing years, numerous initiatives have been challenged on single subject grounds, but the California courts have only sustained three of those challenges.[77] Yet again, there is significant disagreement amongst the justices, with a few calling for a stricter standard for initiatives. For example, in a 1978 case a dissenting justice suggested:

> ...that the single subject rule should be applied more strictly to initiative measures than to legislative bills, and that the "functionally related" test was the appropriate standard by which to measure compliance of initiatives with the rule.[78]

---

74. Yute Air Alaska, Inc. v. McAlpine at 1181.

75. Yute Air Alaska, Inc. v. McAlpine at 1184-1185.

76. Perry v. Jordan (1948), 34 Cal. 2d 87 at 92.

77. See Senate of the State of California v. Jones (1999), 21 Cal. 4th 1142 at 1170.

78. Schmitz v. Younger (1978) 21 Cal.3d 90 cited in Harbor v. Deukmejian (1987), 43 Cal. 3d 1078 at 1099.

With one to three justices dissenting on recent initiative single subject rulings, it is not clear how long the court's "reasonably germane" standard will be upheld.

Arizona is another state that construes the single subject restriction as being the same for initiatives as they are for legislative measures. The Arizona standard was established in *Kerby v. Luhrs* in 1934.[79] That case interpreted the constitution's Article XXI, Section 1 requirement for legislature-proposed constitutional amendments, "If more than one proposed amendment shall be submitted at any election, such proposed amendments shall be submitted in such manner that the electors may vote for or against such proposed amendments separately." In *Slayton v. Shumway*, a 1990 single subject challenge to an initiative, the court determined that *Kerby* provided the proper test for initiatives as well. But in contrast to California, the Arizona Supreme Court justices have demonstrated a remarkable consensus in upholding their longstanding standards of review.

Oklahoma has applied an equivalent standard to initiated amendments and to legislative bills. Article 24, Section 1 of the Oklahoma constitution specifies that:

> No proposal for the amendment or alteration of this Constitution which is submitted to the voters shall embrace more than one general subject and the voters shall vote separately for or against each proposal submitted....

And Article 5, Section 57 specifies that "Every act of the Legislature shall embrace but one subject." The Oklahoma Supreme Court has applied the same general standard to both constitutional amendments and legislative bills. In both types of cases, the standard of review is to determine whether the changes proposed are "germane." In a 1996 challenge to an initiated constitutional amendment related to gambling, the Court stated that:

> the test for gauging multiplicity for subjects is whether the changes proposed are all germane to a singular common subject and purpose or are essentially unrelated one to another.[80]

Similarly, the Court noted in a 1993 single subject challenge to one of the legislature's appropriations bills that:

---

79. Kerby v. Luhrs (1934), 44 Ariz. 208, 36 P.2d 549 at 554.
80. In re Petition No. 363, State Question No. 672 (1996), OK 122; 927 P,.2d 558 at 566.

As our prior cases applying art. 5, section 57 indicate, the most appropriate standard for applying the single-subject rule is germaneness: are the various provisions related to a common theme or purpose?[81]

The Oregon Supreme Court has also applied the same standard across legislative acts and initiative and legislative constitutional amendments, reiterating that the equal standard applied to both sources of legislation in 1997.[82] And in Oklahoma and Oregon, as in Arizona, the supreme court justices have demonstrated a large degree of consensus on the proper standard of review.

It is interesting to note that these five states, where the standards for single subject review are the same for initiative and legislative measures, were all noted as states with consistent standards of review over time. However, while the majority opinion of the supreme courts in Alaska, California, Arizona, Oklahoma, and Oregon all advocate treating initiatives with the same deference accorded to legislative measures, the dissenting justices in the first two states advocate stricter standards of review for initiatives compared to those for the legislature. Based on the dissents in California and Alaska, if change occurs to the standards, it is likely to be to apply stricter standards to the initiative. Again, it appears that if there is a trend, it is for the states' courts to tighten their standards of review for the initiative when they change the standards over time.

Differing Standards for Legislative and Initiative Measures

The previous section noted that justices in the minority in Alaska and California argued against the courts' equal treatment of single subject requirements for initiatives and legislative acts. The majority in two of the state supreme courts have agreed with this principle of separate standards of review. In Montana and Florida the majority has clearly set forth their rationale for treating legislative measures and initiative measures differently, with a more favorable presumption of compliance with single subject requirements afforded to the legislatures. Their rationale focuses on the distinct nature of the initiative process, rather than any explicit provisions in the constitutions that set different standards of review for initiatives and referenda. In Colorado, Missouri, and Washington the supreme courts *articulate* the same standards of review, but in practice their *application* of single subject rules clearly varies based on the source of a proposed statute or constitutional amendment.

---

81. Campbell v. White (1993), OK 89; 856 P.2d 255 at 260.
82. Caleb v. Beesley (1997), 326 Ore. 83; 949 P.2d 724 at 89.

Stricter Review for Initiatives

As previously discussed, the Florida Supreme Court reversed itself and established new, stricter standards for the review of single subject compliance in 1984. In *Fine v. Firestone* the court decided that there was a difference between the legislative "one subject" restriction and the "one subject" restriction for initiative constitutional amendments.[83] In part they justified their new opinion on a new interpretation of the terminology associated with the two single subject provisions — "one subject and matter *properly* connected therewith" for legislative statutes versus "one subject and matter *directly* connected therewith" for initiative amendments. Two other reasons were based on the court's reassessment of the initiative process.

> Second, we find that we should take a broader view of the legislative provision because any proposed law must proceed through legislative debate and public hearing. Such a process allows change in the content of any law before its adoption. This process is, in itself, a restriction on the drafting of a proposal which is not applicable to the scheme for constitutional revision or amendment by initiative. Third, and most important, we find that we should require strict compliance with the single-subject rule in the initiative process for constitutional change because our constitution is the basic document that controls our governmental functions, including the adoption of any laws by the legislature.[84]

In the final paragraph of the *Fine* majority opinion the Court concluded that if the same proposal had been put forward by the legislature, a constitutional revision commission, or a constitutional convention, it might have passed judicial scrutiny, but initiative petitions should be *strictly* scrutinized with respect to the "one subject" requirement.

We noted earlier how the Montana Supreme Court recently reversed its long-time application of the 1914 *Hay* "unity of subject" standard of review for constitutional amendments proposed by initiative.[85] Sections 1 through 7 of Article XIV on "Constitutional Revision" outline provisions for calling constitutional conventions. Section 8 provides for amendment by legislative referendum. Sections 9 and 10 relate to amendment by initiative. Article XIV then concludes with Section 11, entitled "Submission," which states:

> If more than one amendment is submitted at the same election, each shall be so prepared and distinguished that it can be voted upon separately.

---

83. Fine v. Firestone(1984), 448 So. 2d 984, 1998 Fla. at 988-989.
84. Fine v. Firestone (1984), 448 So. 2d 984, 1998 Fla. at 989.
85. Marsh v. Bartlett (1999), 343 Mo. 526; 121 S.W.2d 737.

The court determined that while it was one thing to apply the *Hay* standard when amendments could only be proposed by the legislature, it was now of the opinion that it is an entirely different matter when amendments are proposed by initiative:

> The Montana Constitution [originally] guaranteed that legislators would debate and deliberate upon any proposed constitutional amendment. For present-day constitutional initiatives, however, there is no guarantee that Montana voters will have similar deliberative opportunities...The voter to whom a measure is submitted has a business or occupation other than that of the consideration of legislation. The measure is submitted to the banker, the merchant, the farmer, the lawyer, the housewife.[86]

The Montana Supreme Court has not had the occasion to apply its new standard of review to a "one amendment" challenge to a constitutional legislative referendum. However, the language of the *Marshall* opinion would seem to indicate that the court would judge a legislative amendment more liberally than it would an identical initiative amendment. The court perceived its role as being to protect the banker, the merchant, the farmer, the lawyer, and the housewife from having to vote on overly complex or misleading initiatives, whereas the legislature is assumed to provide that same protection for its own ballot measures.

Different Applications of Standards

The Colorado Supreme Court has employed the same standard in the few years since the single subject limitation was established for initiatives, referring repeatedly to its 1995 test in which subject matter of a measure needs to be "necessarily or properly connected" rather than "disconnected or incongruous" and it looks for a "unifying or common objective" in the different parts of a measure.[87] However, it is not the "test," but rather *when* the test is applied that is significant in some cases. As previously discussed, the Colorado Supreme Court decided that it can review initiative constitutional amendments for single subject compliance *prior to* an election, but that it has no jurisdiction to review legislative referenda that propose constitutional amendments until *after* an election. The Colorado Constitution was amended in 1994 to restrict both legislative amendments and initiative amendments and statutes to a single subject. The legislature indicated the purpose behind this change was "to prevent surreptitious

---

86. Marshall v. State, 1999 MT 33; 975 P.2d 325 at 330.
87. In re Title Public Rights in Waters II (1995), 898 P.2d 1076 at 1079-1080.

measures and apprise the people of the subject of each measure by the title, that is, to prevent surprise and fraud from being practiced upon voters."[88] However, in its refusal to accept pre-election challenges to legislative referenda, the Colorado Supreme Court has clearly discriminated between initiatives and referenda for rationale that appears to be in contradiction to the requirement explicitly stated in the constitution. Whereas the former may be stricken from the ballot as a result of single subject challenges, the latter are immune to pre-election challenges.

Another indication that the Colorado court may treat initiatives more strictly than legislative acts or amendments is found in the high number of initiative ballot titles that are disapproved by the court. The administrative ballot title setting process in Colorado is one of the most rigorous and arguably one of the most equitable processes used in any initiative state. A Ballot Title Setting Board comprised of the Secretary of State, a representative from the Attorney General's Office, and a representative of the Legislative Legal Services Office together determine the ballot title at a hearing that permits interested members of the public to make their opinions heard. Each of these officials is herself elected separately, or is answerable to an official elected independent of the others, in addition to their representation of two branches of the government. While the votes of two out of the three board members are sufficient to pass a title, the decisions are generally unanimous. In contrast, for legislative ballot issues the Colorado General Assembly sets its own ballot titles, although it is generally accomplished by, or with the assistance of, the Legislative Legal Services Office. Yet, even with the central role of the Legislative Legal Services Office in setting initiative ballot titles — the same office that helps draft the legislature's bills and amendments and set titles of all legislative acts — initiative ballot titles are commonly overturned by the Supreme Court for violations of the single subject rule. Literally dozens of initiated measures have been challenged on single subject grounds since the restrictions first went into effect in 1995. In the vast majority of the cases the Title Setting Board's title and judgment that an initiative encompasses a single subject are overturned. Either the Attorney General, the Secretary of State, and the Deputy for Legislative Legal Services are uncharacteristically inept when it comes to determining the validity of initiatives, or the Colorado Supreme Court is extremely strict in its scrutiny of initiatives.

In Washington the initiated statute is at a disadvantage compared to legislative statutes due to the Supreme Court's application of different rules for different "types" of ballot titles. While the court notes that its standard is to liberally construe Article 2, Section 19 of the Constitution that

---

88. CRS 1-40-106.5 (1994 Sup).

specifies "single subject" for all bills, it applies different standards of review depending on whether the ballot title is "general" or "restrictive."

Where the title is general, "any subject reasonably germane to such title may be embraced within the body of the bill." The constitution is not violated even if the general subject contains several incidental subjects or subdivisions. "All that is required is that there be some 'rational unity' between the general subject and the incidental subdivisions."[89]

However, if a title is determined by the courts to be restrictive, it "will not be regarded as liberally and provisions not fairly within it will not be given force... A restrictive title expressly limits the scope of the act to that expressed in the title."[90] As a result of this distinction initiatives are at a disadvantage. The disadvantage arises because the title of a proposed statutory initiative is set by the Attorney General,[91] while the legislature prepares its own titles for referenda. The initiative proponent is dependent upon the Attorney General, and the title he sets, to determine the type of single subject review the Court will apply.

The significance of the different standards of review for the two types of titles was demonstrated in the 1997 Supreme Court case *State v. Broadaway*. An initiative was submitted through the legislature and the legislature ultimately adopted it and passed it as a bill. When the resultant statute was later challenged on the grounds that it violated the single subject requirement, the Supreme Court determined that the statute met the single subject requirements *because* the relevant title was the *legislative* title and not the initiative ballot title. If the official *ballot* title, "Shall penalties and sentencing standards be increased for crimes involving a firearm, and sentences and plea agreements be public records?" had applied, the act would have violated the single subject rule. However, the general legislative title, "An Act Relating to increasing penalties for armed crimes..." was determined to meet the single subject requirement because it was a general title.[92] Even if the standards applied by the court are uniform, the standard of single subject review is ultimately controlled by the title. For the initiative that title is not controlled by the proponent; it is set by the Attorney General and "classified" by the Court.

Finally, the courts have a great deal of leeway in their application of the single subject rule in terms of the "severability" clauses that often apply

---

89. Washington Federation of State Employees v. State (1995), 127 Wash. 2d 544; 901 P.2d 1028 at 1034, citing several other Washington cases, including State v. Grisby, 97 Wash. 2d 493, 498, 647 P.2d 6 (1982).

90. State v. Broadaway (1997), 133 Wash. 2d 118; 942 P.2d 363 at 127.

91. Revised Code of Washington 29.27.060.

92. State v. Broadaway (1997), 133 Wash. 2d 118; 942 P.2d 363 at 124-129.

to statutes and constitutional amendments that are found to violate single subject requirements. In his dissent to the majority opinion in *Missourians v. Blunt*, Justice Rendlin was of the opinion that the court was disqualifying an initiative that showed a great deal more singularity of purpose than a legislative amendment the court had said met the "one subject" requirement several years earlier.[93] Furthermore, he noted that the majority's own opinion clearly demonstrated the one provision of the initiative that they construed as violating the single subject rule because they were "beyond the central purpose and not matters properly connected therewith, was readily severable."[94] But four years later in *Hammerschmidt v. Boone County* the Court demonstrated its willingness to allow for the severance of a section of two different *legislative* bills that it construed as a second subject.[95] In fact, in *Hammerschmidt* the Court even considered whether any provisions within the severed section might be reinstated as falling within the single subject of the allowable portions of the bills. This case provides a distinct contrast to the treatment received by the initiated amendment in the *Blunt* case.

In summary, we see that there are variations in the standards of review used by some courts over time. There are also variations in the standards that some courts apply to their review of initiative measures and legislative measures when it comes to determining what is and is not a single subject — even when the language of the state constitutions themselves provide no basis for the different types of scrutiny. Initiatives are more strictly scrutinized than legislative ballot measures. Furthermore, it appears that the courts are becoming stricter in their review of initiatives, when their standards do change over time. It is also clear that there is a significant degree of disagreement among justices on the standards of review and the application of those standards on the courts' review of initiative ballot measures. What constitutes a single subject is, truly, "in the eye of the beholder."

Conclusion

This paper has demonstrated that the "single subject" and "single amendment" provisions that exist in most of the initiative states' constitutions have a significant impact on the initiative process. It has also suggested that such provisions have a much greater impact on *initiative* lawmaking powers than they have on the state legislatures' lawmaking powers. In the

---

93. Missourians v. Blunt (1990), 799 S.W.2d 824 at 837.
94. Missourians v. Blunt (1990), 799 S.W.2d 824 at 839.
95. Hammerschmidt v. Boone County (1994), 877 S.W.2d 98.

vast majority of these states there are identical or very similarly worded constraints on both the legislative and the initiative processes. However, while the legislatures rarely see a single subject challenge to their bills or ballot measures, single subject challenges are a common, if not a standard hurdle for initiative proponents in several states. Furthermore, the courts often apply a stricter level of scrutiny to initiative measures, based on their own assessments of the risks associated with initiative versus legislative measures. In practice, the states' provisions for judicial review of single subject compliance have placed the judiciary at the center of the initiative process. There are certainly benefits associated with this form of judicial review of initiatives, but the benefits do not come without costs.

The benefits of single subject rules were discussed in Part 1. Certainly the prevention of logrolling and the promotion of informed legislators and voters are widely accepted as desirable ends. Whether the courts should be the guardians against "precipitous and cataclysmic change" when the legislature and/or the citizenry determine that "significant and timely reform" is needed is perhaps more contentious. Only a couple of the states' courts have cited this as a rationale for single subject provisions for initiatives, and for their heightened scrutiny of initiated measures. Still, single subject restrictions have been a traditional method of controlling the legislative process throughout the United States' history.

However, if the judiciary were as active in making single subject judgments in the normal *legislative* process as they are in the *initiative* process, it seems likely that there would have been more concern about the violation of the "separation of powers" provisions that are included in every state constitution. Would the Florida legislature accede to its every bill being examined by the Florida Supreme Court to determine whether the titles were sufficient and whether they adhered to the one subject requirement? Would the Colorado General Assembly be content with the single subject limitations if the Colorado Supreme Court were to routinely review *their* bills and resolutions for compliance, delaying their enactment pending review? The ability of different branches of government to "check" and "balance" the others is one of the basic principle of American government, that works with the separation of power to prevent the concentration of power. It is a question of the *degree* of judicial involvement in the legislative function, not the fact that there is any judicial involvement.

This essay does not conclude that single subject and single amendment provisions need necessarily be abolished. Clearly these limitations on the legislative process serve some valuable ends, and they have not led to a significant amount of involvement of the courts in the powers exercised by the state legislatures. However, the record of judicial decisions in the initiative states reveals that the judiciary does exercise a great deal of power through the single subject provisions that apply to the *initiative* process.

The fact is that in states like Arizona, Colorado, and Florida the supreme courts regularly determine what measures may or may not be proposed and voted upon by the people. To what *degree* should the judiciary itself have the power to determine *whether* a single subject challenge is allowed, *when* that challenge will be heard, and *what standards* the court will apply in determining whether a measure constitutes one subject or one amendment?

In order to ensure that the legislative power of the initiative remains separate from, and not subservient to the judicial power, the role of the courts in the judicial review of initiatives for single subject provisions needs to be clarified. The citizen's initiative power is a legislative power, as is recognized by its inclusion with the legislative article in most states' constitutions, and as many courts have explicitly stated. According to the doctrine of the separation of powers the legislative power must have some degree of independence from the judicial branch. The variation of the state courts' treatment of the single subject rule over time, and across the states would seem to indicate that it would be prudent to develop some more specific guidelines regarding the proper role of the courts in this area. To preserve the separation of the legislative power of the initiative and the judicial power, the exact degree of judicial oversight needs to be determined. If the constitutional and statutory provisions are unclear, then the people and/or the legislatures need to establish clearer standards of review for the single subject and single amendment provisions in the state constitutions. As several ballot measures proposing reform of the judicial branch that have been struck down for violating single subject restrictions demonstrate, the courts are not without their own conflicts of interest.[96]

As it stands now, the initiative power is at the mercy of the court's conception of "oneness" which, as Justice Lewis of the Florida Supreme Court pointed out, changes as often as the justices on the court do. Certainly this contradicts the American conception of law as being both predictable and fair in its application. The extent of the people's power of the initiative should not be a matter that is merely "in the eye of the beholder." The principle of the separation of powers is as essential to the maintenance of a balance of executive, legislative, and judicial powers in the states as it is to the United States as a whole. If it should prove impossible to curb the role of the courts in the initiative process, if the entrée provided by the single subject rule is just too tempting, the states and the citizens would be better off without the single subject rule for initiatives. A few everything-including-the-kitchen-sink type of initiatives might make it to the

---

96. For example, see Aisenberg v. Campbell, Supreme Court of Colorado, November 1, 1999.

ballot, however, the record demonstrates that is a dangerous tactic for initiative proponents, as voters are apt to vote "No" when a measure is too complex. It would be better to have a few overly complex initiatives, than to permit the judiciary to usurp a legislative power.

Section Three

The Courts, the First Amendment and the Regulation of Initiative and Referendum

The state legislatures aren't the only ones whose actions have affected the I&R process—the courts' role must be examined as well.

Much has been written over the years about the role the courts should play in regulating not only what is passed utilizing the initiative process but the role it should play in regulating the process itself. This section contains the observations of two attorneys who have extensive knowledge of the U.S. Supreme Court's role in regulating the initiative and referendum process. Kris Kobach in Chapter 10 provides an in-depth legal analysis of several of the Court's major findings and Paul Grant in Chapter 11 gives the reader a first-hand account of the impetus for several of these cases as well as his own view of what the High Court's rulings mean.

Additionally, Mads Qvortrup in Chapter 12 will discuss the role of the courts in reviewing actual reforms passed utilizing the initiative and referendum process and what effect these decisions have had on individuals wishing to utilize the process.

Also, included in Appendix B of the book is a comprehensive listing of many of the major cases that have had an impact on the initiative and referendum process.

Chapter 10

Taking Shelter Behind the First Amendment: The Defense of the Popular Initiative

By Kris W. Kobach[*]

During the last quarter of the Twentieth Century, many state legislatures across the country watched with dismay as voters made increasingly frequent use of the initiative to circumvent the normal legislative process. Voters employed this mechanism of direct democracy[1] to break legislative deadlocks,[2] to dislodge unpopular but entrenched government programs,[3]

---

[*] I wish to thank Sean Martin for his assistance in conducting research for this project. I am also grateful to the UMKC School of Law and the UMKC Law Foundation for their commitment and support.

1. I use the term "direct democracy" to refer to "initiatives and referendums" even though, technically, these devices of popular law-making exemplify semi-direct democracy. The term direct democracy has taken hold in common parlance and certainly is less of a mouthful. It is also reasonably accurate, for although the initiative and referendum are less direct forms of popular legislating than true direct democracy (town meetings and other face-to-face assemblies, such as the Swiss Landsgemeinde), they seem radically "direct" when compared to the procedures and institutions of representative democracy.

2. Consider California's Proposition 227, which terminated California's bilingual education program. The proposition was passed in 1998 with 61 percent of voters in favor. See Nancy Wride, O.C. Teacher Has a Final: State Schools Chief Runoff, L.A. Times, June 4, 1998 at A1. It broke a legislative deadlock that had lasted for two years in the California legislature, due to the divisive nature of mandatory bilingual education. See Frank del Olmo, Perspective on Proposition 227: A Thoughtful Measure, But Not the Right One, L.A. Times, May 24, 1998 at M5.

3. Efforts to end racial preferences in state hiring and educational admissions exemplify this use of the initiative (where such systems do not enjoy popular support). California's Proposition 209, passed in 1996 with 54 percent in favor, was the first statewide initiative to end such racial preferences. See Dave Lesher, Battle over Prop. 209 Moves to the Courts, L.A. Times, Nov. 7, 1996 at A1. It was followed by I-200 in the State of Washington, which passed with 58 percent of the vote. Tom Brune and Joe Heim, New Battle Begins: Interpreting Law, Seattle Times, Nov. 4, 1998 at B1.

to address issues that legislators were unwilling to touch,[4] and to enact reforms that ran contrary to the interests of sitting legislators.[5] To some degree, each successful initiative represented the erosion of the power of elected representatives. Thus, it was hardly surprising when legislatures across the country began conceiving new regulations on the initiative process in order to curtail the frequency and scope of initiative campaigns and to raise the hurdle necessary for success at the ballot box. Delivering jeremiads on subjects ranging from the potential of fraud in signature collection to the credulity of the electorate, state legislators erected numerous firewalls to contain the putative dangers of direct democracy.

The regulations have come in all shapes and sizes. Some have been sincere efforts to improve the legitimacy of the process, while others have been thinly-disguised attempts to hobble it. From statutes banning the use of paid petition circulators[6] to requirements that circulators be at least eighteen years of age and registered to vote,[7] the signature-gathering process has been a frequent target of legislatures. Such restrictions become particularly arduous when combined with measures increasing the number

---

4. Initiatives to legalize the use of marijuana for medical purposes exemplify this type of effort. It is an understatement to say that elected representatives are usually reluctant to consider legalizing any classified narcotic in any context. Five States passed such initiatives between 1996 and 1998—California and Arizona in 1996; Alaska, Arizona, Nevada, and Washington in 1998 (Arizona addressed the question a second time to overturn a state law passed in the wake of the 1996 initiative, requiring federal authorization for medical marijuana prescriptions). Bob Davis and G. Pascal Zachary, Election '96: Affirmative Action, Shareholder Lawsuits And Tax Increases Are Rejected by Voters, WALL ST. J., Nov. 7, 1996 at A17; Edward Felsenthal and Keith Perine, Election '98: A Record Year for Ballot Initiatives, WALL ST. J., Nov. 5, 1998 at B1. Medical marijuana propositions also appeared on the 1998 ballots in Colorado and the District of Columbia, but the question was invalidated after petition signatures were disqualified in Colorado, and Congress decreed that the votes would not be counted in the District of Columbia. See Keith Perine, Ballot Initiatives Nationwide to Give Voters a Say on Death, Taxes and Drugs, WALL ST. J., Nov. 2, 1998 at A36.

5. There is perhaps no better example of this than the success of initiatives to limit the length of state legislative terms. Eighteen states have enacted such limits via popular initiative. See Martin Kasindorf, No Broad Pattern Evident in Ballot-Initiative Results, USA TODAY, Nov. 4, 1999 at 4A.

6. See COLORADO REV. STAT. § 1-40-110 (1980), invalidated in Meyer v. Grant, 486 U.S. 414 (1988).

7. See COLORADO REV. STAT. § 1-40-112(1) (1998), partially invalidated in American Const. Law Found. v. Meyer, 120 F.3d 1092, 1100-01 (10th Cir. 1997), aff'd, Buckley v. American Const. Law Found., 119 S.Ct. 636, 645 (1999).

of signatures required to place an issue on the ballot[8] or decreasing the time available for signature collection.[9] Other regulations label the signature gatherer with warning signs: "paid" badges worn by the circulator[10] and lists of major financial contributors on the petition itself[11] serve to admonish the would-be signer. Legislative efforts to circumscribe the initiative process have not been limited to the petition-circulating process. Some states have attempted to raise the bar that must be cleared on election day. From supermajority requirements[12] to rules demanding victory in two elections,[13] procedural reforms of this sort can operate to defeat initiative propositions that lack overwhelming support.

---

8. See The War on Initiatives, SALT LAKE TRIB. at A10; Edward Epstein, Stricter Rules Urged for San Francisco Initiatives, SAN FRANCISCO CHRON., Oct. 19, 1999 at A18; Chris Pipho, The Changing State Legislature, 81:4 PHI DELTA KAPPAN, Dec, 1, 1999.

9. See Louis Jacobson, How Much Power to the People?, NATIONAL JOURNAL, Oct. 3, 1998 (discussing 1998 Missouri initiative shortening circulation period from six months to four months). See also COLORADO REV. STAT. § 1-40-108(1) (1998), construed in American Const. Law Found. v. Meyer, 120 F.3d at 1098-99 ("a neutral ballot access regulation….insufficient by itself to require strict scrutiny) (citing Burdick v. Takushi, 504 U.S. 428, 433 (1992) & Timmons v. Twin Cities Area New Party, 117 S.Ct. 1364, 1366 (1997)).

10. See Buckley, 119 S.Ct. at 645 (internal citations omitted).

11. See Lee Condon, Schiff Revives Bill to Identify Petition Pushers, LOS ANGELES DAILY NEWS, Mar. 18, 1999 (discussing efforts of Adam Schiff, a Pasadena Democrat, to reintroduce into the California Senate a bill vetoed by Governor Wilson in 1998). The bill was enrolled on Sept. 8, 1999, and was vetoed on Oct. 10, 1999. S.B. 1219, 1999-2000 Regular Sess. (Cal. 1999).

12. In Wyoming, the passage of a popular initiative requires not a simple majority of votes cast on the ballot issue, but more than 50 percent of the total number of voters participating on election day (in all statewide elections). WYO. CONST. art. 3, § 52. In Mississippi, a similar requirement sets the hurdle at 40 percent of all votes cast. See Reed Branson, Citizen Lawmaking Proves Difficult: 6-Year-Old Miss. Initiative Process Claims No Successes, THE COMMERCIAL APPEAL (Memphis, Tenn.), July 27, 1998 at B1; cf Martin Dyckman, Renovating the Constitution, ST. PETERSBURG TIMES (Fla.), June 22, 1997 at 1D. Some supermajority requirements have been established, and attacked, via initiative. See Mark Baldassare and Cheryl Katz, Orange County Voices: The Swollen Majority: Will Voters Retain the Old Two-Thirds Election Rule?, L.A. TIMES, Dec. 26, 1999 at B19 (describing initiative on California ballot to remove traditional two-thirds supermajority requirement for passage of school bonds).

13. In Nebraska, Legislative Resolution 18CA would require an initial vote of approval and a subsequent vote of ratification to validate constitutional amendments. The measure, which would apply to both legislatively-proposed amendments and popular-initiative amendments, will be on the November 2000 ballot for approval. See Robynn Tysver, In The Legislature, OMAHA WORLD-HERALD, May 28, 1999 at 18.

Defenders of the initiative process have challenged such regulations in the judicial arena, with mixed results. Although the legal strategies and tactics used in such battles have varied widely, virtually all of the challenges have asserted the protection of the First Amendment of the U.S. Constitution.[14] Without question, the First Amendment has proven the most effective constitutional shield available. However, it is far from impenetrable and its breadth has been inadequate to sustain some challenges. First Amendment challenges to regulations of direct democracy have, of necessity, offered considerable room for judicial interpretation. The spare wording of the constitutional text makes no mention of initiatives, ballot issues, signature gathering, or other aspects of direct democracy. Yet the political speech of the initiative process plainly lies at the core of the First Amendment. Over the years, the Supreme Court's jurisprudence in this area has gradually taken shape, but many of its contours remain in doubt and its foundations seem somewhat insecure. In this chapter, I briefly describe the Court's landmark holdings that set the parameters for regulation of the initiative process. I then explore the strengths and weaknesses of these interpretations and suggest a direction for future judicial approaches to the subject. Finally, I explore the limits of the First Amendment as a shield for the initiative process and consider other constitutional approaches to challenging overly restrictive state regulations.

Meyer v. Grant

One of the most salient landmarks of the Supreme Court's initiative jurisprudence is the 1988 decision in *Meyer v. Grant*.[15] In that case, the Court assessed the constitutionality of a 1980 Colorado law making it a felony to pay petition circulators.[16] Voting unanimously, the Court struck the law down on First Amendment grounds. However, the *Meyer* prece-

---

14. "Congress shall make no law respecting an establishment of religion, or prohibiting the free exercise thereof; or abridging the freedom of speech, or of the press; or the right of the people peaceably to assemble, and to petition the Government for redress of grievances." U.S. CONST. amend. I.

15. 486 U.S. 414 (1988).

16. Colorado Rev. Stat. §1-40-110 (1980) provided that: "Any person, corporation, or association of persons who directly or indirectly pays to or receives from or agrees to pay to or receive from any other person, corporation, or association of persons any money or other thing of value in consideration of or as an inducement to the circulation of an initiative or referendum petition or in consideration of or as an inducement to the signing of any such petition commits a class 5 felony and shall be punished as provided in section 18-1-105, C.R.S. (1973)."

dent is not only noteworthy because it established the constitutionality of using paid petition circulators; it also ensconced a number of critical principles that would guide the consideration of future cases.

First, the Court recognized that the circulation of an initiative petition "involves the type of interactive communication concerning political change" and may be classified as "core political speech."[17] This classification is of paramount importance because it entitles petition circulation to the highest degree of First Amendment protection. Where core political speech is involved, the shielding power of the First Amendment is "at its zenith."[18] Normally, a statute that burdens core political speech can withstand constitutional challenge only if the government is able to meet its heavy burden of demonstrating that the statute serves a compelling governmental interest, and the statute is narrowly tailored to serving that interest, or necessary to serve that interest. The Court acknowledged that the state's interest in protecting the integrity of the initiative process was sufficiently weighty. However, the state had failed to demonstrate that the ban on paid petition circulators was necessary. As the Court stated: [W]e are not prepared to assume that a professional circulator — whose qualifications for similar future assignments may well depend on a reputation for competence and integrity — is any more likely to accept false signatures than a volunteer who is motivated entirely by an interest in having the proposition placed on the ballot.[19]

Other provisions of the Colorado Code were sufficient to address the danger of fraudulent signature collection. The code prohibited forged signatures, false or misleading statements relating to a petition, and the paying of someone to sign a petition.[20]

Second, the Court avouched that the Colorado ban on paid circulators restricted political expression in two ways. It limited the number of voices who could project the initiative proponents' message and restricted the total number of hours that they could speak.[21] It also made it less likely that initiative proponents could "garner the number of signatures necessary to place the matter on the ballot, thus limiting their ability to make the matter the focus of statewide discussion."[22] These words are potentially pregnant with meaning for future cases. They imply that, where the initiative power exists, the legislature may not circumscribe the signature collection process in such a manner as to render it unduly difficult for initiative pro-

---

17. 486 U.S. 414, 421.
18. Id. at 425.
19. Id. at 426.
20. Id. at 426-27.
21. Id. at 422-23.
22. Id. at 423.

ponents to succeed in placing their propositions on the ballot. I return to this critical implication below.

Third, the Court affirmed that the availability of alternative modes of communication does not relieve the state of its First Amendment obligations with respect to the method in question. In other words, just because initiative proponents could still utilize unpaid petition circulators and other channels to collect signatures, that did not validate the state's attempt to close this most productive avenue. In the words of the Court, "The First Amendment protects appellees' right not only to advocate their cause but also to select what they believe to be the most effective means for so doing."[23]

Fourth, the Court rejected the state's argument that because the power of the initiative is a state-created right, the state must be allowed to impose any limitations on that right. Or, to put it differently, if the state has the power to eliminate initiatives entirely, shouldn't it also have the lesser power to limit the political discussion in initiative campaigns? The Court repudiated this notion unequivocally.[24] The prerogative to create or abolish the setting in which political speech takes place does not empower a state government to sweep aside the protections of the First Amendment within that setting.

Although this response to the state's argument was correct and consistent with Supreme Court precedent in similar cases,[25] it missed the deeper flaw in the state's argument: the initiative right was not created by the *state*. The initiative right was created by the sovereign in Colorado—it was created by the *people*. The initiative process is a constitutionally-defined process and the popular right to propose initiatives is a constitutional right, as it is in all the other states that possess the initiative. Constitutional rights cannot be created by the state (meaning the state government). In Colorado, as in every other state but one, constitutional amendments can only be adopted by popular referendum.[26] The state legislature has the power to place an item before the sovereign by passing a resolution *proposing* an amendment, but the state legislature cannot *adopt* any amendment. The initiative is therefore not a creation of the government. Nor may it be abolished by the government. If it could be, many state governments would have voted to do away with the initiative long ago.

---

23. Id. at 424.

24. See id. at 424-25.

25. For example, in cases involving limited public forums, the Court has for several decades recognized that the power of the government to create or abolish the forum does not free the government from its obligation to respect free speech rights within the forum. See generally Widmar v. Vincent, 454 U.S. 263 (1981).

26. The one state that does not require referendum approval for constitutional amendments is Delaware.

Buckley v. American Constitutional Law Foundation, Inc.

The next great landmark in the jurisprudence of direct democracy came 11 years later, in the case of *Buckley v. American Constitutional Law Foundation, Inc.*[27] The state of Colorado had once again attempted to limit the petition circulation process, this time with a salvo of regulations. At issue in the case were six specific restrictions: (1) a requirement that petition circulators be at least 18 years old; (2) the limitation of the circulation period to six months; (3) a requirement that, at the time petitions are submitted to the state, petition circulators attach to each petition section an affidavit containing the circulator's name and address, among other things; (4) a requirement that petition circulators be registered voters; (5) a requirement that petition circulators wear identification badges stating their names, their status as "VOLUNTEER" or "PAID," and if the latter, the name and telephone number of their employer; and (6) a disclosure requirement obligating the initiative proponents to reveal information about the petition circulators and the amount of money paid to them.[28]

The U.S. Court of Appeals for the Tenth Circuit found the first three requirements listed above (age limit, six-month period, and affidavit requirement) to be constitutionally-valid regulations of the initiative process, while striking down as unconstitutional the last three requirements (registered-voter requirement, badge requirement with respect to displaying the circulator's name, and disclosure requirement).[29] The Supreme Court reviewed only the last three requirements. While it did not directly affirm the Tenth Circuit's judgment that the first three requirements were constitutionally permissible, the Court did offer considerable indirect support for the Tenth Circuit's conclusions.[30] Thus, state regulations requiring circulators to be of voting age, limiting the circulation period to six months, and requiring

---

27. 119 S. Ct. 636 (1999).

28. Id. at 640-41.

29. See American Constitutional Law Foundation, Inc. v. Meyer, 120 F.3d 1092 (10th Cir. 1997).

30. The Supreme Court stated the following. "As the Tenth Circuit recognized in upholding the age restriction, the six-month limit on circulation, and the affidavit requirement, States allowing ballot initiatives have considerable leeway to protect the integrity and reliability of the initiative process, as they have with respect to election processes generally." 119 S. Ct. 636, 642. "In contrast [to the badge requirement], the affidavit requirement upheld by the District Court and Court of Appeals, which must be met only after circulators have completed their conversations with electors, exemplifies the type of regulation for which McIntyre left room." Id. at 646. See also id. at 645.

at the time of petition submission affidavits containing circulators' names and addresses appear to be on constitutionally-secure footing.

With respect to the three requirements that it did review, the Supreme Court affirmed the holding of the Tenth Circuit. Thus, the Court struck down the law stipulating that petition circulators had to be registered voters. Echoing the theme of *Meyer* regarding the silencing of voices needed to convey the message of initiative proponents, the Court concluded that: "The requirement that circulators be not merely voter eligible, but registered voters...decreases the pool of potential circulators as certainly as that pool is decreased by the prohibition of payment to circulators."[31]

Regarding the badge law, the Supreme Court, like the Tenth Circuit below it, only reviewed the constitutionality of the requirement that petition circulators display their names. It left undecided the question of whether states may force circulators to wear badges indicating their status as "PAID" or "VOLUNTEER" and the identity of their employers. However, the Court's conclusion regarding the name requirement was unequivocal: the requirement was tantamount to a ban on anonymous political speech and therefore violated the First Amendment. "The injury to speech is heightened for the petition circulator because the badge requirement compels personal name identification at the precise moment when the circulator's interest in anonymity is greatest."[32] The Court recognized that circulators may justifiably fear retaliation, harassment, or other adverse reactions from the strangers that they approach. Accordingly, without the option of anonymity, many circulators would be unwilling to engage in this form of political speech.[33]

With respect to the disclosure requirements, the Court upheld Colorado's provisions compelling initiative proponents to report their names and their total expenditures on signature collection, on a monthly basis. As the Court noted, making such information available to the public allows voters to learn who is behind an initiative and how much they have paid to promote it. Accordingly, the government was able to establish sufficient interest in facilitating such public inquiry by requiring the reports.[34]

However, the Court did not buy the state's argument that it was also necessary to require circulators to report their names and the amount of money that each was paid for the collection of signatures. Acknowledging that the state possessed an important interest in deterring fraud and corruption in the initiative process,[35] the Court nonetheless found the extraction

---

31. Id. at 643.
32. Id. at 646.
33. Id. at 645-46.
34. See id. at 647.
35. Id. at 648.

of this information to be unwarranted. "The added benefit of revealing the names of paid circulators and amounts paid to each circulator... is hardly apparent and has not been demonstrated."[36] The state could protect the integrity of the process through other means, such as the Colorado law prohibiting the forging of signatures and the law requiring disclosure of who pays petition circulators and how much.[37] Significantly, the Court noted in passing that "ballot initiatives do not involve the risk of '*quid pro quo*' corruption present when money is paid to, or for, candidates."[38] The Court recognized a salient distinction between the way money influences direct democracy and the way it influences electoral democracy. In the former, money can buy troops and advertising, but it cannot buy votes, because the decision-making body is the electorate. In the latter, money can not only buy personnel and advertising for candidates; it can also buy votes when contributors make hefty campaign donations to legislators and the legislators respond by voting in the way desired by the contributors.

Another aspect of the *Buckley* holding bears mentioning at this point. It concerns the critical questions of *how* the protected political expression occurs and *who* the relevant speaker is when assessing a free speech claim in the petition circulation context. First consider the question of how the protected speech occurs. The *Meyer* Court acknowledged to two forms of protected speech: the speech of the proponent to the public through his circulators, and the speech of the proponent to the public through the ballot. The *Buckley* Court added a third form of protected speech to the list: the speech of the circulators to the citizens they accost.

Regarding the related question of who the relevant speaker is, the *Buckley* Court established beyond a doubt that there are two categories of protected speakers: the proponents of initiatives, who ask petition circulators to carry their messages to the voters; and the circulators themselves, who speak directly to voters when soliciting signatures. Clearly, the speech of the circulators to citizens on the street must be regarded as protected speech for First Amendment purposes. The Court acknowledged this when discussing the badge requirement: the speakers who needed anonymity in order to avoid harassment were the circulators who repeatedly approached strangers to ask for signatures.[39] However, the Court acknowledged that the proponents of an initiative are also speakers with First Amendment rights at stake in the circulation of petitions. Reiterating the approach taken in *Meyer* with the requirement that circulators be volunteers only,

---

36. Id. at 647.
37. See id. at 648.
38. Id.
39. See id. at 645-46.

the Court struck down the requirement that circulators be registered voters. "Both provisions limit the number of voices who will convey the initiative proponents' message and, consequently, cut down the size of the audience proponents can reach."[40] The treatment of initiative proponents as speakers is noteworthy because their speech is indirect, being conveyed by their circulators or by the ballot. Moreover, the Court recognized that the First Amendment protects their ability to speak effectively to a wider audience, not merely their ability to speak.

In this respect, the *Buckley* decision seriously imperiled a number of other states' restrictions on the petition circulation process, making them prime targets for constitutional challenge. At least 10 initiative states plus the District of Columbia require that circulators be eligible electors in the state;[41] and Georgia requires circulators to be state residents.[42] These restrictions similarly reduce the number of voices that may carry a proponent's message to the voters. To be sure, the states would assert a different interest in defense of such restrictions: that of assuring that states retain control of their own affairs by ensuring that participants in the initiative process live in the state. The states would argue that invasions of circulators from out of state threaten the independence of state decision making. Nevertheless, the *Meyer* and *Buckley* precedents would be difficult to overcome, as the holdings plainly cast constitutional doubt on restrictions that limit the pool of available circulators. As Chief Justice Rehnquist noted in dissent, "Today's decision appears to place each of these laws in serious constitutional jeopardy."[43]

The Ambiguities of Meyer and Buckley

With most First Amendment questions, the Supreme Court and lower courts analyze state laws using a level of scrutiny that is identifiable and reasonably well established by prior case law. The various levels of scrutiny range from strict scrutiny (under which the state must demonstrate a compelling public interest and show that the regulation is narrowly tailored,

---

40. Id. at 643-44 (quoting Meyer, 486 U.S. 414, 422-23)(internal quotation marks and brackets omitted).

41. Chief Justice Rehnquist listed the following 19 states, several of which are not initiative states: Arizona, California, Colorado, Connecticut, Idaho, Illinois, Kansas, Michigan, Missouri, Nebraska, New York, Ohio, Pennsylvania, Rhode Island, South Dakota, Virginia, West Virginia, Wisconsin, Wyoming Id. at 661, n. 3 (Rehnquist, Ch. J., dissenting).

42. Id. at 661, n. 4 (Rehnquist, Ch. J., dissenting).

43. Id. at 661 (Rehnquist, Ch. J., dissenting).

or necessary, to serving that interest) to intermediate scrutiny (under which the state must present an important governmental interest and show a substantial relationship between the regulation and that interest) to minimal scrutiny (under which the challenging party must demonstrate that the regulation is not rationally related to a legitimate governmental interest). With particular types of First Amendment questions, the Court's approach may evolve over many decades.[44] During such evolutionary periods, considerable uncertainty may exist. Plainly, the Court's jurisprudence with respect to the First Amendment's protection of the initiative process is fraught with such uncertainty today.

Within the Court itself, there exists considerable ambiguity as to which level of scrutiny should be used. In *Meyer*, the Court explicitly stated that strict scrutiny, also termed "exacting scrutiny," was appropriate when evaluating government restrictions on the core political speech involved in the gathering of petition signatures.[45] Moreover, the Court drove the point home by declaring that "the burden that Colorado must overcome to justify this criminal law is well-nigh insurmountable."[46] However, in *Buckley*, this well-established standard began to blur. Justice Ginsburg, writing for the majority of the Court, insisted in a footnote that the Court was applying strict scrutiny: "Our decision is entirely in keeping with the 'now-settled approach' that state regulations imposing 'severe burdens' on speech... must be narrowly tailored to serve a compelling state interest."[47] Yet the majority appeared to be applying a standard akin to intermediate scrutiny later in the same opinion. Agreeing with the state that its interest in protecting the initiative process from corruption was sufficient, the Court described the interest not as a "compelling" one, but as merely a "substantial interest" and an "important interest."[48] These terms described the threshold normally associated with intermediate scrutiny. In his concurrence, Justice Thomas noted that the majority opinion appeared to "dilute" the standard of scrutiny by only requiring that Colorado's reporting provision be "substantially related to important governmental interests."[49]

---

44. For example: The Courts' analysis of speech on public property took the better part of the twentieth century to evolve. See DANIEL A. FARBER, THE FIRST AMENDMENT 167-72 (1998).

45. Grant, 486 U.S. at 421.

46. Id. at 425.

47. Buckley, 119 S. Ct. 636, 642, n. 12 (internal brackets and quotation marks omitted). The majority opinion also noted that exacting scrutiny was appropriate when evaluating financial disclosure requirements, as the court had done in 1976 in the landmark campaign finance case of Buckley v. Valeo (424 U.S. 1). 119 S. Ct. 636, 647.

48. Id. at 648.

49. Id. at 623 (Thomas, J., dissenting).

Although the *Buckley* Court chose not to examine the three Colorado regulations that had been approved by the Tenth Circuit, the Court's indirect endorsement of these restrictions suggested that the Supreme Court was willing to contemplate a level of review that was well below strict scrutiny. Arguably, at least two of these restrictions would not have survived strict scrutiny, had it been applied. The 18-year age requirement for circulators hardly seems to be the least restrictive age level at which petition circulation may be allowed. Can it seriously be argued that 16-year-old citizens are incapable of describing ballot issues? If so, one must ignore the legions of high school debaters who regular evince their policy acumen in classrooms across the country. Moreover, it is difficult to expostulate that the state has a compelling interest in regulating the political maturity of circulators when the initiative proponents' self interest provides more-than-sufficient incentive to monitor this area themselves. A circulator who is too immature to explain the issues is, by definition, not a useful circulator to the initiative proponent. Thus, the necessity requirement of strict scrutiny is not met.

The part of the reporting requirement that the Tenth Circuit upheld (requiring proponents to report their expenditures on signature collection) may also be more susceptible to challenge than the majority suggested. Justice Thomas questioned the majority's assumption that the state's compelling interest is compelling at all points in the initiative process. "[W]e recognized in *Meyer* that 'the risk of improper conduct . . . is more remote at the petition stage of an initiative.' Similarly, I would think, at the very least, the State's interest in informing the public of the financial interests behind an initiative proposal is not compelling during the petition stage."[50] The affidavit requirement is the only Colorado regulation at issue that clearly survives strict scrutiny. It is a minimally restrictive means of realizing the state's compelling interest in preventing fraudulent signatures.

Whether the Supreme Court's apparent watering-down of the standard was an illusion created by imprecise word choice in the *Buckley* opinion or it reflected a deliberate shifting of the goalposts, it is critical that the Court actually apply strict scrutiny when reviewing regulations of the initiative process in the future. The political discussion between circulator and signer is core political speech in the most fundamental sense — dialogue between ordinary citizens about political issues. And the larger discussion between proponent and public is the *sine qua non* of democratic government — an endeavor not to mobilize the public behind a personality, but to persuade them to *govern themselves* in a particular way.

---

50. Id. (internal citation omitted).

The Confusion of First Amendment Issues and Ballot Access Issues

The primary reason that the Tenth Circuit allowed the 18-year age restriction and the six-month circulation period to stand was that the court openly *declined to apply strict scrutiny* in evaluating these regulations. Instead of treating these challenged regulations as regulations on speech, the Court decided to characterize them as "ballot access" regulations. This was not a merely semantic distinction; it was a critical shift of category that virtually ensured that the state's regulations would be upheld.

The Supreme Court has produced a substantial body of case law concerning the regulation of *election* ballots — that is, ballots used to elect candidates to office.[51] In such cases, candidates challenging ballot access regulations have primarily asserted First Amendment rights of association. Getting one's name on a ballot is not usually treated as an act of free speech; rather it is typically framed as an act of association with the party of one's choice. The Court has recognized that with candidate elections, there inevitably must exist a significant amount of regulation as to who can have his or her name on general election ballots. If there were no restrictions on ballot access and anyone could simply declare that he wanted his name to appear on the general election ballot, party primaries would become virtually meaningless; and voters might routinely see general election ballots with ten or more candidates running for the same office. The Supreme Court has recognized the danger of voter confusion and candidate fraud in the absence of ballot access restrictions. "As a practical matter, there must be a substantial regulation of elections if they are to be fair and honest and if some sort of order, rather than chaos, is to accompany the democratic process."[52] The Court's understanding that it must allow the states room to enact regulation of election ballots "to reduce election- and campaign- related disorder" has led it to articulate a specialized form of analysis in ballot access cases.[53] The Court applies a sliding scale when scrutinizing candidates' free association claims in this context: if the Court believes that a law substantially burdens access to the ballot then it uses strict

---

51. See, e.g., Timmons v. Twin Cities Area New Party, 520 U.S. 351 (1997) (upholding a state's ban on multi-party, or "fusion" candidates); Burdick v. Takushi, 504 U.S. 428 (1992) (upholding a state law that completely prohibited write-in votes in primary and general elections); Anderson v. Celebrezze, 460 U.S. 780 (1983) (striking down a state's early filing deadline for independent candidates for President).

52. Storer v. Brown, 415 U.S. 724, 730 (1974).

53. Timmons, 520 U.S. 351, 358.

scrutiny; if the Court does not regard the burden to be significant then it exercises a lower degree of scrutiny. In the latter instance, the state need only present an "important regulatory interest;" and its regulations need only be reasonable and nondiscriminatory.[54] This lower level of scrutiny is somewhere between minimal and intermediate. Regardless of its precise location on the scrutiny spectrum, it is a relatively low hurdle for states to clear.

Without any explanation, the Tenth Circuit lifted this sliding scale approach from the context of election ballots and associational rights and inserted it into the context of initiative ballots and free speech rights.[55] Strangely, the Tenth Circuit offered a litany of Supreme Court quotations referring to "the election process for state offices" and "the electoral process."[56] But, because a vote on an initiative is not an "election," the Tenth Circuit needed to explain why these precedents were relevant. It also needed to provide some justification for extending the sliding scale approach to petition circulation cases when the Supreme Court in *Meyer* had stated unequivocally that regulations of the petition-circulating process were subject to strict scrutiny. The Tenth Circuit offered no such explanation or justification.[57]

This judicial failure was significant. There are three critical distinctions between ballot access regulations in the electoral context and regulations of the initiative process. First and foremost, different constitutional rights are stake. Ballot access cases invariably involve either the right to associate freely or equal protection claims concerning candidates' ability to place their names on election ballots. In contrast, initiative cases typically involve the free speech rights of proponents and circulators. For decades, the Supreme Court's First Amendment jurisprudence has made it abundantly clear that free speech rights enjoy the highest degree of constitutional protection, where core political speech is involved.

Second, the likelihood of corruption is considerably greater in the electoral context. The election of candidates to office intrinsically entails the accumulation of power in the hands of individual office holders. Power corrupts. And individuals seeking personal power face often engage in corrupt practices or behave fraudulently in the quest for such power. In contrast, initiatives do not elevate individuals to office. To be sure, it is frequently the case that particular interests are helped or hurt by the passage of a given initiative. And political leaders often use their support of ini-

---

54. Id.

55. American Constitutional Law Foundation v. Meyer, 120 F.3d. 1092, 1098 (10th Cir. 1997)

56. Id. at 1097-98.

57. See id.

tiatives to win popularity for themselves.[58] But initiative votes do not confer formal power on specific individuals in the direct manner that elections do. The benefits of the policies advanced by the initiative process are almost always diffused widely. Indeed, initiatives that are not perceived as beneficial by broad sections of the electorate are unlikely to succeed at the polls. It is the concentration of benefits inherent in the election process that invites corruption and abuse.

Third, by definition, initiatives involve the circulation of petitions by ordinary citizens. The drive for signatures necessitates political speech. This is not the case in the electoral context, where the overwhelming majority of candidates for office do not utilize petitions to get on the election ballot. Candidates for the Presidency aside, virtually all major party candidates simply pay filing fees that entitle them to a place on the ballot. No persuasion of fellow citizens is required. Accordingly, free speech issues are typically either completely absent or only marginally present in electoral ballot access context.

Even more perplexing than its use of electoral ballot access precedents to resolve free speech claims in the initiative context was the Tenth Circuit's attempt to distinguish between the registered voter restriction and the minimum age restriction. In applying the sliding scale approach to Colorado's requirement that petition circulators be registered voters, the Circuit Court noted correctly that "when a statute allows some people to speak but not others, the principles of equal protection and free speech are intertwined."[59] The court went on to note that there were at least 400,000 unregistered voters in Colorado who were being prevented from participating in the core political speech of petition circulation. The court also recognized the related burden on the speech rights of proponents: the "exclusion of unregistered circulators also limits the number of voices to convey the proponent's message, limiting the audience the proponents can reach...."[60] Therefore, the Tenth Circuit concluded, because this amounted to a substantial burden on First Amendment rights, the regulation would be assessed under strict scrutiny.[61] Holding that the state could present no compelling interest in defense of the regulation, the court struck it down.

The same arguments applied to Colorado's minimum age requirement for circulators. From the circulators' perspective, equal protection and free speech rights were at stake. Hundreds of thousands of citizens under the age of eighteen were being prevented from participating in core polit-

---

58. For a discussion of such "initiative entrepreneurs," see KRIS W. KOBACH, THE REFERENDUM: DIRECT DEMOCRACY IN SWITZERLAND 134-36, 241 (1993).

59. American Constitutional Law Foundation v. Meyer, 120 F.3d. 1092, 1100.

60. Id.

61. Id.

ical speech. Similarly, from the proponent's perspective, the exclusion of this group of circulators limited the number of voices to convey the proponent's message. Strangely, the Tenth Circuit seemed oblivious to these similarities. Instead, the court seized upon the fact that youth is a temporary disability. The court stated that the age requirement "merely postpones the opportunity to circulate."[62] Therefore, the court surmised, lesser scrutiny was appropriate. In doing so, the Tenth Circuit ignored the fact that, from the proponent's perspective, the burden on speech was not temporary and was no less substantial than the exclusion of unregistered circulators. Moreover, from the circulator's perspective, the burden on speech was arguably *greater*, not less. An unregistered person could choose to register immediately if he felt that the initiative campaign was important enough to warrant his registration. However, a person under eighteen could not choose to become older. From the circulators' perspective, the burden on speech may have been temporary, but it was unchangeable.[63]

Plainly, it was inappropriate for the Tenth Circuit to hijack the sliding scale approach from the electoral ballot access cases and apply it to a free speech challenge in the initiative context. The factors warranting a more deferential approach to state regulations in electoral ballot access cases are absent in initiative cases. The appropriate judicial analysis would apply strict scrutiny to any government regulation restricting the free speech rights of proponents or circulators. Unfortunately, the Supreme Court did not offer any opinion on the Tenth Circuit's mishandling of the standard of review; so this question remains shrouded in uncertainty.

The Limits of the First Amendment Shield

What about restrictions on the initiative process that do not infringe upon the free speech rights of circulators or proponents, but greatly circumscribe the usefulness of the initiative device nonetheless? Restrictions

---

62. Id. at 1101.

63. The Tenth Circuit also asserted, without citing any supporting precedent, that age restrictions on the right to vote need not face strict scrutiny. Therefore, since "Plaintiffs have not demonstrated that persons under eighteen have a stronger interest in circulating than they do in voting," id., the court saw no reason to apply strict scrutiny. This line of reasoning was highly problematic. First, it is irrelevant to the sliding scale approach that the court purported to be using. The level of scrutiny was supposed to be decided by the burden on First Amendment rights, not by a comparison of speech interests with voting interests. Second, persons under eighteen arguably do have a stronger interest in circulating than in voting. The Constitution explicitly protects their speech rights in the First Amendment. Yet it expressly excludes them from the constitutional right to vote in the Twenty-Sixth Amendment.

of this sort include supermajority requirements for the adoption of ballot initiatives, requirements demanding victory in two success popular votes, and requirements demanding a minimum number of "Yes" votes equal to a majority of the voters participating in a prior election for statewide office. In such cases, the First Amendment offers no shelter. The First Amendment prevents states from silencing initiative proponents, but it presents no constitutional obstacle to requirements that set the victory threshold at an extremely high level.

Another category of restrictions makes the signature-collection race more difficult to run without preventing any discrete group from participating. This category includes geographic distribution rules governing the collection of signatures. Thirteen states have such distribution rules, which force proponents to draw a large number of petition signatures from sparsely populated, rural counties. Such distribution rules exert a demonstrable effect on the number of propositions that qualify for the ballot. During the period from 1950 to 1992, states without distribution requirements saw an average of 48 propositions qualify for the ballot, whereas states with distribution requirements saw an average of only 22 propositions qualify for the ballot.[64]

The other common method by which states render the signature collection race more arduous is through compression of the allotted time or elevation of the required signature threshold. Colorado's relatively short, six-month circulation period was reviewed and upheld by the Tenth Circuit in the *Buckley* case. Most of the other initiative states stipulate circulation periods that are much less restrictive. Of the 24 states that have the initiative process at the state level, 17 states allow proponents a year or more to amass the required signatures. And four of these states impose no time limit on petition circulation whatsoever.[65] In Switzerland, the country with the most experience in the direct democracy game, proponents of national constitutional initiatives are allowed 18 months to collect their

---

64. David B. Magleby, Direct Legislation in the American States, in REFERENDUMS AROUND THE WORLD: THE GROWING USE OF DIRECT DEMOCRACY 225-27 (David Butler & Austin Ranney eds., 1994).

65. The signature collection periods for each state are as follows: Alaska, 1 year; Ariz., 20 months; Ark., unlimited; Cal., 150 days; Colo., 6 months; Fla., 4 years; Idaho, 18 months; Me., 1 year; Mass., 64 days; Mich., 180 days; Miss., 1 year; Mo., 18 months; Mont., 1 year; Neb., 1 year; Nev., 11 months for constitutional initiative, 10 months for statutory initiative; N.D., 1 year; Ohio, unlimited; Okla., 90 days; Or., unlimited; S.D., 1 year; Utah, unlimited; Wash., 6 months for direct statutory initiative, 10 months for indirect statutory initiative; Wyo., 18 months. Illinois, the remaining state with the initiative device, is not included in this list because its severe subject matter limitations effectively discourage the appearance of any initiatives on the ballot.

signatures.[66] The signature thresholds vary widely among the states, from 2 percent of the population in North Dakota to 15 percent of registered voters in Wyoming.

As I noted above, the Supreme Court in *Meyer* offered propitious words for a future First Amendment challenge to unreasonably short circulation periods. The *Meyer* Court stated that one way in which Colorado's ban on paid circulators restricted political expression was by "[making] it less likely that [proponents] will garner the number of signatures necessary to place the matter on the ballot, thus limiting their ability to make the matter the focus of statewide discussion."[67] Short circulation periods, in combination with moderate or high required signature thresholds, similarly reduce the likelihood of success in petition circulation. Accordingly, they too constrain proponents' ability to make their propositions the focus of statewide discussion. Thus, the stage would seem to be set for a First Amendment challenge to a short circulation period based on *Meyer's* recognition that having one's issue on the ballot, and therefore subject to statewide discussion, is a form of political expression. The Tenth Circuit brushed aside such a challenge to Colorado's six-month circulation period with little analysis,[68] and the Supreme Court never reviewed the question directly in *Buckley*. So how might another constitutional challenge to an extremely short signature circulation period be framed?

At the outset, the success of such a challenge would depend on the Court's willingness to stand by its statement in *Meyer* and acknowledge the full implications of its own words. Presented with such a case, the Court might then qualify the *Meyer* language by pointing out that, practically speaking, an initiative state must erect some hurdles to govern which proponents are entitled to place their propositions on initiative ballots. Otherwise, there would be no way of separating those ideas with broad public support from those with very little support. By definition, all hurdles make it more difficult to place one's proposition on the ballot. Therefore initiative states must, of necessity, allocate access to this form of political expression to some proponents while denying it to others. Unless the Court is willing to say that *all* of these hurdles constitute a substantial infringement on core political speech and therefore trigger strict scrutiny (a position that it is unlikely to take), it will need to come up with a method of dis-

---

66. Kris W. Kobach, supra note 58, at 42 (1993).

67. Meyer, 486 U.S. 414, 423.

68. Without citing any evidence in support of its assertion, the Tenth Circuit simply declared that, "Although some measures might fare better under a longer or indeterminate period, the current deadline is not a significant burden on the ability of organized proponents to place a measure on the ballot." American Constitutional Law Foundation v. Meyer, 120 F.3d. 1092, 1099.

tinguishing between major and minor restrictions on the petition circulation process, or it will have to treat all such restrictions to a lower standard of review.

If the Court were to come up with a test for distinguishing between major and minor hurdles in the circulation process, it would almost certainly be a relatively subjective and amorphous test. There are no clear thresholds in circulation periods, required signature thresholds, or geographic distribution rules. Moreover, the various potential combinations of the three types of restrictions create an infinite and complex set of possibilities. How could a court determine whether the combination of a short circulation period (say, three months) with an easy threshold (say, 2 percent of registered voters) and no distribution rule is more or less burdensome than a combination of a moderate circulation period (1 year) with a moderate threshold (5 percent of registered voters) and an onerous distribution rule? Any attempt at judicial line drawing in this area would inevitably be arbitrary, subjective, and malleable.

A more useful framework for analyzing such restrictions on the circulation process would employ a hybrid jurisprudence of free speech and equal protection doctrines. The *Meyer* decision plainly established that political expression is at issue, and therefore the protections of the First Amendment are operative. However, any challenger of restrictive circulation periods or burdensome distribution rules must acknowledge that the state is entitled to ration access to this forum for political expression. The question must then be asked, "On what basis are some initiative proponents being excluded?" The state in question would answer that its rules discriminate on the basis of the popularity of the propositions. And that may indeed have been the state's intent when the rules were set. However, the Equal Protection Clause of the Fourteenth Amendment[69] is not solely concerned with discriminatory intent; it is also concerned with discriminatory *effect*. And the practical effect of unduly restrictive circulation periods is not that they reward the most popular propositions. Rather, they reward the proponents with the most resources to invest in petition circulation. Forcing initiative proponents to accumulate the necessary signatures in an extremely contracted period effectively limits the initiative device to those proponents with enough money to hire an army of circulators. Propositions coming from sponsors with modest resources stand little chance of gaining the necessary signatures in time, no matter how popular the proposals may be.

Thus, the appropriate constitutional challenge might be framed as a hybrid equal protection and free speech claim. Short circulation periods,

---

69. "…nor shall any state…deny to any person within its jurisdiction the equal protection of the laws." U.S. CONST. amend. XIV, § 1.

combined with moderate or high signature collection thresholds, limit access an important forum of political expression on the basis of wealth. Traditionally, equal protection challenges only trigger strict scrutiny when a suspect classification (such as race) is used by the state, or when the regulation has the effect of denying a fundamental constitutional right (such as the right to vote). The Supreme Court has never regarded classifications based on wealth as suspect, and it is unlikely to treat the right to have one's proposition on the ballot as a fundamental right. Consequently, under traditional equal protection doctrine, a challenge to a short circulation period would only engender minimal scrutiny. However, given the hybrid nature of the constitutional challenge and the fact that this area of constitutional jurisprudence is far from settled, the Supreme Court might recognize that at least intermediate scrutiny is appropriate. If the Court did so, then the prospects for a successful constitutional challenge would improve considerably.

In any event, it must be noted that an unduly short circulation period is vulnerable even under minimal scrutiny. In its case before the Tenth Circuit, Colorado asserted three state interests underlying its six-month circulation period: preserving the integrity of the state's elections, maintaining an orderly ballot, and limiting voter confusion.[70] To be sure, these are all legitimate governmental interests. However, it is difficult to see how making the petition circulation race more difficult to complete is rationally related to any of these interests. The integrity of the initiative process is not threatened by a circulation period that offers a reasonable chance of success to a proponent with a popular idea but limited resources. If "integrity" is assumed to mean the absence of fraud and corruption, it is unclear how forcing proponents to accelerate their campaigns and use more hired circulators furthers that interest. The orderliness of the ballot is a product of its organizational structure, not the number of issues on it. And voter confusion is a function not of the *number* of questions that make the ballot, but of the *complexity* of the individual issues. In other words, an initiative ballot containing two complicated questions is more "confusing" than a ballot containing ten simple questions. The ten-question ballot may be more taxing to complete, but it is not more confusing. Even minimal scrutiny demands a rational connection between the asserted interests of the state and the regulations that the state enacts. Arguably, there was no such connection in Colorado's case.

In conclusion, it is clear that the First Amendment has been, and will remain, the primary constitutional shield available to users of the initiative process. The Supreme Court's decisions in *Meyer* and *Buckley* created

---

70. American Constitutional Law Foundation v. Meyer, 120 F.3d. 1092, 1099.

important precedents. And these precedents serve as a platform from which future First Amendment challenges to state regulations may be launched. However, the Court was somewhat equivocal in its application of strict scrutiny in *Buckley*, and undoubtedly this unique area of constitutional law will continue to evolve. The First Amendment shield cannot ward off every blow delivered by state legislatures seeking to impede the initiative process. Some restrictions, such as supermajority requirements, will meet with no barrier in the U.S. Constitution. Others, such as abbreviated circulation periods, will push the limits of the First Amendment shield. In such cases, a hybrid approach utilizing the Equal Protection Clause may offer constitutional shelter. Hopefully, this hybrid approach will be tested, and the Court will eventually clarify the *Buckley* holding as to when strict scrutiny is appropriate. As the Court itself has opined in the past, "Liberty finds no refuge in a jurisprudence of doubt."[71] Neither does democracy.

---

71. Planned Parenthood of Southeastern Pennsylvania v. Casey, 505 U.S. 833, 844 (1992).

Chapter 11

The First Amendment Limits State Regulation of Initiatives and Referenda

By Paul Grant

The Supreme Court has twice directly addressed the limits of state power to regulate citizen initiatives and referenda. These two fairly recent decisions are: *Meyer v. Grant*, 486 U.S. 414 (1988) (*"Meyer"*), and *Buckley v. American Constitutional Law Foundation*, Inc. (*"Buckley"*)[1], 119 S.Ct. 636 (1999). Both establish First Amendment protection for I&R processes.

Meyer is a powerful and clean decision, based on clearly articulated First Amendment principles. *Buckley* is much less clear, suggesting on its surface that future cases should rely on *ad hoc* analysis without any clearly defined principles as guidance. Upon closer scrutiny, however, the Court's actual findings in *Buckley* can be shown to rely on principles which were clearly defined in earlier cases, including *Meyer*. I was involved in both *Meyer* and *Buckley*, in various capacities,[2] and, with that experience in mind, will attempt to offer some background and insight into what these two decisions have established.

In 1984, I and other Coloradans joined together to support an effort to amend Colorado's Constitution via the citizen initiative process. We sought to eliminate transportation monopolies in Colorado by ending Colorado's treatment of transportation companies as [competition-shielded] public utilities. In our petitioning efforts, we were confronted with the typical difficulty of motivating volunteers to do the difficult job of soliciting tens of thousands of signatures from strangers in public places. It was obvious that paid petitioners would be better able to deal with the difficult job of persuading strangers to stop, take the time to consider the petition, and

---

1. Which should not be confused with an important earlier case dealing with campaign finance regulations, the case of Buckley v. Valeo, 424 U.S. 1 (1976).

2. In *Meyer v. Grant*, I was the lead plaintiff as well as a witness at trial. In *Buckley v. ACLF*, I was a witness at trial, provided research at trial, was co-counsel and argued before the Tenth Circuit, and authored a principal brief before the Supreme Court.

sign it. The problem was that paid petition circulation was a felony offense in Colorado. Paid petitioning had been prohibited by statute since the 1940s.

The felony prohibition against paid petition circulation seemed to me to be an obvious infringement on political speech and action, rights protected by the First Amendment. But Colorado did not agree. Thinking nonetheless that Colorado must recognize a distinction between political speech and the act of holding a petition clipboard while voters sign the petitions, I devised a scheme to pay "petition advocates" to stand alongside the "volunteer" petition circulator. Petition advocates were paid based on their success in persuading voters to sign petitions held by volunteer circulators. Petition advocates and petition circulators could switch roles from time to time, but we only paid for their success as advocates.

Colorado's Secretary of State and Attorney General were not impressed at our creativity - in fact, they must have been offended. The Attorney General inserted an undercover operative into our petition operation, an agent who took our money for "petition advocacy", and then testified against us at a hearing conducted by the Secretary of State. The Secretary referred us to the AG for felony criminal prosecution.

By that time, I had lost my sense of humor in the matter and decided to take our First Amendment challenge of Colorado's insipid regulation into federal district court. We were surprised in the trial court to find that our petition activities were not protected by the First Amendment. We were surprised again in the Tenth Circuit Court of Appeals (*Grant v. Meyer*, 741 F.2d 1210 (10th Cir. 1984)), when a panel of that court adopted the district court opinion. Judge Holloway wrote a wonderful dissent to that initial Tenth Circuit opinion, in which he saw plenty of First Amendment problems with Colorado's regulation. Later, when the Tenth Circuit decided to rehear the case, *en banc*, Judge Holloway wrote a powerful opinion reversing the initial Tenth Circuit decision. *See Grant v. Meyer*, 828 F.2d 1446 (10th Cir. 1987).

We were very fortunate the Tenth Circuit took our case *en banc*, because that is a fairly rare occurrence. Had we petitioned the Supreme Court after our initial loss at the Tenth Circuit, the Supreme Court would most likely never have considered our case. But, since we prevailed with the Tenth Circuit holding Colorado's statute unconstitutional, the case was then well-positioned for the Supreme Court to review the decision. They quite often do accept appeals when a state statute is found unconstitutional, apparently out of "respect" for state authority. Why First Amendment rights are more important when the state loses in the court below, than they are when the citizens lose, I do not pretend to understand. But that seems to be the approach taken too often by the Court in deciding which cases to take.

The Supreme Court had no difficulty unanimously deciding that Colorado's felony ban on paid petitioning curtailed the "core political speech" activity of petition proponents. *Meyer v. Grant*, 486 U.S. 414 (1988). The Court recognized that restricting petitioning to volunteers would reduce the number of voices who would be heard in favor of a message, thus restricting First Amendment-protected political expression. The Court applied "strict scrutiny" to this state regulation of speech and determined Colorado could not justify this interference with protected speech.

Colorado, however, did not accept its loss gracefully. The Secretary of State made public speeches criticizing the Supreme Court's interference with Colorado's regulatory schemes, complaining that the Supreme Court did not understand the problems caused by paid petitioners. She helped persuade state legislators in 1993 to enact comprehensive new regulations, some again aimed at suppressing paid petitioning. New statutory provisions required paid petitioners to wear an identification badge while petitioning, providing the petitioner's name and his status as a paid petitioner. Colorado also imposed a monthly reporting requirement for petition sponsors, requiring monthly reports of all items paid to paid circulators, along with the paid circulators' names and home addresses.

Colorado professed to need to identify "problem petition circulators," so that they could be investigated and prosecuted for improper petitioning techniques, and for *improper arguments*. Colorado apparently assumed that only paid petitioners would present problems, since the regulations only applied to paid circulators.

The American Constitutional Law Foundation (ACLF) immediately brought suit in the U.S. District Court for Colorado to challenge the new regulations. Also challenged were some long-existing statutes, including Colorado's requirements limiting petition circulation to registered voters and prohibiting persons under 18 from petition circulation.

The District Court found Colorado's identification badge requirement for paid petitioners offensive to the First Amendment, along with the monthly reporting requirement that required identification of paid petitioners by name and address. All other regulations were upheld.

The Tenth Circuit reviewed cross-appeals of the District Court decision, affirming the two findings of unconstitutionality, plus adding a third: Colorado's restriction on petitioning to registered voters also violated the First Amendment. *ACLF v. Meyer*, 120 F.3d 1092 (10th Cir. 1997). The Court recognized, as had the Supreme Court in *Meyer v. Grant*, previously, that restricting the persons allowed to petition, in this case to registered voters, limited the number of persons who can advocate signing the petition, thus restricted core political speech. This restriction on political discussion could not be justified under the Supreme Court's *strict scrutiny* standard of review.

Yet, the same court did not apply strict scrutiny to the age requirement and found no constitutional problem with Colorado prohibiting persons under 18 from circulating petitions.[3] The Court considered this discrimination on the basis of age to be "neutral" and "temporary," and since states can prohibit minors from voting, they can also prohibit them from circulating petitions (*i.e.*, engaging in core political speech). Since this Court acknowledged that circulating petitions is a form of political advocacy, and it acknowledged that the Bill of Rights "is not for adults alone," it is hard to understand how the Court could uphold this restriction on "core political speech" on the basis of age. But it did, and the Supreme Court expressed (in *dicta*) its implicit support for this conclusion. *See Buckley v. ACLF*, 119 S.Ct. 636, 642 (1999). Apparently, age does determine one's right to engage in political expression, and minors are not mature enough to have full First Amendment rights.

The Tenth Circuit provided a somewhat muddled analysis of the issues before it, mixing "candidate ballot access" case precedents (which are typically described as implicating voting and political association rights) with free speech case precedents. This was what Colorado hoped to achieve, since the Supreme Court has frequently held that states have wide latitude in regulating ballot access of candidates. In ballot access cases, states are allowed to burden First Amendment, protected voting and political association rights, so long as the burdens are not "too severe." *See Burdick v. Takushi*, 112 S.Ct. 2059 (1992).

These ballot access standards of review had not previously been applied to political speech cases. That distinction led to Justice Thomas' separate concurrence in *Buckley v. ACLF*, where he argued that the challenged measures all affected political speech, could not survive strict scrutiny, and no showing of a "severe burden" was necessary. *Buckley v. ACLF*, 119 S.Ct. at 649-650.

The *Buckley* Court unfortunately adopted much of the language and approach of the muddled "ballot access," "reasonable regulation of election processes" analysis utilized by the Tenth Circuit. The state's "need" for a regulation is compared to the "severity" of the burden imposed on First Amendment rights, and somehow a Court is supposed to know how much regulation is too much interference with First Amendment rights, and how much interference is okay.

States can now argue that courts should not apply strict scrutiny to regulations on initiative and referenda processes, unless a severe burden is shown—and no state ever acknowledges that its regulations impose any significant burden, let alone a severe burden. Who can explain what standard should be used to measure this burden? There is language in *Buckley* which says that no "litmus paper test" will separate permissible from

---

3. This prohibition included criminal penalties for willful violations, a point neither the Tenth Circuit nor the Supreme Court considered significant enough for comment.

impermissible regulations of the initiative process. Sometimes strict scrutiny should be applied; sometimes not. That sounds like a formula for *ad hoc*, arbitrary decision making by the courts, where some burdens will be found "too severe," and others not, based on the value judgments of judges. Instead of the traditional "strict scrutiny" test of regulations burdening political speech, where nearly all burdens on political expression are found unjustifiable, the Court suggests a new "severe burden" test, where the degree of burden is in the eye of the beholding judge.

The founders of this nation greatly feared this type of arbitrary power, based on their own experiences, labeling arbitrary power the "law of tyrants." They did not trust judicial discretion; they did not believe that judicial discretion should be arbitrary, and that the enforcement of rights should be left to arbitrary decision-making. Chief Justice John Marshall described judicial discretion as "judgment guided by law." It is not clear that our current Supreme Court has the same degree of commitment to making decisions based on clearly-defined law.

The *Buckley* Court did unfortunately use the "no litmus paper test" language, but it is also true that not all the justices who concurred in the judgment concurred with that approach. *Buckley*, 119 S.Ct. at 650 (Thomas, J. concurring) (Restrictions on core political speech all plainly impose a severe First Amendment burden, requiring strict scrutiny analysis; no coherent distinction between severe and non-severe burdens can be culled from prior cases dealing with voting and associational rights). The *Buckley* "incoherent standard" approach should be abandoned in the future. I&R proponents will be arguing for a clearer and cleaner definition of principles in future cases.

Buckley's actual analysis does not in fact seem to follow its own stated rules. It is important to read *Buckley* closely to see how the Court applied its standards there. Three regulations were examined. All three were found unconstitutional.

Colorado's requirement that limited petition circulation to registered voters was struck down because, like the restriction against paid petitioners in *Meyer v. Grant* (486 U.S. 414 (1988) (*Meyer* held strict scrutiny was the correct test)), it decreased the pool of available circulators, hence limiting the number of voices who would convey the proponents' message. *Buckley*, 119 S.Ct. at 643-644.

Colorado's voter registration requirement also reduced the chances of proponents to achieve ballot status, and thus make their measure a matter of statewide discussion, again impacting political discussion. *Id.*, at 644. Colorado failed to justify its burden. *Id. Buckley* followed *Meyer* (on this issue), which was a strict scrutiny case. The fact that it was easy to register to vote in Colorado, did not make the burden on speech "not severe." *Id.*

Colorado's paid circulator *identification requirement* was found to burden speech by inhibiting participation in the petitioning process. *Id.*, at 645. Petitioning is akin to handbill circulation. *Id.* But the burden on petitioning is more severe than the burden on handbill authors in *McIntyre* (which applied strict scrutiny to a requirement that handbills disclose authorship), since petition circulation involves more face-to-face communication, at "the precise moment when the circulator's interest in anonymity is greatest." *Id.*, at 646. Colorado lacked sufficient cause to justify this burden. *Id.*

Colorado's monthly reporting requirements required disclosure of the name and address of each paid circulator, as well as the amount paid each circulator. The *Buckley* Court appears to have held that strict scrutiny applies to disclosure requirements (following *Buckley v. Valeo*), since such requirements discourage participation, and that these requirements failed the test. *Id.*, at 648. ("We agree with the Court of Appeals appraisal... Colorado's reporting requirements, to the extent that they target paid circulators, fail exacting scrutiny"). Why was this a "severe burden"? Who can say?

So, although *Buckley* purports not to establish any bright line test to determine which initiative regulations are unconstitutional burdens on First Amendment rights, *Buckley* itself applied the precedence of strict scrutiny cases and the logic of strict scrutiny analysis to three different regulations.

Buckley, therefore, exhibits the continuing vitality of the First Amendment as a substantial barrier to any state regulation which inhibits participation in the initiative petitioning process, to speech-burdening regulations (as long as the speakers are adults) making it less likely that proponents will qualify their measure for the ballot and for the ensuing statewide discussion, and to any regulation which restricts who (unless they are minors) may participate in the petitioning process.

What *Buckley* also accomplished with its discussion of "reasonable regulations" versus severe burdens, was to water-down the apparent importance of First Amendment principles in the initiative and referendum context. This will only encourage more state regulations and interference with the fundamental rights involved in citizen initiatives and referenda.

There was a time when the Supreme Court conveyed the message that the democratic freedoms of the First Amendment were indispensable, and that that priority gave First Amendment liberties *a sanctity and a sanction not permitting dubious intrusions. Thomas v. Collins*, 323 U.S. 516, 530 (1945). Contrary to recent Supreme Court ballot access decisions involving voting and associational rights, where the Court holds that the character and magnitude of the burden should be measured against the State's interest in regulating, the *Thomas* Court recognized that "*it is the character of the right, not of the limitation*, which determines what standard governs the choice" ["where individual freedom ends and the State's power begins"]. *Thomas v. Collins*, 323 U.S. at 529-530.

The state's interest in regulating has in recent years obviously grown more important to the Supreme Court, illustrating just how the Court participates in eroding constitutional protections over time.

Buckley did not address the argument that I&R proponents are now presenting in other cases, in other courts, the argument that the initiative process involves a form of First Amendment-protected "petition for redress of grievances," and that the early stages of the initiative process (where measures are drafted, titles set, and signatures are collected) are, therefore, strictly private political action where state intrusions should be subject to the most exacting scrutiny. A revolution was fought to establish petition rights; thus no state intrusion is warranted. This approach, if adopted by the courts, may assist the courts in distinguishing between regulations which interfere with the exercise of fundamental rights, and permissible regulations which reasonably regulate an election process—regulations such as a requirement for a certain number of signatures before a measure qualifies for the ballot, a turn-in date for petitions to allow the state to count signatures, etc.

Buckley relies on "core political speech" and anonymous speech and compelled financial disclosure cases and does not offer explicit instruction as to how to evaluate First Amendment claims presented in other challenges to initiative and referendum regulations. Courts are now unfortunately left on their own to devise analytical approaches for many different types of regulation.

What most states resort to in attempting to justify their regulations, is what Colorado attempted in *Meyer* and *Buckley*: to avoid any meaningful scrutiny for any of its regulations by simply denying that any of the challenged regulations imposed any real burden on First Amendment rights. The Supreme Court did not accept Colorado's view in either case. The state's view of those burdens should never receive serious weight—not any more than did George III's views in America in 1776. It is against the state that I&R proponents seek protection. You don't ask the fox if the chickens are in danger and you don't ask the tyrant whether he is being oppressive.

Colorado also attempted in *Buckley* and in *Meyer* to persuade the Court that its regulations supported the reliability or integrity of the initiative process, or that its regulations served administrative efficiency. These arguments failed, in large part because Colorado did not—and could not—show that its concerns could not be served by less burdensome regulations.

Conclusion

State officials regulating I&R processes are like all government agents: they will fight to preserve their power. Citizen I&R threatens institutional state power by asserting citizen sovereignty. The battle between state regulators and I&R proponents will continue, with the courts caught in the middle.

The Supreme Court has sent mixed signals as to how important it considers the rights involved in citizen initiative and referenda processes. If courts allow and contribute to state suppression of citizen I&R, citizen discontent with government will be deprived of a vital outlet for expression. Unrelieved pressures can result in unforeseen eruptions.

America's founders demanded their rights of political participation and expression, to invoke the sovereignty of the people. They fought and won a revolution against the most powerful nation on earth — to gain their freedom and establish their sovereignty. Those who would ignore this history should consider the risks.

Chapter 12

The Courts v. the People: An Essay on Judicial Review of Initiatives

By Mads Qvortrup

Sometimes they are the unaccountable elitists in robes who meddle in politics where they do not belong. Sometimes they are the bulwarks of liberty and the champions of the citizens against abuses of power.[1] The role of the courts is controversial — and has always been controversial. Judges in all democratic countries are used to the vilification as well as the praise that goes with adjudicating on controversial issues, which divide the electorate. Yet in an age when all political authority is supposed to derive from the people — at a time when voters increasingly are permitted to vote in referenda and initiatives[2] — the growing power of the judges is a startling development. What is especially startling is that the courts increasingly are encroaching upon decisions made by the citizens themselves — and that they feel that their encroachments are democratically justified. This development calls for a justification of the courts increasing tendency to strike down decisions made by the people.

In 1997, the Ninth Circuit Court, in *Jones v. Bates*, ruled that the average voter could not have understood proposition 140 (a ballot-measure

---

1. The standard case for judicial review has been stated thus by Arend Lijphart: "one can argue that a written and rigid constitution is still not a sufficient restraint on parliamentary majorities, unless there is an independent body that decides whether laws are in conformity with the constitution. If parliament itself is the judge of the constitutionality of its own laws, it can easily be tempted to resolve any doubts in its own favour. The remedy that is usually advocated is to give the courts...the power of judicial review — that is, the power to test the constitutionality of laws passed by the national legislature." Arend Lijphart, *Democracies: Patterns of Majoritarian and Consensus Government in Twenty-One Countries* (New Haven: Yale University Press, 1984), p. 192. The classical case for judicial review is developed by Alexander Hamilton in "Federalist Paper No. 78."

2. The number of initiatives appearing in statewide ballots increased from 67 in 1992, to 68 in 1994, to 92 initiatives in 1996. Elisabeth Gerber, "Pressuring Legislatures Through the Use of Initiatives: Two Forms of Indirect Influence," in Shaun Bowler, Todd Donovan and Caroline Tolbert (eds.), *Citizens as Lawmakers* (Columbia: Ohio State University Press, 1998), p. 191.

Table 1. Initiatives Adopted, Challenged and Invalidated in California, Oregon and Colorado

Initiatives adopted	127
Initiatives challenged by the courts	69 of 127 (54%)
Initiatives invalidated by the courts	33 of 69 (55%)*

* Nine cases are pending.

---

which imposed life time term limits on certain state positions). *Jones v. Bates* is but one of many recent examples of judicial intervention in the initiative process. In the past decade over half of all voter-approved initiatives (in the states which most frequently use the initiative) have been challenged in the courts (54%), and in more than half of the cases (55%), have the courts invalidated part or all of the challenged initiative (See Table 1).[3]

This trend raises a number of important problems: how should the courts adjudicate on laws enacted directly by the people? Should the Courts apply 'strict scrutiny' assuming the voters alleged lack of knowledge? Or, should the courts accord special deference to laws enacted by the citizens? Citizen lawmaking is arguably different from legislation by representatives. Citizens do not— and cannot— devote their entire lives to deliberations and discussions[4]. Some scholars have seen this as an argument for stricter scrutiny of laws enacted directly by the people.[5]

---

3. It should be noted that invalidation, to a large extent, is correlated to the subject matter of the initiative. Tax initiatives and environmental protection initiatives have been far less likely to be invalidated than initiatives that target minorities or political speech. Five out of 8 initiatives affecting minorities have been invalidated in part of in entirety (3). All initiatives concerning campaign finance reform have been invalidated. Only one of seven initiatives dealing with tax issues has been invalidated. See Kenneth Miller, "The Role of the Courts in the Initiative Process: A Search for Standards." Paper delivered at the Annual Meeting of the American Political Science Association, 2-5 September 1999, p. 3.

4. Some have argued that new technology could alter this conclusion, see Ian Budge, *The New Challenge of Direct Democracy* (Cambridge: Polity Press, 1996). Richard Katz has challenged this position, new technology "may make instantaneous communication possible to millions of people...but it cannot add hours to the day. Assuming citizens would sit eight hours a day for five days a week...[the] town meetings could only hear from 2400 citizens a day assuming one minute each (hardly adequate time for a rational argument to be expressed)...In purely political terms the vast majority of citizens would not speak." Richard Katz, *Democracy and Elections* (Oxford: Oxford University Press, 1997), p.96

5. Julian Eule, " Judicial Review of Direct Democracy," *Yale Law Journal*, vol. 99, no. 7, May 1990.

In a recent article Mihui Pak reached the conclusion that:

[d]ue to the lack of procedural safeguards requiring deliberation and thought in the initiative process and the absence to a concrete body, the courts ought to look for indications of 'considered evaluation', construe initiatives narrowly and apply strict scrutiny when reviewing popularly enacted measures.[6]

This article challenges Pak's conclusion. It is argued that his conclusion is fundamentally flawed as it is derived from empirically disputed premises unsupported by political scientists.

The Case for Judicial Review of Direct Legislation

There is (paradoxically) an abundance of democratic arguments for limiting popular decision-making for the sake of the citizens themselves. James Madison opined in *The Federalist No. 63* that:

There are particular moments...when the people stimulated by some irregular passion, or some illicit advantage, or misled by the artful misrepresentations of interested men, may call for measures which they themselves will afterwards be the most ready to lament and condemn.[7]

The Federalist saw judicial review as one of the remedies, which would protect "the people against their own temporary errors and delusions."[8] The courts could, in Hamilton's words, be "a safeguard against the effects of occasional ill humors in the society."[9]

The problem of judicial review of direct legislation is thus particularly warranted. For while initiatives may appear to be the unabridged will of the people they are, in fact, a threat to democracy. For, or so it is argued, the "[p]eople [is] under- or misinformed, lost, bewildered, overly self-inter-

---

6. Mihui Pak, "The Counter-Majoritarian Difficulty in Focus: Judicial Review of Initiatives," 32 *Columbia Journal of Law and Social Problems*, 273, 1999.

7. James Madison, "The Federalist Number 63," in James Madison, Alexander Hamilton, and John Jay, *The Federalist Papers* (London: Penguin, 1987), p. 371.

8. Ibid.

9. Alexander Hamilton, "The Federalist Number 78," in James Madison, Alexander Hamilton, and John Jay, *The Federalist Papers* (London: Penguin, 1987), p. 441.

ested, or simply apathetic."[10] It would, therefore, seem that the judges carefully should assess whether the enacted measures in every case *really* represent the will of the "people." For, as Swiss philosopher Jean-Jacques Rousseau once wrote, "We always want what is advantageous for us but we do not always discern it. The people is never corrupted, but it is often misled."[11] A case can, consequently, be made for a standard of review, which ensures that initiatives are a reflection of the popular, will. That is the courts should—following the Supreme Court in *Greene v. McElroy*—apply "strict scrutiny," that is "in areas of doubtful constitutionality... [there should be] careful and purposeful consideration by those responsible for enacting... our laws."[12]

The problem is, however, that the courts have adjudicated differently on ballot initiatives. Some state courts have shown considerable deference to initiatives, whereas federal courts "appear more willing to invalidate initiatives."[13] The explanation might be that federal judges, who typically have lifetime tenure, and hence enjoy a large measure of insulation from public opinion, are more wary about offending the voters than judges who have to face the electorate—as is the case for state-judges.[14] The sitting judges of the highest courts in all but two of the states that permit initiatives (Maine and Massachusetts) are ultimately held accountable to the voters for their decisions. It is not difficult to understand that these judges have been reluctant to strike down initiatives.[15]

This difference in the pattern of adjudication raise important questions, which go to the very heart of the justification for judicial review. Alexander Hamilton argued, in *Federalist Paper 78*:

---

10. Jim Rossi, "Participation Run Amok: The Costs of Mass Participation for Deliberative Agency Decision-Making," *Northwestern University Law Review*, vol. 92, 1997, pp. 215-16.

11. Jean Jacques Rousseau, *The Social Contract* (London: Penguin Books, 1968), p. 73.

12. Greene v. McElroy, 360 U.S. 474, 507 (1959). Yet the fundamental question is if the courts can discern the true intentions of the voters. Judge Cornelia Kennedy has challenged this view: "Since the court cannot ask voters why they voted that way, a court has no way of ascertaining what motivated the electorate," Kinksey v. City of Jackson, 663 F2d, 662 (5th Cir.1981), quoted in Eule, cit op., p. 1561.

13. Craig Holman and Robert Stern, Judicial Review of Ballot Initiatives, In Depth Studies at http://www.iandrinstitute.org/

14. Kenneth Miller, "The Role of the Courts in the Initiative Process: A Search for Standards." Paper delivered at the Annual Meeting of the American Political Science Association, 2-5 September 1999, p. 3.

15. Julian Eule, "Judicial Review of Direct Democracy," p. 1579.

[that to] avoid an arbitrary discretion in the courts, it is indispensable that they should be bound down by strict rules and precedents which serve to define and point out their duty in every particular case that comes before them.[16]

The observed variation in the patterns of adjudication is a far cry from Alexander Hamilton's ideal.

This lack of standards is a fundamental problem, which ought to be resolved through the adoption of a common standard of judicial review of initiatives. The question is if "strict scrutiny" — as advocated by Pak — is a legitimate principle of adjudication, i.e., if judicial review of initiatives can and should be based on the premise that the voters are ignorant of the contents of the laws that they enact.

Judicial review of initiatives is a controversial issue among judges. Some judges have found it illegitimate that the least democratic of the political institutions can overrule the decisions of the people. As one judge has put it:

[a] system which permits one judge to block with a stroke of a pen what 4,736,180 state residents voted to enact tests the integrity of our constitution.[17]

Others have noted that initiatives ought to be treated exactly as enactments by elected legislators.[18] Still others believe that initiatives should be scrutinized more closely than laws enacted by legislatures, as the voters (allegedly) lack the cognitive ability to reach informed decisions. Pak is a proponent of the latter view.

The question is not whether judicial review of even the most popular measures is permissible.[19] The question is rather if the judges can adjudicate on the basis of the premise that the voters are ignorant of the measures that

---

16. Alexander Hamilton, "Federalist Paper 78," in James Madison, Alexander Hamilton, and John Jay, *The Federalist Papers* (London. Penguin Classics, 1987), p. 442.

17. Coalition for Economic Equality v. Wilson, 110F 3d, 1431, 1437 (9th Cir. 1997).

18. The Supreme Court seems to prefer this interpretation. In *Citizens Against Rent-Control/Coalition of Fair Housing v. The City of Berkeley*, it ruled that it is, "irrelevant that the voters rather than a legislative body enact[s] [the law] because the voters may no more violate the constitution by enacting a ballot measure than a legislative body may by enacting legislation." Citizens Against Rent Control/Coalition of Fair Housing v. City of Berkeley, 454, U.S. 290, 295 (1981). This ruling seems to be consistent with the precedent established in Pacific States Telephone and Telegraph Co. v. Oregon (223 U.S. 118 (1912), in which the Supreme Court ruled that Oregon's use of the initiative to enact a gross-receipts tax was consistent with the principle of republican government.

19. On this see Eule, 1990.

they assent to in initiatives. Are the courts, in other words, justified in striking down direct legislation on the grounds that the voters lack the competence to decide issues while they, the "judges are viewed as better positioned to deliberate?"[20] Are the voters as incompetent as Pak assumes? This is not primarily a legal question, but an empirical question, which requires us to consult the findings of political scientists rather than legal precedents.

Reasoning Voters

Studies of electoral behavior have traditionally been based on the assumption that decision-makers had to possess encyclopedic knowledge of the issues.[21] Contemporary political scientists have challenged this assumption in recent years, by emphasizing that voters cope with information demands by using information short cuts.[22] The voters do not need in depth (encyclopedic) knowledge about the issues to make informed decisions. Reasoning voters are approximately rational, trying to come to terms with decisions about which they are vaguely informed, that is they seek to decide rationally "with limited information and processing capacity."[23] The reasoning voter is thus a description of "voters [who] actually do reason about parties, candidates and issues" by investing their votes in collective goods on the basis of "costly and imperfect information under conditions of uncertainty."[24]

As contrasted with private investors these "public" investors have less incentive to gather costly information[25]. They therefore look for short cuts, that is for ways in which they can make optimal decisions on the basis of

---

20. Pak, cit op., p. 245.

21. For a review see Shaun Bowler and Todd Donovan, *Demanding Choices* (Ann Arbor: University of Michigan Press, 1998), pp. 21-42. The traditional view of the ignorant voter derives from the Michigan-school's study of the American voters in the 1950s. See Angus Campbell et al., *The American Voter* (New York: John Wiley, 1960). The empirical validity of this model was already challenged in the 1970s. See Norman Nie, Sidney Verba and John Petrocik, *The Changing American Voter* (Cambridge: Harvard University Press, 1979).

22. For a review see Franz Urban Pappi, "Political Behaviour: Reasoning Voters and Multi Party Systems," in Robert Goodin and Hans-Dieter Klingemann, *The New Handbook of Political Science* (Oxford: Oxford University Press, 1996), pp. 255-275.

23. P. Snidermann, R.A. Brody, and P.E. Tetlock, *Reasoning and Choice* (New York: Cambridge University Press, 1991), p. 18.

24. S.L. Popkin, *The Reasoning Voter* (Chicago: Chicago University Press), pp. 7-10.

25. For a classical discussion of the information problem see Anthony Downs, *An Economic Theory of Democracy* (New York: Harper, 1957).

inexpensive information. These insights have recently entered the sub-area of initiative and referendum studies through the seminal work by Arthur Lupia. Lupia writes:

> As an alternative to the costly acquisition of encyclopedic information, voters may choose to employ information shortcuts. For example voters can acquire information about preferences or opinions of friends, co-workers, political parties or groups, which they may then use to infer how a proposition will affect them.[26]

In a study of the 1990 insurance initiatives Arthur Lupia thus demonstrated that apparently ill-informed voters, who had knowledge of the insurance industry's preference about insurance regulation initiatives had opinions which were nearly identical to those of well-informed voters (within three percent or less).[27]

These findings have been corroborated in a recent study by Shaun Bowler and Todd Donovan, in which the authors show that "voters can and do think about and decide upon propositions in ways that make sense and in ways that take advantage of readily available information."[28] One of the most frequently cited cues is elite endorsements. The voters do not study the proposals in detail, they rather base their decisions on elite cues. The voters in Washington's term-limit initiatives in 1991 thus took their cues from Speaker Tom Foley's position on the issue. Foley's position had a dramatic effect on the "probability of supporting the initiative, depending on feelings toward Foley. Those with negative feelings toward Foley [were] almost twice as likely to vote for the initiative [which Foley opposed]."[29]

These findings do not prove that voters deliberate, nor that they evaluate policies from an objective perspective. Yet the findings indicate that the voters have the cognitive ability to respond to the steep information demands presented to them, and that they are likely to reason and vote in accordance with their preferences.

---

26. Lupia, supra 13, p. 63.

27. Arthur Lupia, "Short-cuts versus Encyclopedias: Information and Voting Behavior in California's Insurance Reform Elections," in *American Political Science Review*, vol. 88, 1994, p. 71.

28. One of the paradoxical findings in these studies has been that voters can use information from advertisements. Campaign spending does not— according to these findings— induce the voters to vote for the richer side. Advertisements rather provide the voters with cues, which enable them to make up their minds. See Bowler and Donovan, supra 12, p. 165.

29. Jeffrey Karp, "The Influence of Elite-Endorsements in Initiative Campaigns," in Shaun Bowler, Todd Donovan and Caroline Tolbert (eds.), *Citizens as Lawmakers* (Columbia: Ohio State University Press, 1998), p. 161.

Pak finds— quoting Thomas Cronin— that very few voters read the ballot pamphlet. In contrast, "legislators spend weeks in committees reviewing the law and debating its impact."[30] It would follow from this that representative government is preferable to citizen lawmaking.[31] This conclusion is, however, debatable, as it is based on empirically inaccurate data. A recent study reports that 54% of the voters read the ballot pamphlet. The pamphlet is thus the most cited source of information, ahead of newspaper editorials (47%), TV-editorials (33%) and friends (22%).[32] Moreover surveys indicate that the voters not only rely on shortcuts, but that they, in fact, have a considerable knowledge of the issues; "53% of the Colorado voters said they were somewhat informed and an impressive 37% said they were very informed."[33] It seems, therefore, difficult to sustain the objection that the voters lack the competence to decide on ballot measures.

Pak's line of reasoning seems to be based on a Burkean notion of the legislator. Burke wrote:

> Your representative owes you not his industry alone but his judgment; and he betrays, instead of serving, you if he sacrifices it to your opinion.[34]

Yet it is questionable if this elitist conception of democracy is defensible, or even realistic. James Buchanan and Gordon Tullock notes that:

> [I]n the face of observable pressure group activity with its demonstrable results on the outcome of specific issues presented and debated in legislative assemblies, that behavioral premise that calls the legislator to follow a selfless pursuit of the 'public interest' or the 'general welfare' as something independent of and apart from private economic interest is severely threatened.[35]

Recent studies support Buchanan and Tullock's observations; legislators are less than fully informed when they cast their votes. They often

---

30. Pak, cit op., p. 254.

31. For a similar conclusion see David Magleby, *Direct Legislation. Voting on Ballot Propositions in the United States* (Baltimore: Johns Hopkins University Press, 1984), p. 181.

32. Bowler and Donovan, cit op., p. 56.

33. Dan Smith, Paper presented at The National Initiative and Referendum Conference, The Washington Court Hotel, Washington D.C., 6-8 May 1999.

34. Edmund Burke, "Speech to the Electors in Bristol," in Edmund Burke, *Works*, vol. 1 (London: Bohn's Standard Library, 1902), p. 447.

35. James Buchanan and Gordon Tullock, *The Calculus of Consent* (Ann Arbor: University of Michigan Press, 1962), p. 283.

vote on bills they may not have read. In the main their decisions are anchored in pressure from constituents, committee chairs and party leaders.[36] This lack of knowledge among the elected representatives should— according to some— have implications. William Riker and Berry Weingast have thus made a case for stricter judicial scrutiny of laws enacted by legislatures, on the grounds that the representatives fail to represent the majority of the people.[37]

These studies, which are based on empirical evidence, make it difficult to sustain Pak's case for "strict scrutiny" of the initiative process. If the outcomes of initiatives were produced by voter ignorance, as argued by Pak, then a case for strict scrutiny could have been made. However voters enact laws "as if" they understand the issues. The view that "initiatives…trigger a harder judicial look" (as the voters are less knowledgeable than the legislators) is, therefore, ill founded.[38]

Implications

The refutation of Pak's case for a stricter judicial review of ballot propositions does not, of course, render judicial review impermissible. It is the duty of the courts "to declare all acts contrary to the manifest tenor of the Constitution void"[39]. But there is nothing inherent in initiatives, which justifies they almost routinely are challenged—and invalidated—in the courts. The courts should give initiatives the same deference that they accord to measures enacted by the legislatures. That the majority of the initiatives enacted by the voters in the Western states have been nullified by the courts, indicates that the judges have failed to appreciate this. However, just because a law is enacted by the people, it should not be sacrosanct if it violates the Constitution.

There is always a question of legitimacy involved when the courts strike down the enactments of the people themselves. Judicial review might be legally permissible, but the political implications of judicial review of initiatives are different from the political implications of judicial review of laws enacted by the legislatures. The citizens—we might assume—are

---

36. John Kingdon, *Congressmen's Voting Decisions* (Ann Arbor: University of Michigan Press, 1989).

37. William Riker and Berry Weingast, "Constitutional Regulation of Legislative Choice: The Political Consequences of Judicial Deference to Legislatures," *Virginia Law Review*, vol. 74, 1998, p. 74.

38. Julian Eule, "Judicial Review of Direct Democracy," *99 Yale Law Journal*, 1990, p. 1545.

39. Alexander Hamilton, cit op., p. 438.

more likely to be outraged when judge strikes down a measure enacted by themselves, than when a judge strikes down a law enacted by another member of the "power elite."[40]

The judiciary has been described as "the least democratic of the three branches of American national government."[41] That the courts (especially the federal courts) are the least accountable of the institutions in America's political life makes it imperative that the courts restrict their interference in political life lest the legitimacy of the whole political system would be impaired.

The voters may be unaware and unmoved when laws enacted by the legislatures are declared void by the courts— they might even applaud the decision. But judicial challenges of ballot measures are (politically) birds of a different feather. Judicial review of initiatives— especially popular ones— risks engendering the perception that the citizens have been subverted, and is likely to result in an even higher level of political discomfort.[42] The scheme proposed by Pak— and enforced in *Jones v. Bates*— will not only undermine the principle that the "will of the people" is the touchstone of political legitimacy, it will also increase the already alarming distrust in the political system. Indeed this resentment has recently been shown in the citizens' reaction against judges who defied the wills of a majority of the voters. The electoral defeat of Rose Bird, California's chief justice (who struck down several initiatives) is but one of a number of judges who have suffered the consequences of nullifying the will of the people.

Conclusion

The increasing use of the initiative has resulted in an increasing number of propositions being challenged in the courts; 54% of the successful initiatives in the Pacific states are challenged, and 55% of these are invalidated in part or in totality by the courts. This trend raises the question if the courts should give more or less deference to legislation enacted direct-

---

40. Mads Qvortrup, "The Constitutional Implications of the Use of the Referendum." Unpublished Doctoral Dissertation, University of Oxford, Chap. IV.

41. Jess H. Choper, cited in Pak, cit op., p. 238.

42. "A distinguishing feature of politics in the 1990s is a pervasive sense of public distrust of, frustration with, and alienation from government…A recent Gallup-Poll showed that only 20% of respondents said that they can trust the federal government all or some of the time— half the percentage during the Watergate scandal." Caroline Tolbert "Changing Rules for State Legislatures: Direct Democracy and Governance Policies," in Shaun Bowler, Todd Donovan and Caroline Tolbert (eds.), *Citizens as Lawmakers* (Columbia: Ohio State University Press, 1998), p. 172.

ly by the people. Pak argues— along with Eule— that a case can be made for "a harder look" at initiatives. The voters, he claims (without offering empirical proof), lack the knowledge required to decide on these issues. Moreover their, alleged, lack of knowledge result—according to Pak— in the enactment of laws that are inconsistent with the preferences of the voters. The brief analysis of the scholarly evidence regarding voter knowledge presented in this paper does not support the premises underlying Pak's argument. Indeed, Pak's conclusion is inconsistent with recent scholarship by, Lupia, Bowler and Donovan, which has established that voters use "information short-cuts" to cope with the information demand. Moreover Pak's conclusion is inconsistent with Smith's survey findings which show that an overwhelming number of the voters felt that they are well informed.

These results undermine Pak's case for strict scrutiny of citizen-enacted legislation. The evidence does not, to be sure, undermine the case for judicial review of direct legislation, but it undermines the case for judicial intervention on the grounds that the people are unable to reach informed decisions. Judicial review is still permissible, indeed, desirable. If constitutions are to play any part in limiting government, then someone must decide when they have been breached and how they should be applied. The courts are ideally suited to play this part. But an overly zealous judiciary, which almost routinely strikes down laws enacted by the people is not a necessary consequence of judicial review. On the contrary, an interventionist judiciary risks engendering the perception that the "elite" is unresponsive to the wishes and the views of the citizens.

"The courts," wrote Hamilton, are "designed to be an intermediate between the people and the legislature in order, among other things, to keep the latter within the limits assigned to its authority." That the courts currently show a considerably greater propensity to strike down initiatives indicates that the courts themselves perhaps have overstepped the limits assigned to their authority.

Section Four

The Government's
View of Regulation

No discussion is ever complete without hearing from all sides. It should be noted that the Institute extended an invitation to the authors of many of the major laws regulating the I&R process giving them an opportunity to provide a first hand account as to why the regulation was necessary —they all declined.

However, this section does provide observations on the necessity or fallacy of regulating the I&R process from two individuals who have been intimately involved in the oversight of the process—Secretary of State Bill Jones from California, the largest state with I&R, and Attorney General Don Stenberg of Nebraska, where many attempts to regulate the process have originated.

Additionally, Jenni Drage of the National Conference of State Legislatures provides an in-depth overview of some the I&R legislation that has been considered over the last few years. More information regarding attempts by the state legislatures to regulate the I&R process can be found by visiting the Institute's legislative section at http://www.iandrinstitute.org.

Chapter 13

Preserving the Democratic Legacy of the American Frontier: Limiting Regulation of the People's Initiative and Referendum Process

By Don Stenberg

The spirit and legacy of the American frontier were derived from common struggles and shared experiences as the country grew and developed. Thus, whether attributed to the prairie populism of the Great Plains or the Yankee independence of New England, the adoption of the initiative and referendum process across the country may be seen as part of the democratic legacy and independent spirit of the American frontier. The preservation of this legacy, and the careful regulation of the petition process it entails, are challenges for the new century. At issue is just how much regulation of the process is desirable or necessary.

At a time when horses were more common than cars, the people of Nebraska, like those of nearly half the states, set up a potent check on the power of its elected Legislature, and claimed for themselves the power of direct democracy known as the Initiative and Referendum. They did so with these words:

> [T]he legislative authority of the State shall be vested in a Legislature ... The people reserve for themselves, however, the power to propose laws, and amendments to the constitution, and to enact or reject the same at the polls, independent of the Legislature, and also reserve power at their own option to approve or reject at the polls any act ... passed by the Legislature. Neb. Const. art. III, § 1.

This assertion of power by the electorate did not go unchallenged. In Nebraska, as elsewhere, the Legislature has not stopped trying to reign in this competing legislative power since it was reclaimed by the first and second generation citizens of the State. Year after year, and legislative session after session, bills have been introduced to restrict the petition process. In recent years, these proposals have been introduced in the name of "fraud prevention" as well as the alleged protection of the public from rascally varmints known as "circulators"—the likes of which haven't been seen in the State since the days of horse thieves and cattle rustlers.

Just what are the proper limits of regulation of the Initiative and Referendum process? What safeguards are necessary to protect its integrity, and which ones just frustrate the process? During my service as Nebraska's Attorney General I have repeatedly challenged legislative attempts to hamper the Initiative and Referendum process. In so doing, I utilized a judicial standard developed by the Nebraska Supreme Court nearly eight decades ago. This "facilitation" standard serves the people of Nebraska well, and could be a model for evaluating legislative attempts to regulate the Initiative and Referendum process elsewhere.

In *State ex rel. Brant v. Beermann*, 217 Neb. 632, 350 N.W.2d 18 (1984), the Nebraska Supreme Court reviewed the State's constitutional provisions creating the Initiative and Referendum process. The court described the important nature of the process and recounted components of the "facilitation" standard for reviewing legislative attempts to regulate the process:

> By the foregoing constitutional provisions the people of the State of Nebraska have reserved the power to propose and enact laws independent of the Legislature. Consequently, the Legislature and the electorate are concurrently equal in rank as sources of legislation. *Provisions authorizing the initiative should be construed in such a manner that the legislative power reserved in the people is effectual. See Klosterman v. Marsh*, 180 Neb. 506, 143 N.W.2d 744 (1966); *State ex rel. Morris v. Marsh*, 183 Neb. 521, 162 N.W.2d 262 (1968); *Adams v. Bolin*, 74 Ariz. 269, 247 P.2d 617 (1952). *Such right reserved in the people of Nebraska is so precious and jealously guarded* that the Governor cannot veto measures initiated by the people. *See* Neb.Const. art. III, §4.
>
> "*The right of initiative is precious to the people and is one which the courts are zealous to preserve to the fullest tenable measure of spirit as well as letter.*" *McFadden v. Jordan*, 32 Cal.2d 330, 332, 196 P.2d 787, 788 (1948). "To preserve the full spirit of the initiative the submission of issues to the voters should not become bogged down by lengthy litigation in the courts...." *Perry v. Jordan*, 34 Cal.2d 87, 91, 207 P.2d 47, 49 (1949).
>
> Provisions concerning the initiative, the legislative power reserved to the people, should receive liberal construction to effectuate the policy proposed and adopted by the initiative as a part of the democratic process. *See State v. Davis*, 418 S.W.2d 163, (Mo. 1967); cf. *State ex rel. Boyer v. Grady*, 201 Neb. 360, 269 N.W.2d 73 (1978) (powers of the initiative and referendum regarding municipalities are to be liberally construed to permit, rather than restrict, the power and to attain, rather than prevent, its object).

Id. at 636, 350 N.W.2d at 21 (emphasis added). *See also State ex rel. Morris v. Marsh*, 183 Neb. 521, 545, 162 N.W.2d 262 (1968) (*"The powers reserved to the people by initiative and referendum acts have long been regarded as sacrosanct....*") (emphasis added).

As evidenced by the foregoing case law, the Nebraska Supreme Court has long construed the constitutional provisions dealing with initiative and referendum petitions as precious and fundamental rights reserved by the people free from interference by the Legislature, save only the legislative right to pass laws which *facilitate* the initiative and referendum process. *Stenberg v. Beermann*, 240 Neb. 754, 485 N.W.2d 151 (1992); *State ex rel. Morris v. Marsh*, 183 Neb. 520, 524-25, 162 N.W.2d 262, 265, 266 (1968); *Klosterman v. Marsh*, 180 Neb. 506, 513, 143 N.W.2d 744, 749 (1966); *State ex rel. Winter v. Swanson*, 138 Neb. 597, 598, 294 N.W. 200, 201 (1940); *State ex rel. Ayres v. Amsberry*, 104 Neb. 273, 276-77, 177 N.W. 179, 180 (1920), *vacated on other grounds*, 104 Neb. 279, 178 N.W. 822 (1920).

The word "facilitate" is a common term and is always defined as meaning to make easy or less difficult; to free from difficulty or impediment. 35 C.J.S. Facilitate, pgs. 487, 488 (1960); *Black's Law Dictionary*, p. 531 (5th ed. 1979). *Accord Amsberry*, 104 Neb. at 276. The Nebraska Supreme Court has held that a law to "facilitate" the operation of the people's initiative power must either prevent fraud or render intelligible the purpose of the proposed law or constitutional amendment. *State ex rel. Winter v. Swanson*, 138 Neb. 597, 294 N.W. 200 (1940). *See also State ex rel. Stenberg v. Beermann*, 240 Neb. 754, 485 N.W.2d 151 (1992). The Court's resolve to declare unconstitutional any statute which does not facilitate the initiative and referendum process was set forth as follows:

> Bearing upon the question of the construction of the statute, we have to consider also the language of the initiative and referendum amendment to the Constitution as follows: "This amendment shall be self-executing, but legislation may be enacted especially to facilitate its operation." Const., art. III, sec. 1D. Under this provision, *legislation permissible must be such as frees the operation of the constitutional provisions from obstruction or hindrance. Any legislation which would hamper or render ineffective the power reserved to the people would be unconstitutional.*
>
> *Laws to facilitate the operation of the amendment must be reasonable, so as not to unnecessarily obstruct or impede the operation of the law.*

State ex rel. Ayres v. Amsberry, 104 Neb. at 276, 277, 177 N.W. at 180 (emphasis added).

Additionally, the Court has stated, "The amendment under consideration reserves to the people the right to act in the capacity of legislators.

The presumption should be in favor of the validity and legality of their act. The law should be construed, if possible, so as to prevent absurdity and hardship and so as to favor public convenience." Id. at 287, 177 N.W. at 180 (emphasis added).

Legislation which is claimed to "facilitate" the people's initiative and referendum process must be "reasonable." *Stenberg v. Beermann,* 240 Neb. at 756. Among the considerations in making this determination is whether it "tends to insure a fair, intelligent, and impartial result on the part of the electorate." *Id.* Furthermore, *"Any legislation which would hamper or render ineffective the power reserved to the people would be unconstitutional." State ex rel. Ayres v. Amsberry,* 104 Neb. at 276-277. Thus, "reasonable" fraud prevention measures must meet this overriding standard. Laws causing absurd and unnecessary hardships do not facilitate the process. *Id.* at 277. In short, "Laws to facilitate the operation of the [petition process] amendment must be reasonable, so as not to unnecessarily obstruct or impede the operation of the law." *Id.* In addition, the Nebraska Constitution "reserves to the people the right to act in the capacity of legislators. *The presumption should be in favor of the validity and legality of their act. The law should be construed, if possible, so as to prevent absurdity and hardship and so as to favor public convenience." Id.* at 277-278 (emphasis added).

Thus, when all the facets of the Court's standard are considered, it is clear that only a narrowly tailored anti-fraud provision, which does not impede the process more than necessary to prevent fraud, could be said to facilitate the people's initiative process. In other words, in order to be "reasonable" under the Court's established standard, a fraud prevention statute must go no further than necessary to prevent fraud. This standard is intentionally high, and is similar to the least restrictive means test applied under the First Amendment.

A number of important corollaries under the "facilitation" standard may be identified:

1. Provisions authorizing the initiative should be construed in such a manner that the legislative power reserved in the people is effectual. *State ex rel. Stenberg v. Moore,* 258 Neb. 199, 210-211, 602 N.W.2d 465 (1999); *State ex rel. Brant v. Beermann,* 217 Neb. 632, 350 N.W.2d 18 (1984); *State ex rel. Morris v. Marsh,* 183 Neb. 521, 162 N.W.2d 262 (1968); *Klosterman v. Marsh,* 180 Neb. 506, 143 N.W.2d 744 (1966).
2. Permissible legislation must be such as frees the operation of the constitutional provisions from obstruction or hindrance. Any legislation which would hamper or render ineffective the power reserved to the people is unconstitutional. *State ex rel. Stenberg v. Moore,* 258 Neb. 199, 210-211, 602 N.W.2d 465 (1999); *State*

ex rel. Ayres v. Amsberry, 104 Neb. 273, 177 N.W. 179 (1920), *vacated on other grounds,* 104 Neb. 279, 178 N.W. 822 (1920).

3. Statutory enactments may not directly or indirectly limit, curtail, or destroy the rights of initiative and referendum, which are expressly declared to be self-executing. The legislature may only facilitate the initiative process. If the legislature hinders these rights, the statutes are unconstitutional and void. *State ex rel. Brant v. Beermann,* 217 Neb. 632, 350 N.W.2d 18 (1984); *Klosterman v. Marsh,* 180 Neb. 506, 143 N.W.2d 744 (1966); *State ex rel. Ayres v. Amsberry,* 104 Neb. 273, 177 N.W. 179 (1920), *vacated on other grounds,* 104 Neb. 279, 178 N.W. 822 (1920).

4. Laws to facilitate the operation of the Initiative and Referendum Process must be reasonable, so as not to unnecessarily obstruct or impede the operation of the law. *State ex rel. Stenberg v. Beermann,* 240 Neb. 754, 485 N.W.2d 151 (1992); *State ex rel. Ayres v. Amsberry,* 104 Neb. 273, 177 N.W. 179 (1920), *vacated on other grounds,* 104 Neb. 279, 178 N.W. 822 (1920).

5. The word "facilitate" is a common term and is always defined as meaning to make easy or less difficult; to free from difficulty or impediment. 35 C.J.S. Facilitate, pgs. 487, 488 (1960); *Black's Law Dictionary,* p. 531 (5th ed. 1979).

6. A law to "facilitate" the operation of the people's initiative power must either prevent fraud or render intelligible the purpose of the proposed law or constitutional amendment. *State ex rel. Stenberg v. Beermann,* 240 Neb. 754, 485 N.W.2d 151 (1992); *State ex rel. Winter v. Swanson,* 138 Neb. 597, 294 N.W. 200 (1940).

7. Only a narrowly tailored anti-fraud provision, which does not impede the process more than necessary to prevent fraud, could be said to facilitate the people's initiative process. *State ex rel. Stenberg v. Moore,* 258 Neb. 199, 210-211, 602 N.W.2d 465 (1999); *State ex rel. Stenberg v. Beermann,* 240 Neb. 754, 485 N.W.2d 151 (1992); *State ex rel. Ayres v. Amsberry,* 104 Neb. 273, 177 N.W. 179 (1920), *vacated on other grounds,* 104 Neb. 279, 178 N.W. 822 (1920).

8. Legislative regulation of the process must not unreasonably or unnecessarily burden the people's reserved initiative and referendum rights even in the name of fraud prevention. Where less onerous or less restrictive means are available to accomplish the same purpose, a more onerous or more restrictive restriction is unnecessary and unreasonable. *State ex rel. Stenberg v. Moore,* 258 Neb. 199, 214, 602 N.W.2d 465 (1999); *State ex rel. Stenberg v. Beermann,* 240 Neb. 754, 485 N.W.2d 151 (1992). *State*

ex rel. Ayres v. Amsberry, 104 Neb. 273, 177 N.W. 179 (1920), *vacated on other grounds,* 104 Neb. 279, 178 N.W. 822 (1920).

9. The Initiative and Referendum provisions reserve to the people the right to act in the capacity of legislators. The presumption should be in favor of the validity and legality of their act. The law should be construed, if possible, so as to prevent absurdity and hardship and so as to favor public convenience. *State ex rel. Stenberg v. Moore,* 258 Neb. 199, 213, 602 N.W.2d 465 (1999); *State ex rel. Stenberg v. Beermann,* 240 Neb. 754, 485 N.W.2d 151 (1992); *Klosterman v. Marsh,* 180 Neb. 506, 143 N.W.2d 744 (1966); *State ex rel. Ayres v. Amsberry,* 104 Neb. 273, 177 N.W. 179 (1920), *vacated on other grounds,* 104 Neb. 279, 178 N.W. 822 (1920).

10. The presumption in favor of the validity of the signatures of voters is not dependant upon the signing of a voter's full name. *State ex rel. Stenberg v. Beermann,* 240 Neb. 754, 485 N.W.2d 151 (1992); *State ex rel. Morris v. Marsh,* 183 Neb. 521, 162 N.W.2d 262 (1968).

Using these legal standards I successfully challenged a statute which attempted to make it a criminal offense for a petition circulator to cross county lines. *State ex rel. Stenberg v. Beermann,* 240 Neb. 754, 485 N.W.2d 151 (1992). I also successfully challenged a statute imposing a burdensome matching requirement between numerous items of information on the petition form and voter registration records. *State ex rel. Stenberg v. Moore,* 258 Neb. 199, 602 N.W.2d 465 (1999).

As issues arise in the future as to the proper level of petition regulation, some basic questions must be kept in mind. Is the regulation broader than necessary to prevent fraud? Are other anti-fraud measures already in place? Would the regulation facilitate the Initiative and Referendum process or hinder it? The rights of the people under the Initiative and Referendum process are fundamental constitutional rights. Statutory regulation of such rights must be narrowly drafted, and it must facilitate rather than hinder the exercise of the people's rights.

As William Jennings Bryan urged, in his address to the Nebraska Constitutional Convention in 1920, "[W]e have the initiative and the referendum in Nebraska; do not disturb them. If defects are discovered, correct them and perfect the machinery...Make it possible for the people to have what they want...we are the world's teacher in democracy;...the world looks to us for an example. We cannot ask others to trust the people unless we are ourselves willing to trust them." *Journal of the Nebraska Constitutional Convention,* vol. 1, p. 326-327.

Chapter 14

Initiative and Reform

By Bill Jones

Is the initiative today in need of reformation so that it more perfectly embodies what the people want and are there good ways of doing so? The answer is definitely yes to both questions.

One of the most remarkable things about that remarkable modern contribution to government, the popular initiative, is that the arguments for and against it have been fueled by the same passions from the beginning until today. These same arguments go directly to the current questions of whether or not the initiative is in crisis and needs immediate regulation.

In California, the initiative, referendum, and recall reforms found their most passionate advocate and detractor in the same family. Hiram Johnson, governor and zealous Progressive, championed the "direct democracy" which the new reforms would instill into state politics gone rotten with the corruption of special interest money. His father, though, saw such "direct democracy" as pernicious itself. It would not be a cure but a disease. Grover Johnson declared, "The voice of the people is not the voice of God, for the voice of the people sent Jesus to the Cross."

The argument's two poles were marked from that time forward. The initiative, which was designed to more freely announce and implement the people's will, could just as easily become the tyrannical and fickle instrument by which representative government was undermined. Today the arguments have taken slight turns in the road. The concern of many initiative supporters is that it has itself become corrupted by the very special interest influence on government that the reform set out to curb or eliminate entirely. On the other hand, those who favor curbing the initiative itself now see it as unchecked, heedless, even reckless. Both groups focus on the power of money to direct this potent tool. The president of Colorado's state Senate said recently, "Now if you have $400,000 you can get your issue on the ballot with paid circulators and into law with 30-second sound bites. That's not a true citizens' initiative." His opposite, the director of the National Conference of State Legislatures offered, "There is a fear that this is direct democracy run amok." He was echoed by the chairman of Oregon's state Senate Judiciary Committee, "For $100,000 you can put just about anything you want on the ballot in Oregon...A democ-

217

racy is not intended to be efficient or quick. It is a slower, deliberative process."

Which perspective is closest to the truth? In the answers lies whether the initiative remains as it began in the early part of the 20th century as we enter the 21st century. Has the people's will, the grand effort at 'direct democracy' been thwarted? Has the infection of special interest money now spread to the initiative itself, transforming a reform into merely another method by which special interests wield power? Are the proposals to reform the reform really getting at an evil or creating one?

My own experience with the initiative process was instructive. I was the author of California's "Three Strikes, You're Out" law, which in addition to being legislatively introduced was also placed on the ballot as Proposition 184 because voters clearly did not trust the legislature to keep the measure's purpose undiluted. It provided for maximum life sentences for delineated classes of repeat serious felons. It was approved in 1994 by 71.8% of California's voters, who were determined to take action after a repeat felon killed a child. It was a textbook example of the people's will working through the initiative process. It was also a clear example of the people's mistrust of their legislature.

From that perspective, I believe a short history lesson about the initiative's inception in California and what it attempted at the outset and achieved may shed light on the current controversy. It is a controversy, though, which will remain active as long as some form of initiative is part of governance in 24 states. It will do so because the fundamental controversy is the fundamental argument about the nature of our form of government.

The Past Is Prologue

What is an initiative? It is a method of lawmaking. It is voted on directly by the citizens. It cannot, in most instances, be altered by the legislature once enacted. Or if altered, a supermajority of two thirds of the legislators is required. Changes in initiative enacted statutes or constitutional additions must be submitted to the voters for approval.

There are two kinds of initiative. The first is statutory which enacts an addition or alteration to the body of statutes of California. The second is constitutional. This form of initiative changes the basic law of the state, the constitution. Both forms of initiative are open to challenge by judicial interpretation.

There were at the beginning two methods of initiative. The first was direct. A measure was submitted by its proponents to the people and voted on in a general election. The second was indirect. A measure was qualified by collection of signatures of registered voters, 5% of the last vote for Governor. The proposed initiative was submitted to the legislature for consideration before going on the ballot. The legislature had 40 days to enact the proposal without change or amendment. If the legislature did not amend or change the proposal, it was not placed on the ballot and became law. Neither type of initiative could be vetoed by the Governor.

The initiative in California was born of decades of simmering outrage that the central institution of representative government, the legislature, was owned by special interests, specifically the Southern Pacific Railroad. "In those days," wrote a newspaper reporter in 1896, "there was only one kind of politics and that was corrupt politics. It didn't matter whether a man was a Republican or Democrat. The Southern Pacific Railroad controlled both parties…"

But by the turn of the century, the Progressives, a dissident group within the Republican Party, had managed to bring legislation by direct vote of the people to Los Angeles. In 1904 the Progressives secured the pledges of a majority of the state legislature to support the ideas of initiative and referendum. But through adroit manipulation, the Southern Pacific Railroad and its allies blocked any implementation of these reforms for seven years. It took the notorious trials of several major labor leaders, government officials, and corporate executives starting in 1906 to change both public opinion and galvanize uncorrupted members of the legislature.

The election of a dynamic Progressive, Hiram Johnson, in 1910 was the catalyst for a host of long bottled up reforms. Johnson introduced a package of twenty-three constitutional amendments that were to be submitted to the voters the next year. Senate Constitutional Amendments 22 and 23 created the initiative, referendum, and recall.

On October 10, 1911 the voters approved twenty-two of the amendments in a special election by a vote of 168,744 to 52,093. It was a rousing triumph for the reformist movement. It expressed public repudiation of special interest power and a willingness to embark on the new experiment in "direct democracy." California at that time was just the tenth state to enact these methods of lawmaking.

But, although the very modernist Progressives would have blanched at the proposition, what Hiram Johnson had done was hearken to an older vision of government. It was, moreover, a vision rejected at the time of the Founding in favor of representative democracy. When the French Revolution, carried to excess not just during the Terror in 1794, but even during its relatively benign period starting in 1789, embraced this idea of governance, it demonstrated that the Founders' rejection had been wise indeed.

What the Progressives sought was a practical solution to a thorny and frighteningly intractable problem: the iron control by an un-elected, unrepresentative group of men over the institutions of representative government.

The Progressives did not seek abstract ideas or hypothetical projects in the face of this problem. Yet what they championed, as Grover Johnson feared, potentially carried one of the most dangerous object lessons of antiquity, plebescitary democracy or mob rule. It had, however, been sanitized and made attractive during the mid-18th century by Rousseau. His formulation was the "general will" and it fascinated the French revolutionaries and repulsed the Founders.

It is the "general will," changed and renamed, which exists today as the initiative. When enacted it had over six decades of democratic experience behind it. This was undoubtedly the leavening that made what the Founders feared palatable to the people. So the paradox is that Progressives had sought a concrete solution to a specific problem.

They put in place the most theoretical model of lawmaking ever conceived. And it has worked very well in practice in California.

The General Will

It was Rousseau's central conceit that the people, not as electors, voters, or citizens, contained specific and direct notions about governance. On particular questions, taxes or education, for example, the people's views might be uninformed, contradictory, or even incoherent. Yet, through various means, the people's intent, the "general will" would be known and no institution could impede or alter this intrinsically perfect lawmaking.

Key for Rousseau, and his adherents, was that society and society's formal institutions were corrupt and corrupting. It was vital therefore that the general will be free to express itself and not be deformed by some mediating institution.

This concept of how laws should be made, how a state should be governed, was antithetical to the American Founding. The Founders believed that passions were easily aroused, ignorance was rampant, and the people were always susceptible to fear, coercion, and foolishness.

The Founders' answer lay in representative institutions which would mediate and educate the people.

But what if these institutions themselves were corrupt, not in the inherent way Rousseau imagined, but by the very tangible agencies of bribery, threat, and even attempted assassination as they were at the dawn of the Progressive era? The recourse lay, as it always had, in the people themselves. It was to the people and their goodness and rightness on matters relating to the governance of the state, that the Progressives turned.

The arguments today really amount to a dispute about how best to reveal the "general will." Can the influence of corrupting institutions be curtailed or eliminated from expressions of the general will? Can the general will be put more clearly, more transparently before the people for a vote?

I believe both can be done simply, as I will discuss shortly.

The People in Action

Once enacted, the people of California lost no time in putting the new tool to use. In November 1912, three direct initiatives appeared on the ballot dealing with subjects that would remain popular until today. One set out to consolidate city and county governments in large metropolitan areas, another to outlaw bookmaking, and the third to create a single tax for all levels of government. The initiatives were rejected.

In 1914 the largest number of initiatives ever to appear on a single ballot, seventeen, were presented to the voters. Interestingly, many commentators have noted that while the impetus for the initiative was government corruption, none of the early measures were directed at corruption. Instead, taxes, liquor, gambling, wages, and various bond issues preoccupied voters.

It seemed initially that what Hiram Johnson had urged was taking place. The initiative was not being used to supplant the elected state government but to supplement it. When representative institutions became a perceived impediment to the people's wishes, they could be bypassed. Dr. Eugene Lee of the University of California, Berkeley said the Progressives intended, when pressed "to make every man his own legislature."

From 1912 until June 1998, 1,043 initiatives were prepared for circulation. Most, 1,024, were direct initiatives. Of these 272 qualified for the ballot. They received the requisite number of signatures of registered voters.

Only 87 initiatives have actually been approved, though. They were split between 31 constitutional amendments, 52 statutory revisions. The remaining 4 were mixes of constitutional amendments and statutes.

Obviously, the voters have not approved every utopian or fanciful scheme presented to them. Sixteen initiative measures failed to stiffen Prohibition. During the Depression, Californians rejected the "Thirty Dollars Every Thursday" pension initiative twice. Sunday business closings, a ban on smallpox vaccinations, requiring Bibles in public classrooms, outlawing ocean net fishing, all failed. But in a recent election, an initiative to stop the export of horsemeat from California passed, as did legalizing the medicinal use of marijuana, and a candidate ballot designation scheme that even its proponents rightly thought unconstitutional.

Before the 1980s, California voters approved of only about a third of the initiatives on the ballot. But as the 1990s began, the number of measures submitted and qualifying rose. Likewise, the voters approved nearly half of the initiatives on the ballot in 1990.

The mere numbers, though, don't reflect how profoundly the initiatives have shaped California's government and politics. From education to taxes, gambling and term limits, criminal law and procedure are all now driven by enactments through the initiative process.

It is a development that most Californians applaud. In 1998 a Field Poll revealed that by 74% to 7% the public believes the initiative process, even with flaws, is a valuable tool. In part this is due to a widespread distrust of government and a cynicism about the motives of elected officials.

How Initiatives Function

There are competing theories, therefore, about why initiatives are being used more and more often to direct not merely quixotic policy demands, like banning horsemeat export, but the most divisive questions. One theory, originating in demographics, is that while legislative districts are drawn based on population, a large segment of that population is not voting or being represented as fully other groups. California today is half minority, young, and transient. People move freely and often. Districts in some parts of the state also contain substantial numbers of non-citizens who are ineligible to vote at all.

In elections during this decade particularly, the older, stable, non-minority population has voted proportionally in greater numbers that the overall population. One striking example of this tendency was reported in 1998 in the *San Francisco Chronicle*. In the November 1996 General Election, four Democrats were elected in four Assembly districts in Los Angeles County. The total number of votes cast was 169,410. In sharp contrast, one Republican was elected in a single Assembly district in northern California. The total number of votes cast for him was 181,799. The legislature, according to this interpretation, represents the overall population of the state, voting and nonvoting, while the initiative is used by the more heavily voting older, non-minority citizens.

In support of this theory proponents can cite initiatives to restrict services to illegal immigrants, make English the required language in public schools, and end preferential race and gender based state laws. But the evidence of voter-approved initiatives easily supports a counter view. Californians have also enacted measures to create an open state primary, limit spending on and contributions to legislative races, establish lower auto insurance rates, increase the minimum wage, and a welter of taxes on tobacco products that fund anti-smoking programs.

It is as likely that the increasing number of initiatives submitted for qualification and the increasing numbers of initiatives being approved by voters indicates a profound dissatisfaction with the legislature. For over thirty years, California has had a full-time legislature. But one of the most frequent criticisms of this full-time institution is that it fails to adequately answer many of the problems facing the state. The 1990 term limits initiative, Proposition 140, which restricted members of the Senate to two four-year terms and the Assembly to three two-year terms, was a direct response to this voter dissatisfaction.

So, categorizing the initiative as the captive of any group or bloc of voters is difficult to do without mangling the facts.

It is equally clear that Grover Johnson's fear was unfounded. In the eighty or so years since the initiative reform went into effect, the people of California have shown themselves to be remarkably clear-eyed and prudent about the measures they adopt. There has been no mob rule.

A Flawed Reform?

Still, critical arguments, some with much merit, have been raised about the initiative and where it may be going. While every commentator has a favorite list of faults, they generally fall into half a dozen broad categories.

First, the initiative undermines the basic practice of representative government. The legislature may willingly put off difficult or controversial measures if the voters can take them up by initiative. Proposition 13, for example, the landmark reform of property tax over twenty years ago, was virtually untouchable by the legislature. Term limits for legislators likewise was an issue the legislature could not, either as individuals or institutionally, consider coolly.

If the evidence is looked at with any objectivity, there is no proof that the use of the initiative has adversely affected representative government. The legislature acts on what it perceives to be popular and institutionally unthreatening. The people act in what they perceive to be their interests. Rather than threaten representative government, the initiative in practice has formed a functional symbiosis with it.

Second, the initiative may become the instrument of choice for special interests and thrust unsound policies before the voters and into law. There is reason to agree with some of this criticism. But a limited relativism is at work in all-popular government. The people may very well enact unwise proposals, just as their representatives do on occasion. Unwise policy choices are the people's prerogative. It is not the business of others to prevent the people from being unwise on occasion if they so choose, to paraphrase Oliver Wendell Holmes. Or what appears to one to be foolish may seem the epitome of good judgment to another.

Third, the increasing use of initiatives is expanding the sheer length of the ballot. Voters experience intellectual and psychological fatigue when they have to wade through a long ballot clogged with even longer initiatives, some amounting thousands of complicated sentences. A ballot pamphlet can reach over one hundred pages in length. As John Allswang, who teaches at California State University at Los Angeles quipped, "The average American doesn't read that much serious nonfiction in a year."

It is true that more initiatives are cropping up on the ballot, but as the process's early history shows, even a very long list of initiatives has been digested and intelligently voted on. At present, the fear that the initiative may overwhelm the ballot is unfounded.

Fourth, direct democracy ignores the legislature. This is so. It was generally intended to be so. It means in practice that the debate, compromise, reconsideration and argument that attend every piece of legislation are absent when an initiative is voted on. In theory this is a valid and disturbing situation. In fact, though, the voters of California have somehow managed very well to sort through dross and foolishness over the years. Enacting just 87 initiatives is about one a year since the reform went into effect. The voters are hardly flooding the constitution and statutes with daffy initiative based schemes.

Fifth, the initiative, as a tool of special interests now, has priced itself out of the reach of most grassroots efforts. There is much truth to this observation. The answer, though, does not lie in curbing the people's access to the initiative but in making it more fully reflect their will.

And finally, with such a welter of measures and arguments in the ballot pamphlet and on the ballot itself, the average voter is incapable of dealing with the various proposals. The typical voter lacks enough information, analytical training, and time to cast a responsible ballot. The director of a public affairs group, the Democracy Center lamented, "Everyone, left and right, is pandering to public emotion and simplicity, because that's how the game is played."

This last criticism of the initiative, which lies behind many others, is at best condescending and at worst a call for rule by experts. It would be more persuasive if the initiative's history and current practice, aside from a few egregious instances, showed repeated patterns of voter confusion. The record is strikingly clear, though. The voters have acted with much sophistication when presented with initiative proposals. Whether or not groups or business disagrees with the voters' preferences is beside the point.

Thus, when reviewed closely, much of the criticism directed at the initiative does not have a great deal of force.

But it is undeniable, though, that the initiative, the citizen's cudgel to force change that the legislature ignores, is now financially beyond the reach of most citizen groups. It has indeed become the chosen instrument of organized, professional, commercial entities to put their favored laws before the voters.

The High Cost of Populism

Two developments may signal a real change in how initiatives function. These developments also form the basis for most of the proper suggested reform regulation.

One major change, still being processed by both politicians and citizens alike, was the recent Supreme Court decision in *Buckley v. American Constitutional Law Foundation, Inc.* (cite omitted). All I need to say here, since it is discussed elsewhere more extensively, is that the *Buckley* ruling has created confusion about initiative circulation and certainly increased the commercialization of the process. These are both detrimental to the people's experiment with direct democracy. Action by the legislature may sort out the first set of problems but the rush of business enterprises into initiative circulation and creation has just begun in earnest.

The second development is a symptom of the first. Money, enormous amounts raised and spent, is now the engine of the initiative generally. In 1996, $141,274,345 was spent in California to put twenty-seven initiatives on the June primary or November general election ballots. The trend has only accelerated. By the November 1998 ballot, nearly $200 million was spent by three groups: gambling interests, the utility industry, and tobacco companies. One initiative alone, Proposition 5, which dealt with the scope and regulation of Indian gaming, accounted for nearly half of that incredible sum of money.

It is apparent that this sea change in who uses and how initiatives are used is the reason for the trenchant analysis that many initiatives are now the creatures of special interests. It is a cruel irony, if accurate. The noble hopes of Johnson and the other Progressives have been utterly spun around. And the people are the losers, now just as they were at the beginning of this century. But, the bright side to this development, as the many failed initiatives abundantly demonstrate, is that merely spending more money does not mean the people will vote for a measure.

One newspaper recently did a step-by-step progression of an initiative from idea to the end of the campaign. The total cost for this effort ranged from $2.7 million to $29.7 million. This is not the grassroots effort of "Mr. Smith Goes to Washington." It is a business, focused and continuous. A pessimistic sponsor of environmental initiatives said recently, "The day when ordinary citizens can mount an initiative is over."

And in that climate, it is easy to see how voters may be confused and mislead more and more. Proposition 36, for example, established the California Lottery. The initiative was written and financed by Scientific Games and when the measure passed, Scientific Games became the sole supplier of lottery tickets, a lucrative victory. Would the voters have endorsed the lottery fully knowing that the sponsor of the initiative would be its major beneficiary? In fact, voters liked Proposition 36 because it did create a lottery with the promise of rich payouts and pledged a large portion of the money to California's public schools. Yet, would widespread appreciation of the sponsor's financial stake have altered the outcome? It certainly could have done so.

An extreme example of what may become more common in the future happened in 1998. Proposition 225 was adopted in the June primary. It 'instructed' California's state and federal legislators to propose and vote for a specific amendment to the United States Constitution that would adopt congressional term limits. If an incumbent legislator failed to support such an amendment, then a derogatory ballot label would be printed next to their name, "Disregarded Voter Instruction on Term Limits."

Proposition 225 was quickly christened 'The Scarlet Letter Initiative.' The proponents suddenly realized, after the initiative was qualified for the ballot, that it was unconstitutional. It attempted to prescribe additional requirements to be elected to Congress that would violate Article V of the United States Constitution. Article V grants exclusive power to propose and ratify constitutional amendments to state legislatures and Congress acting as deliberative bodies. It does not allow such amendments to be ratified by popular vote. Nor does it allow initiatives that compel or coerce legislators to vote in a certain way on constitutional amendments.

But it was too late for the Proposition 225 proponents. They circulated another initiative and even went so far in their ballot argument purportedly in favor of Proposition 225 to say that "passage of this measure will likely result in needless and costly litigation." It passed even so with 53% of the vote. It was promptly challenged in court and promptly struck down.

Could this confection of confusing initiatives have been avoided? Yes. Can a repetition be avoided in the future? Yes. Both solutions require cautious reform of the current initiative process.

Reforming the Reform

I start with two basic premises when it comes to changing the initiative process. These premises are fixed. First, any proposed new regulation of initiatives must be simple. Second, any new regulations must be few.

The ultimate aim of any reform of this cherished lawmaking tool is to make the people's will more apparent. And frankly, from a practical standpoint, unless the people are thoroughly convinced that the initiative process is hopelessly tainted by special interests, very few regulations will be acceptable. Every poll and every election re-affirms the people's basic approval of the initiative process.

One "reform" that should *not* be adopted is "mediation" of disputed initiatives rather than permitting judicial scrutiny. Proposition 187 was enacted in 1994 with nearly 59% of the vote. It would have restricted or curtailed various services to illegal immigrants in California. Challenged in lower federal court, it was on appeal to the 9th Circuit Court of Appeals when a new governor decided that rather than let a full legal interpretation be made, the disputed initiative would be handed over to mediation and the result would be binding on the same people of California who naively assumed they were exercising their lawmaking power. As the former chief deputy attorney general correctly said, "Mediation will dilute the people's right to the initiative process."

With these basics in mind, let me offer the following improvements. They will, taken together, reveal the people's will on any given question. Several grow out of the report by the California Constitution Revision Commission after its exhaustive and productive examination of our state government.

First, the constitution is the foundational document of our state government. To add, subtract, or alter it should be done with the fullest potential voter participation. It is in this sense that initiatives aimed at the constitution are intrinsically different from statutory initiatives. Therefore, constitutional initiatives should only appear, except in very special circumstances, on the November or general election ballot.

The reason for this recommendation is that the record is clear for special and primary elections in the past quarter of a century. Voter participation has declined in these elections to the point that often not even a plurality of the electorate casts ballots in them. As the Commission pointed out, since 1984 the turnout for primary elections has not exceeded 48% of the electorate. By contrast, the general election in November is consistently above 50% of registered voters.

If we are going to make changes to our fundamental governing document, reason and prudence dictate that we also try to draw in the historically greatest number of voters. It may also be worth examining the question of raising the qualifying percentage of raw signatures to place constitutional initiatives on the ballot from the current 8% of the total votes cast for Governor in the last election to perhaps 10% or even 12%. In 1998 a constitutional initiative qualified for the ballot by obtaining 693,230 valid signatures. This may be too few Californians when the object is our constitution.

Second, after an initiative has qualified for the ballot, the initiative proponents should have the ability to correct, modify, or alter the initiative after the legislature holds the currently mandated informational hearings. This ability would be purely voluntary. The initiative proponents could submit their proposal to legislative scrutiny without being obligated take any advice that was offered. It would be a way for proponents to correct errors, solidify shaky arguments against later judicial challenge, and clarify their own intent. Such an opportunity for legislative advice would both bring legislators back into the issue at hand and preserve the freedom and autonomy of the initiative proponents.

Third, California's Government Code Section 12172 already provides for the Secretary of State to do an analysis of initiatives if the proponents wish. This is a reasonable net to catch poor draftsmanship and to comment on obvious mistakes like Proposition 225 before everyone needlessly goes to the time and expense of putting matters right.

Finally, one of the major areas of the initiative process that requires urgent attention is that of the paid initiative petition circulator or "bounty hunter." I have sponsored a number of legislative solutions in this area. One key measure would prohibit bounty hunters from being paid on a per signature basis. This aspect alone of their activity accounts for an inordinate amount of fraud and criminal activity. I strongly believe, because of the initiative's power and purpose that the role of bounty hunters in the collection of initiative signatures needs to be closely monitored.

Basically, I believe from examination and actual experience, my own and the people of California, that the initiative process is far less in need of regulation than some believe. Any regulation of it should be undertaken with reluctance and only with the clear aims of letting the people have their say directly, simply, and effectively.

While the heated arguments about the initiative process will go on, the assertions of its frailty or sickness are greatly exaggerated.

Chapter 15

State Efforts to Regulate the Initiative Process

By Jennie Drage*

The job of regulating the initiative process is not an easy one. State legislatures are placed in the position of having to craft regulations for a popular and increasingly vibrant political process. Many observers and most legislators believe that representative and direct democracy can effectively coexist, and even complement each other. However, use of the initiative has changed dramatically in recent years, and the existing regulations are not always able to effectively address the initiative as it is practiced today.

The most obvious change is that the use of the initiative increased dramatically during the 1990s, and all indications are that this trend will continue into 2000. There are more initiatives in circulation and on the ballot than ever before. In Colorado, for example, there were 19 initiatives on the ballot in the 1970s, 15 in the 1980s, and 35 in the 1990s. Second, there is also more money involved the initiative process than ever before. A third characteristic of the late 20th and early 21st century initiative is the evolution of the initiative as a for-profit business, particularly in the area of signature gathering. All of these are changes that the legislature must grapple with, and as these changes grow increasingly evident, so, too, does the volume of legislation addressing the initiative.

Legislation addressing the initiative process is generally drafted with an eye to preventing corruption or the appearance of corruption in the process. For example, the Legislative Declaration preceding the general provisions for initiative and referendum in Colorado reads, "It is not the intention of this article to limit or abridge in any manner the powers reserved to the people in the initiative and referendum, but rather to properly safeguard, pro-

* Jennie Drage is a policy specialist with the National Conference of State Legislatures. NCSL is a bipartisan, non-profit organization. NCSL's mission is to improve the quality and effectiveness of state legislatures, foster interstate communications and cooperation, and ensure legislatures a strong, cohesive voice in the federal system. NCSL does not take a position on initiative and referendum.

tect, and preserve inviolate for them these modern instrumentalities of democratic government" (Colo. Rev. Stat. § 1-40-101).

Colorado has, in fact, been at the forefront of efforts to regulate the initiative process. The General Assembly has experimented with a number of reforms over the last decade and a half, although not always successfully. The first major reform was attempted in the mid-1980s. In response to a perception that the possibility for corruption existed when workers were paid to gather signatures on initiative petitions, the General Assembly prohibited payment for the circulation of initiative petitions. The U.S. Supreme Court struck down that measure in 1988, saying that petition circulation was "core political speech" and thus protected by the First Amendment (*Meyer vs. Grant*, 486 U.S. 414). In 1999, in the *Buckley vs. American Constitutional Law Foundation* case, the U.S. Supreme Court struck down several initiative regulations enacted in Colorado in 1993, including the requirement that petition circulators be Colorado registered voters, that they wear an identification badge bearing their name, and that initiative proponents report the names and addresses of circulators and the amount paid to each.

Colorado's experience illustrates the difficulty state legislatures encounter in trying to regulate the initiative process. They walk a fine line in attempting to protect the integrity of direct democracy without infringing on First Amendment rights.

The 1999 legislative sessions saw more than 150 bills in 31 states that addressed the initiative process. That number is greater than the number of states (24) that have the initiative, because 13 states (Alabama, Connecticut, Delaware, Georgia, Hawaii, Iowa, Louisiana, Minnesota, New Jersey, New York, Pennsylvania, Rhode Island and Texas) considered legislation that proposed granting to the people the power of the initiative. Most of these bills failed, but Minnesota's House File 484 met with some success. It was passed by the House of Representatives, and should be taken up by the Senate in the 2000 session.

Of the 24 initiative states, only six (Florida, Massachusetts, Michigan, North Dakota, Ohio and Oklahoma) did not consider any bills addressing the initiative process. The 127 bills in the remaining 18 initiative states addressed everything from increasing or decreasing the number of signatures required on a petition, to requiring a two-thirds vote to pass wildlife initiatives. Only 19 of the 127 bills were passed. The bills that were passed addressed the content of voter information pamphlets (Arizona, Montana, Utah), voter registration and residency requirements for petition circulators (Arizona, Idaho, Missouri, Oregon, Utah), petition sufficiency (Arkansas, Montana), campaign finance (Arkansas, Montana, Utah), fair campaign practices (Nevada), ballot titles (Oregon), petition filing deadlines (Oregon), signature verification (Oregon, South Dakota) and signature requirements (Oregon).

With 49 bills, Oregon accounted for more than a third of the initiative-related legislation introduced in 1999. Only five of those bills were passed by the legislature. One was Senate Bill 806 (Chapter 262), which deletes the requirements that election petition circulators be registered voters and that the signature sheet contain a notice indicating whether the person circulating the petition is paid. This particular measure came as a response to the U.S. Supreme Court ruling in *Buckley vs. ACLF*, regarding the previously discussed Colorado requirements. In fact, a number of states passed similar measures that were designed to bring their statutes into line with this opinion, including Arizona (House Bill 2656/Chapter 353), Idaho (House Bill 153/Chapter 47), Missouri (House Bill 676) and Utah (House Bill 129/Chapter 45). All of these measures, with the exception of Oregon's, add a new requirement in place of the previous registered voter requirement: that circulators be residents of the state, or that they be qualified to register to vote. The Oregon House passed a bill establishing that requirement (House Bill 3252), but the bill did not pass the Senate.

Another bill passed by Oregon in 1999 was Senate Bill 867 (Chapter 793), which attempts to clarify the initiative language that appears on the ballot and help prevent voter confusion in the voting booth. It increases the limit on the number of words that may be used in the caption of the ballot title from 10 to 15, increases from 15 to 20 the limit on words in the explanation of a "yes" or "no" vote, and prohibits describing the current provisions of a law in such a way that would incorrectly lead voters to believe that approving the proposed measure would repeal those provisions.

A third measure passed in Oregon, Senate Joint Resolution 3, would extend the time period allowed for the secretary of state to verify signatures on petitions. It would change the deadline for filing initiative petitions from four to five months before the election. This measure was passed by the legislature and will appear on the 2000 primary ballot. Another measure passed in the 1999 session that will appear on the 2000 primary ballot is House Joint Resolution 21. It would increase the number of signatures required to propose an initiative for a constitutional amendment from the current 8 percent to 12 percent of the number of votes cast in the most recent gubernatorial election.

House Bill 3053 (Chapter 1021), the final measure passed in Oregon, changes the formula for statistical sampling of the number of signatures on petitions. Previously, the secretary of state deducted 2 percent of the signatures submitted in order to account for duplication. HB 3053 requires the secretary of state to use a duplication factor of at least 8 percent. Proponents of this measure asserted that the 2 percent fixed duplication factor was no longer accurate, given current signature gathering processes.

Among the 44 bills considered but not passed in Oregon were several addressing campaign finance reporting requirements, measures requiring more detailed explanations of the fiscal impacts of a measure, and a number of measures establishing a citizen review process for measures that qualify for the ballot.

Alaska considered two bills related to the initiative, neither of which passed. House Bill 45, which was passed by the House and may come up for consideration by the Senate in 2000, would change the geographic distribution requirement for signatures from two-thirds of election districts to three-fourths of state House districts. The other would have required a two-thirds vote to pass wildlife initiatives.

Arizona considered four initiative-related bills in 1999, two of which passed. The two that passed were House Bill 2113 (Chapter 294) and House Bill 2656 (Chapter 353). HB 2113 requires that the voter information pamphlet must contain a fiscal impact statement not to exceed 300 words concerning any measure or amendment on the ballot. The statement is to be prepared by Joint Legislative Budget Committee staff. HB 2656 removes the requirement that petition circulators be registered voters and stipulates that they must be qualified to register to vote.

Arkansas considered six bills addressing the initiative, and passed three. Those passed were Senate Bill 702 (Act 877), which provides the immediate right to petition the Arkansas Supreme Court to review the secretary of state's determination of sufficiency of an initiative petition; Senate Joint Resolution 9, which gives the Supreme Court the jurisdiction to determine the sufficiency of initiative and referendum petitions; and House Bill 1052 (Act 1006), which requires that the use of state funds by a state agency, board or commission to oppose or support a ballot measure be reported to the Legislative Council if the amount exceeds $100. Senate Bill 10, which passed the Senate but not the House, would have established a procedure for the recall of elected officials.

Lawmakers in California considered eight bills addressing the initiative process. Just one passed, only to be vetoed by the governor. Senate Bill 1219 would have required that all petitions contain a statement as to whether the circulator is paid or volunteer, as well as the name and address of the committee circulating the petition. The other seven bills in California addressed various aspects of the initiative process, and included one that would have required a two-thirds vote to pass initiated constitutional amendments and one that would have required the state to reimburse cities and counties for all costs of duties performed by elections officials related to initiative petitions.

Colorado considered four bills related to initiative process in 1999, none of which passed. One would have granted powers of initiative and referendum to county electors, another would have prohibited state agencies from expending any public funds to collect political funds, a third would have created the Colorado Elections Commission and transferred all elections-related functions from the secretary of state to the commission, and the fourth addressed striking signatures on recall petitions.

Idaho considered three bills and passed one. House Bill 153 (Chapter 47) repeals the requirement that petition circulators be registered voters and requires that they be Idaho residents and at least age 18. The two that did not pass would have required reporting of contributions of more than $200 by committees in support of or in opposition to an initiative or referendum measure.

Maine considered eight initiative-related bills. Seven died in the 1999 session, and one was carried over into the 2000 session. The bill that carried over, Legislative Document 1908, would establish that paid signature gatherers are the employees of the person, firm or organization responsible for signature collection. This measure would guarantee to circulators of petitions the protection of Maine's labor and workers' compensation laws. Employers would be responsible for the payment of unemployment insurance, workers' compensation insurance and withholding taxes.

Mississippi considered six initiative-related bills in 1999, none of which passed. Three would have changed the signature requirements for initiative petitions, one would have required a 60 percent vote on measures resulting in a loss of state revenues of more than $100 million, another would have made invalid certain initiatives resulting in loss of state revenues and another would have removed the constitutional provisions authorizing initiative constitutional amendments.

Of the six initiative-related bills considered in Missouri in 1999, only one passed. House Bill 676 addresses numerous aspects of election law, among them several provisions relating to initiative and referendum:

- makes the act of knowingly signing an initiative or referendum petition with a false name, more than once, or without registering to vote punishable by up to one year in prison and a $10,000 fine;
- requires a petition circulator to designate in the upper right-hand corner on each petition page the county where signatures are collected;
- invalidates any signatures from voters registered outside the designated county;
- dictates that petition circulators must register with the secretary of state and invalidates any signatures collected by circulators who have not registered;
- invalidates signatures that are crossed out on petitions;
- requires election authorities to complete their verification of each petition signature by the last Tuesday in July;
- requires the secretary of state to certify a petition by the 13th Tuesday before the general election;
- and makes filing a false withdrawal statement with the secretary of state, claiming a voter wants to withdraw his or her signature

from a petition, punishable by up to one year in prison and a $10,000 fine.

Montana considered 10 bills addressing the initiative process in 1999, and passed three of them. The three passed were House Bill 468 (Chapter 117), requiring financial disclosures by persons who employ paid signature gatherers; House Bill 502 (Chapter 374), clarifying the content of arguments for and against ballot measures for inclusion in the voter information pamphlet; and House Bill 508 (Chapter 191), giving the attorney general the authority to deny certification of a ballot measure that does not meet the statutory prerequisites for submission. Among the bills not passed were four that would have increased the number of signatures required to place an initiative measure on the ballot, two that would have altered the geographic distribution requirements for signatures, and one that would have established new requirements for fiscal impact statements regarding proposed initiatives.

Nebraska considered seven initiative-related bills, most of which will carry over into the 2000 session. One was passed in 1999—Legislative Resolution 18 CA—that provides that, if conflicting measures proposing constitutional amendment submitted to the people in the same election are both approved, the one receiving the highest number of affirmative votes shall be referred again to the people for ratification.

Nevada passed Assembly Bill 130 (Chapter 497) in the 1999 session, which repeals a provision that prohibited a person from making a false statement of fact concerning a candidate or ballot question. A second bill which did not pass would have changed the deadline for submitting initiative petitions to allow more time for signature verification.

South Dakota passed Senate Bill 33, the only initiative-related bill the Legislature considered in 1999. It creates a procedure for challenging initiative petitions if any person doubts the validity of signatures on the petition.

Utah passed all three of the initiative-related bills considered in 1999. House Bill 110 (Chapter 109) requires the sponsors of an initiative who use paid petition circulators to file a report stating the amount of money paid per signature. House Bill 143 (Chapter 115) allows the Legislature to make technical corrections to initiatives submitted to the Legislature, and to prepare a legislative review note and fiscal note for the proposed measure. House Bill 129 (Chapter 45) removes the requirement that initiative petition circulators be registered voters and stipulates that they must be Utah residents.

Washington considered four initiative-related bills in 1999, but passed none. The bills would have permitted legislators to send a letter to constituents declaring their positions on ballot propositions; established a geographic distribution requirement for signatures; and required a notice on the petition as to whether the signature gatherer is paid or volunteer.

Wyoming considered two bills addressing the initiative process, but did not pass either one. One would have removed the requirement that the secretary of state publish proposed initiated constitutional amendments in a newspaper in each county of the state. The other would have required a two-thirds vote to pass initiatives that propose to allow, limit or prohibit the taking of wildlife.

Two states considered, but did not pass, measures that could add flexibility to the initiative process. An example is California Senate Bill 384. It would have required initiative proponents to submit petitions to the secretary of state once they obtained 15 percent of the required number of signatures. The secretary of state would then schedule a public hearing to be held within 30 days. After the public hearing, the proponent would be allowed to make substantive changes to the text of the initiative and begin collecting signatures again. Oregon's House Bill 3487 proposed a similar process. It would have created a 12-member citizen initiative review committee to hold hearings to review proposed initiative measures that have qualified for the ballot, identify the issues raised by each measure, and issue a report to the public and the news media. The chief petitioner then would be permitted to amend the measure without filing an additional petition or changing the ballot title, as long as the proposed amendment would not substantially change the substance of the proposed initiative.

In summary, state legislatures were hard at work during the 1999 session, attempting to craft regulations that protect the integrity of the initiative process without infringing on rights guaranteed by the First Amendment. It is a difficult balancing act, but one that has proven necessary since the popularity and vitality of the citizen initiative first skyrocketed in the 1990s.

The 2000 legislative sessions undoubtedly will see further efforts to regulate the initiative process.

Section Five

Regulation of Initiative and Referendum in Other Countries

It is always helpful in any discussion to have a benchmark to work from. In discussing the regulation of the initiative and referendum process in the United States and the effects of these regulations on the process, it might be helpful to understand the effect of regulation on I&R in other countries. In this section, Mads Qvortrup takes a look at this issue and how the regulation between the U.S. and other countries differ.

Chapter 16

Regulation of Direct Democracy Outside the USA: Impressions, Tendencies and Patterns from Overseas

By Mads Qvortrup

Referenda—and especially initiatives—are rare in most Western democracies (see Table 1). Referenda have only become centerpieces of the political systems in Switzerland and—since the 1970s—in Italy. The legislative initiative is practically unknown outside America. Only in New Zealand can the citizens initiate legislation—but they have done so only once[1]. The Swiss can merely propose constitutional amendments, but these are often defeated (the voters have endorsed a mere 12 out of a total of 104 proposed constitutional initiatives).[2]

These differences between America and the rest of the world have led observers to the conclusion that there are "two worlds" of the referendum. One where their potential for making or unmaking policies is ever present in the minds of the legislators or lobbyists, and, on the other hand, a "second world" where referendums only are used infrequently usually to set the seal of legitimacy to a controversial policy change or a change of the regime.[3]

The comparative rarity of the referendum in the "second world" has, moreover, led observers to the conclusion that that the referendums in these polities are unimportant and devoid of controversy; in short, that the referendum in these polities is a democratic curiosity with few—if any—practical implications. Nothing could—in a sense—be further from

---

1. Citizen Initiated Referenda Act 1993. The signature-requirement is 10 percent of the eligible voters.

2. It should, however, be noted that the constitutional initiative has been used to pass laws, which in other polities would have been enacted by ordinary statutes. Wolfgang Luthardt, *Direkte Demokratie. Ein Vergleich in Westeuropa* (Baden-Baden: Nomos, 1994), p. 43.

3. David Butler and Austin Ranney, "Summing Up", in *Referendums: A Comparative Study of Practice and Theory* (Washington, DC: AEI, 1998), p. 222.

Table 1. Provisions for Types of Referendums in Constitutions in Western Polities

Country	Referendum Provision	Const. Amendment	Facultative	Min. Abr. Ref	Initiative
Australia	Yes	Sec. 128(23)	—	—	—
Belgium	No#	—	—	—	—
Denmark	Yes	§.88, 29(6)	§.20(1)	§.42(4)	—
Finland	Yes	Art. 22A(1)	—	—	—
France	Yes	Art. 89(0)	Art. 11(8)	—	—
Ireland	Yes	Art. 46(17)	—	Art. 27(0)	—
Italy	Yes	—	Art. 123, 132	Art. 71*, 75(38)	—
Norway	No	—	—	—	—
Sweden	Yes	—	Ch.8. §4, 15(1)	—	—
U.K.	—	—	—	—	—
New Zealand	—	Sec. 189(6)	—	—	CIRA.1993(1)
Austria	Yes	Art. 44(1)	—	Art. 48*	—

Referendum Provision = Provisions for referendums mentioned in the constitution.
Const. Amendment = Optional Referendum for constitutional amendments.
Facultative = Provisions for facultative referendums on non-constitutional measures.
Min.Abr.Ref = Minority-veto, abrogative referendum, or other constitutional provisions for semi-direct democracy.*

The numbers in the parentheses show the number of referendums, which have been held under this provision. 53.3 percent of the *countries of the world* have constitutional provisions for referendums. The countries are, in addition to the ones already mentioned, Afghanistan, Albania, Algeria, Angola, Antigua-Barbuda, Argentina, the Bahamas, Bangladesh, Blears, Botswana, Bulgaria, Cameroon, Cape Verde, the Central African Republic, Chile, the Comers, the Congo, Cuba, Dominica, Egypt, El Salvador, Ecuador, Equatorial Guinea, Ethiopia, Gabon, Gambia, Georgia, Greece, Granada, Guatemala, Guinea-Bissau, Guyana, Hungary, Iceland, Iran, the Ivory Coast, Jamaica, Japan, Kazakhstan, Kiribati, Latvia, Lithuania, South Korea, Liberia, Liechtenstein, Luxembourg, Madagascar, Mali, Malta, Mauritius, Mongolia, Morocco, Myanmar, Nauru, Niger, Pakistan, Panama, the Philippines, Poland, Portugal, Romania, Russia, Rwanda, St Kitts and Nevis, St Lucia, St Vincent, Samoa, Sao Tome and Principe, Senegal, Sierra Leone, Singapore, Somalia, Spain, Sri Lanka, Surinam, Switzerland, Syria, Togo, Tunisia, Turkey, Vanuatu, Venezuela, Vietnam, Ukraine, and Uruguay, See Mads Qvortrup, "Are Referendums Controlled and Pro-Hegemonic?" in *Political Studies*, forthcoming Spring 2000.

the truth. Referenda are, to be sure, rare. This does not, however, imply that they are unimportant. In fact, it sometimes seems that the fewer the referendums the wider their implications; that is, their infrequency is inversely correlated with their consequences. Norway's referendum (in 1972) on membership of the EEC (the precursor of the EU) led to a break-up of the party-system,[4] as did the referendums on the electoral system in Italy in 1993.[5] The French referendum on a reform of the Senate and local government in 1969 led to the resignation of president Charles de Gaulle and James Gallaghan's Labor government was forced to resign following the unsuccessful referendums on devolution for Scotland and Wales in 1979.[6]

No American plebiscites have had implications for the party-system and no governor has resigned following a defeat of an initiative. In short, no American plebiscites have (with the exception of Prop. 13 in 1978) had consequences which even remotely resemble the effects of referendums in Europe.

Most American referendums and initiatives have few — if any — constitutional implications. The reverse is true in Europe where practically all referendums have considerable constitutional and political implications.[7] It is — given these effects — somewhat odd that the referendum is practically unregulated in these polities.

Regulation of I&R

Regulation can take many forms. Some forms of regulation might be inevitable in a democratic system, the act of voting, the location of the polling stations, and the size of the ballots are issues which necessarily must be regulated. These issues are often uncontroversial — and will not be discussed in this chapter. The forms of regulation which will be discussed are the — often controversial — restrictions which often are imposed on the initiative and referendum process (henceforth the I&R process). These restrictions — which often are introduced to ensure a fair outcome — are[8]:

- Restrictions on signature gathering

---

4. Tor Bjørklund, *Om Folkeavstemninger* (Oslo: Universitetsforlaget, 1997), p. 175.

5. Richard Katz, "The 1993 Parliamentary Electoral Reform," in Carol Mershon and Gianfranco Pasquino (eds.), *Ending the First Republic* (Boulder: Westview Press, 1995).

6. Vernon Bogdanor, "Western Europe," in David Butler and Austin Ranney (eds.), *Referendums Around the World* (1994).

7. Mads Qvortrup, "Constitutional Implications of the Use of the Referendum." Unpublished D.Phil thesis, University of Oxford.

8. See Elisabeth Gerber, *The Populist Paradox. Interest Group Influence and the Promise of Direct Democracy* (Princeton: Princeton University Press, 1999), pp. 37-58.

- Limits on campaign contributions
- Limits on campaign spending
- Pre-election judicial review
- Post-election judicial review
- Single-issue restrictions
- Super-majorities
- Disclosure laws
- Higher signature requirements

Most of the 23 American I&R states have imposed several of these restrictions on the citizens.[9] The reverse is true in Europe and Australia where only one or two of the restrictions are in force. Pre-legislative review has been a dominant feature in Italy,[10] but nowhere else.[11] Supermajorities are known from Denmark, Britain (in the latter case only in the 1979 devolution referendums) and Italy,[12] and most recently from Canada (the Clarity Act stipulates that the voters in any future secession referendum must provide a clear expression of the will of a clear majority[13]). A similar requirement is being debated in Israel at the time of writing. The super-majority provisions have led to the defeat of several laws in Italy and to the defeat of the devolution proposal for Scotland in 1979.[14]

None of the polities have imposed restrictions on Campaign spending (with the notable exception of the Canadian province of Quebec[15] and Britain[16]). In both Ireland and Canada the courts dismissed challenges to

---

9. Caroline J. Tolbert, Daniel H. Lowenstein and Todd Donovan, "Election Law and Rules for Using Initiatives," in Shaun Bowler, Todd Donovan and Caroline J. Tolbert (eds.), *Citizens as Legislators. Direct Democracy in the United States* (Columbus: Ohio State University Press, 1998), 27ff.

10. Pier Vincenzo Uleri, "Italy: Referendums and initiatives from origins to the crisis of a democratic regime," in Michael Gallagher and Pier Vincenzo Uleri (eds.), *The Referendum Experience in Europe* (London: Macmillan, 1996).

11. For a study of pre-legislative review of American initiatives see James D. Gordon and David B. Magleby, "Pre-legislative Review of Initiatives and Referendums," *Notre Dame Law Review*, vol. 64, 1989, pp. 313-34.

12. Mads Qvortrup, *Ensuring Legitimacy. Guidelines for Referendums in Israel* (Ministry of Justice, Jerusalem, Israel, March 2000), p. 18.

13. Clarity Act 2000, Art. 2.2.

14. Vernon Bogdanor, "The 40 Per Cent Rule," in *Parliamentary Affairs*, 1980, pp. 249-63.

15. *The Constitution Unit: Report of Commission on the Conduct of Referendums* (London: Constitution Unit, 1997), p. 61.

16. Parliament is currently debating "The Political Parties, Elections and Referendums Bill—Bill 34 1999-2000." Which will restrict campaign spending to £500.000 for political parties. See Oonagh Gay, "The Political Parties, Elections and Referendums Bill," Research Paper 00/3, House of Commons, London, 2000.

limit expenditures in ballot-campaigns, arguing — in both cases — that such restrictions are incompatible with the constitutional provisions for freedom of speech.[17] In Australia the High Court (Supreme Court) has, on similar grounds, invalidated provisions to restrict broadcasting of political commercials on radio and television during the campaign.[18]

Not all countries are as unregulated as Ireland, New Zealand, Australia and the Scandinavian countries, however. The British Broadcasting Act of 1990 — which was introduced by the Conservative Thatcher government — bans all political advertising on ITV (the commercial channel) and local radio stations.[19] Yet most polities have conspicuously few regulations of the process of (semi) direct democracy.

The "classical" exception to the rule is the *Quebec Referendum Act of 1978*. The official objective of the act was to guarantee the democratic nature of referendums by promoting equality between the two sides. Moreover the act was intended as a mechanism for providing information to the two sides. As the Canadian Supreme Court later noted:

> In its egalitarian aspect the Act [was] intended to prevent the referendum debate being dominated by the most affluent members of society. At the same time, the act [promoted] an informed vote by ensuring that some points of view are not buried by others. This highly laudable objective, intended to ensure fairness of the referendum on a question of public interest, [was] of pressing and substantial importance in a democratic society.[20]

In order to prevent distortion of campaigns by wealthy individuals the act requires that, so called, referendum committees use a special fund to cover the expenses they incur during the campaign. Each committee may spend up to $1.00 per eligible voter. The state contributes to the committees' funds an amount set by the National Assembly. The committees may then raise other funds up to the $1.00 limit. Individual citizens may donate a maximum of $3,000 to each committee, while firms and legal persons are not allowed to contribute funds. This act was, however, ruled unconstitutional by the Canadian Supreme Court in 1997.[21] The Court argued that the Quebec Referendum Act was inconsistent with the Canadian Charter

---

17. Geoffrey Marshall, "The Referendum: What, When, How?" in *Parliamentary Affairs*, 1997, p. 211.

18. Australia Capital Television Pty Ltd. v. Commonwealth of Australia, No. 2, 1992, 108 A.L.R. 577.

19. Broadcasting Act 1990, S.8 (2) (a).

20. Libman v. Quebec (Attorney General) [1997] 3.S.C.R-569, 1.

21. Libman v. Quebec (Attorney General) [1997] 3.S.C.R-569.

of Rights and Freedoms, which protects the freedom of expression and association.

However, the Court acknowledged the need for spending limits. The act was objectionable because it gave the political parties a virtual monopoly on information. The Act would be consistent with the Charter if funds were allocated to civic groups. The *Assemble National* enacted a new law incorporating the Courts recommendations in 1999.[22] The new act remains — the rulings notwithstanding — the only example of restrictions on the referendum process. It remains a truism that plebiscites tend to be unregulated.

The comparative lack of regulation does not, however, imply that the politicians are unaware or categorically opposed to regulations. The Israeli opposition party, Likud, sought to introduce campaign spending limits, qualified majorities and regulations of broadcasting in the debate about the introduction of the referendum in Israel in 1999[23]. Israel is not an exception. The following quote from a front-page article from the English newspaper *The Guardian* indicates that regulation of referendums also is a heated topic in a country, which only has held one nation-wide referendum:

> Labour yesterday proposed tight spending limits on future referendum campaigns which would effectively thwart attempts by maverick Euro-Skeptics like billionaire Yorkshire businessman Paul Sykes to bankroll a campaign against the EU's single currency. The move came on a day when a group of business leaders, headed by Lord Marsh, a Labour cabinet minister in the 1960s, launched a £1 million-plus Business for Sterling campaign designed to offset what they claim is a multi-million pound pro-Euro campaign funded from the EU information budget. Labour's proposals would not stop Lord Marsh, his allies at the wealthy Institute of Directors or the 100,000 strong Federation of Small Businesses from campaigning. But it would limit their individual donations to £500,000 — 10% of the proposed national maximum allowed to parties...Mr. Sykes said last night: "the suggestion that individuals would be limited in what they could spend to promote a cause they believed in would be anti-democratic. It's meant to stifle debate.[24]

This "threat" possibly explains why the government — via the introduction of the Political Parties, Elections and Referendums Bill — decid-

---

22. Loi sur les elections et les référendums dans les municipalities, L.R.Q, C.E-2.2.

23. Evelyn Gordon, "When a Majority is Special," *The Jerusalem Post*, 19 December 1999.

24. "Labour calls for spending curb on referendum campaigns," *The Guardian*, 12 June 1988, A1.

ed to ignore the Neill-committee's recommendation that limits on campaign spending should be avoided. The danger of being outspent by opponents of the single currency was tangible — and unwelcome for the government.

The opposite is true in America. The state governments in America have been prone to regulate the initiative lest the people should employ this device to introduce legislation opposed by the legislators.

The fundamental question is why politicians have failed to introduce restrictions. Are there political reasons for this unwillingness to introduce restrictions? Or is the unwillingness to introduce restrictions a result of different political cultures — as argued by some students of public administrations. Public administration scholars have contended that there are striking contrasts between approaches to public policy in the United States and in Western Europe. West European civil servants usually enjoy an extreme close and co-operative relationship with non-governmental representatives (e.g. business, trade unions, etc.). In America, however, the regulatory process is — for historical reasons — highly legalistic and contentious. These differences have led to the result that issues, which in Europe would be resolved through corporatist bargaining, are sought resolved through legislation in the United States.[25]

The failure to introduce restrictions on the referendum process seems to reflect the fact that it is the governments in Europe and Australia who typically sponsor the legislation, which is submitted to the voters. Neither the government, nor business and trade union leaders have an incentive to introduce restrictions that make the enactment of *their* law more difficult. The voters' can — at most — veto proposals drafted and enacted by the legislators.

Proposals for restrictions of campaign spending have only occurred in the aftermath of a defeat of a government sponsored measure or when the governments feared that interest groups had raised enough money to wage a successful campaign against a government initiated proposal.[26] There is a lot to be said for this public policy interpretation, yet it is clearly less applicable in an analysis of the regulation of I&R than in an analysis of, say, environmental policies or occupational safety.

However, the regulation of I&R is clearly different from regulation of public policy issues; occupational safety regulation directly involves the citizens. I&R regulation merely affects the voter on polling day. Yet it

---

25. For a general introduction to this "school" see inter alia, David Vogel, *National Styles of Regulation* (Ithaca: Cornell University Press, 1986).

26. Ben Seyd, *Electoral Reform in New Zealand. Lessons for the UK* (London, The Constitution Unit, 1998).

might be argued that the same logic applies to the two cases: groups with vested interests fend for themselves. Those who—for institutional reasons—are in a privileged position make every possible effort to maintain in that position. The cultural differences impose one set of restrictions on the legislators' actions. Other restrictions are imposed by constitutional restrictions. Or, as rational choice scholars have argued; the actors' behavior is shaped by the rules of the game.[27] It might be argued that the extent to which the process is regulated depends on whether the citizens can propose legislation or whether they can merely veto legislation proposed by the elected legislators.

The main difference between 'the two worlds of referendums' is that plebiscites in the 'second world' primarily perform the role of being a check on the government (or the majority in parliament in multi-party systems)[28]. Most referendums in the ' second world' of the referendum are constitutionally obligatory referendums on fundamental constitutional changes, changes that—for constitutional reasons—only are implemented if the people endorse them[29]. These provisions are typically inserted in the constitutions as checks against the governments and parliamentary majorities.[30]

The elected lawmakers in the United States have an incentive to restrict citizen involvement, i.e. an incentive to create obstacles to prevent citizens from enacting legislation, which is against the interests of the legislators. European and Australian legislators, by contrast, have an incentive to reduce obstacles in order to increase the probability of the successful passage of their own proposals (proposals which follow a process of elite bargaining).[31] These well-endowed and influential groups have no interest in introducing limits on campaign spending, nor would they benefit from public disclosure laws. Indeed, such regulations might add to the citizens' distrust in the political class, and hence increase the risk of a no-vote in a referendum on a law initiated by the political class. For, as Austin Ranney once noted:

27. See Dennis C. Mueller, *Constitutional Democracy* (Oxford: Oxford University Press, 1996).

28. Mads Qvortrup, "A.V. Dicey, The Referendum as the People's Veto," in *History of Political Thought*, Vol. XX, Issue 3, 1999, pp. 531-546.

29. David Butler and Austin Ranney, "Summing Up," in David Butler and Austin Ranney (eds.), *Referendums. A Comparative Study in Practice and Theory* (Washington, DC: AEI, 1978), p. 222.

30. Mads Qvortrup, "A.V. Dicey, The Referendum as the People's Veto," in *History of Political Thought*, Vol. XX, Issue 3, 1999, p. 531.

31. Jan-Erik Lane and Svante Erson, *Politics and Society in Western Europe* (London: Sage, 1996).

it is much harder to buy an election if everyone knows that the effort is being made; grossly excessive contributions and expenditures may well provoke a backlash among the voters and cause them to vote the other way. Hence... full publicity is one of the best guarantees available against the excessive influence of money on election outcomes."[32]

This logic is not restricted to the second world of referendums. David Olson's study of the 1991 Washington term-limit initiative (I-533) campaign illustrates how lavish one-sided pending brings attention to an initiative and to the group backing the proposal.

Early on in the campaign the "yes-side" was well ahead in the polls. Contributions came from a hitherto unknown organization *Citizens for Congressional Reform* (CCR). By mid-October the media reported that the CCR was located outside Washington and that businessmen connected to the GOP bankrolled it. The widespread support evaporated following the revelation and the measure was defeated by an 8% margin.[33] Knowing which side of an issue parties, groups and elites are promoting might allow for more voters to decide where they stand on an issue, we might think of it as "the who's for it (who's against it) cue."[34]

Disclosure laws might reveal who's behind an issue. This is the reason that governments — who typically are backed by organized interests — are reluctant to introduce disclosure laws. Disclosure laws expose the governments to unwelcome scrutiny of the true beneficiaries of the proposed changes. A government proposing a legislative change is — for obvious reasons — rarely interested in this attention. It is, therefore, not surprising that disclosure laws are unknown outside the USA (again with the notable exception of Canada).

This conclusion goes some way in explaining why the people's representatives in American states (who typically seek to prevent the passage of initiatives) are in favor of regulation (that would expose the financial backers of initiatives) and why legislators in Europe and Australia (who seek to ensure passage of their own proposals) are opposed to disclosure laws. Public knowledge of the vast amounts spent by proponents in, say, the

---

32. Austin Ranney, "Regulating the Referendum," in Austin Ranney (ed.), *The Referendum Device* (Washington, DC: The American Enterprise Institute, 1981), p. 92.

33. David Olsen, "Term-Limits Fail in Washington: the 1991 Battleground," in G. Benjamin and M. Malbin (eds.), *Limiting Legislative Terms* (Washington, DC: Congressional Quarterly Press, 1992).

34. Shaun Bowler and Todd Donovan, *Demanding Choices: Opinions, Voting, and Direct Democracy* (Ann Arbor: Michigan University Press, 1998), p. 38.

controversial referendums on European integration (the yes side typically outspends the no side by a factor of ten to one[35]) is likely to raise suspicion, which increase the probability of a rejection of the proposal.

Towards a Pattern of Campaign Regulation

That the governments outside the USA are less enthusiastic about regulation — if not positively hostile to it — is not a consequence of idealism or theoretical convictions, it is rather a result of the fact they have other incentives than American state legislators.

The government in New Zealand did not consider restrictions on the process in the first referendum on the electoral system in 1992 (a referendum in which the government campaigned for the continuation of the first-past-the-post electoral system), but the government was suddenly in favor of restrictions in the second referendum when the people, in 1993, had to choose between electoral systems which all were opposed by the government.[36]

Yet, as skeptics are sure to point out, this explanation does not cover all cases. Indeed, it does not explain the two notable anomalies; the *Quebec Act*, which, in fact, was passed by the PQ-government (a party that fought desperately for the passage of the 1980 proposal for, so-called, Sovereignty Association)[37] and the *Political Parties, Elections and Referendums Bill*, proposed by a political party with an overwhelming majority in the House of Commons. Why is Tony Blair pressing for the introduction of restrictions on campaign spending in the UK? Possibly because the *PQ* and *New Labour*, credibly enough, believe that the "no" side in the referendums would be bankrolled by, respectively, Anglo-Canadian interest groups from Ontario and the other English-speaking provinces[38] and wealthy Euro-skeptics.

The debate over the introduction of regulations of referendums in Israel is another example, which point in the same direction. The Likud Party —

---

35. See generally David Butler and Uwe Kitzinger, *The 1975 Referendum*. 2nd edition (London: Macmillan, 1995).

36. John Henderson, "New Zealand Referendums, 1992 and 1993," in Alan Simpson (ed.), *Referendums: Constitutional and Political Perspectives*, Occasional Publication No. 5 (Department of Politics, Victoria University of Wellington), p. 143 ff.

37. Michael Burgess, "Constitutional Reform in Canada and the 1992 Referendum," in *Parliamentary Affairs. A Journal of Comparative Politics*, vol. 46, n. 3 (July 1993).

38. Maureen Davis, "Self-Determination and Referendums," in Allan McCartney (ed.), *Asking the People. The Referendum and Constitutional Change* (Edinburgh: USGS, 1992), pp. 4-7.

which initiated the referendum in Israeli politics, did not consider restrictions before it lost office in 1999. After the election the party fundamentally changed its attitude. The party's constitutional spokesperson, Meir Sheetrit, now warned that regulation was necessary because the "government in power would most likely win a vote because it would be able to set the question and control much of the campaign in the run-up to a national poll."[39] These arguments did not convince the Government — perhaps because they tacitly agreed with Mr. Sheetrit.

The outlined pattern does not amount to a universal law of political science. It is, rather a tendency. However the tendency is not — so it seems — a result of the frequency of the number of referendums.

The number of polls held in Switzerland and Italy approach the number of polls held in the Pacific states, yet the direct democracy processes in these countries are comparatively unregulated; no restrictions on campaign spending and campaign expenditures have been introduced in either of the two countries, disclosure laws are unknown and regulation of media access is non-existent[40]. This is possibly because these countries are dominated by referendums and not by initiatives (less than 1/4 of the polls in Switzerland are constitutional initiatives),[41] whereas initiatives are more common than referendums in the United States.[42]

The difference in the level of regulation is thus a function of the institutional provisions for one of the two main forms of direct democracy. The process is regulated in polities where initiatives are common, whereas the reverse is true in polities where the citizen's involvement is restricted to participation in referendums.

The restrictions depend upon the governments' interests: The initiative creates an incentive for regulation. The referendum creates an incentive against regulation of the I&R process.

It is, of course, true that different political and administrative cultures exist in America and the other countries. We should never underestimate these differences, yet it seems that the politicians' incentives are a more obvious reason for the differences in the schemes of regulation.

---

39. David Zev Harris, "Barak: Golan Referendum must be held," *Jerusalem Post*, January 7, 2000.

40. Silvano Möckli, *Direkte Demokratie* (Bern: Haupt, 1994), p. 287.

41. Alexander Treschel and Hanspeter Kriesi, "Switzerland: The referendum and the initiative as a centerpiece of the political system," in Michael Gallagher and Pier Vincenzo Uleri (eds.), *The Referendum Experience in Western Europe* (London: Macmillan, 1996), p. 194.

42. David Magleby, "Direct Legislation in The United States," in David Butler and Austin Ranney, *Referendums around the World. The Growing Use of Direct Democracy* (London: Macmillan, 1994), pp. 230-231.

Last Thoughts

These impressions do not amount to a general theory of direct democracy regulation. The patterns of regulation vary considerably. Yet a pattern can be discerned; America is easily the most regulated country. Not because the American politicians are more prone to regulate than Europeans and Australians but because regulation makes it more difficult for the people to co-legislate and pass laws opposed to the wills of the legislators (and the interest groups). The politicians in Western Europe, on the other hand, have an incentive not to regulate the process, as this would increase the probability of defeats of their own proposals. In short referendums are seldom accompanied by regulation. What all this amounts to is a simple—yet undisputed—law of political science: politicians always seek to maximize their own influence—if necessary at the expense of others.

The Extension of Politics by Other Means

By Peter Schrag

The essays in this book leave little doubt that if you give legislators half a chance, they will try to restrict access to a competing political process that, in any number of ways, impinges not just on their discretion—their ability to conduct their business without voter-imposed mandates limiting their choices, and sometimes on the prerogatives of powerful interest groups (hunters in the Western states, for example)—but also on their careers and self-interest. The most pervasive of those career-restricting measures, of course, have been legislative term limits, which have been written into the constitutions of 18 states, in all but one case through voter initiatives. But there are countless others as well, particularly in the area of campaign finance reform. Some of those reforms have been struck down by the courts (under the same First Amendment principles, incidentally, that the courts have used to strike down attempts to limit the commercialization of the initiative process). But there's not much question that the impulse exists and that, as Paul Jacob notes, legislators are rarely known to make access easier or otherwise expand the process. In the likely event that the use of the initiative process expands in the years ahead, legislative efforts to impose restrictions on it are likely—though hardly certain— to expand as well.

But having said that, the most obvious thing in any debate about legislative and judicial attempts to regulate the initiative process is that there are no normative criteria beyond the Constitution's general protections for due process, free speech and minority rights. The great latitude that the courts permit in California—say in their interpretation of what qualifies as a single subject—would probably be rejected out of hand in Florida where the courts are far more aggressive in their scrutiny. Most states permit some sort of post-election legislative amendment, even repeal, of statutory initiatives, but California does not. Some give legislatures a chance to act before a measure goes on the ballot; some do not.

The list of unresolved questions runs on and on: What's a reasonable threshold for signatures—how many should be required in what period of time and what's a reasonable relationship between them? Who should have the authority to write the ballot title and summary, elements that are often crucial in close elections, and what checks should there be on that authority? In many cases, the first action in a court comes from a dispute over how the appropriate state official has captioned a measure. What constitutes a single subject? And what is the difference between amending the constitution by initiative (permitted in states like California) and revising it by initiative, which is not permitted? Is the initiative itself a normative element of American democracy? And if so, is it central or only peripheral? It may well be true, as Anne G. Campbell writes, that in striking a recent reapportionment initiative from the ballot, the California Supreme Court has become stricter in its application of the single subject standard — indeed the court itself seemed to invite such a conclusion. But that change can easily be regarded (as it may well have been by the court) as a welcome correction to a line of decisions that were too liberal.

Campbell has correctly outlined what sometimes appears to be a double judicial standard, accompanied by weaselly rationales, under which initiatives are subject to stricter single-subject review than are legislative statutes But that double standard also has political, if not legal, rationales. The conventional legislative process, for all the logrolling that sometimes accompanies it, is usually subject to a whole range of institutional checks that the initiative is not — committee hearings, two house agreement, executive veto, as well as the intrinsic legislative impulse to compromise and accommodate as many sides and interests as possible. None of that occurs in direct legislation, which is a winner-take-all process that, by its very nature, is rarely respectful of political minorities. In making their decisions, the voters have no technical experts at their disposal; they don't have the time to read the fine print, sometimes running to many thousands of words of legal language, behind the advertising that initiatives lend themselves to; don't have to record their votes, much less confront those who believe they've been damaged by those votes; can't be run out of office if they make serious errors; are not accountable for the consequences to their fellow citizens or the public weal. Those differences have led some scholars — the late Julian Eule of UCLA most prominent among them — to argue that in the absence of other checks, the courts should apply *stricter* scrutiny to initiatives than they do to conventional legislation.[2]

More fundamentally, any discussion about whether regulating and restricting the initiative and referendum process is good or bad depends in great part on the underlying assumptions about the relative strengths and weaknesses of the initiative and referendum. If you like I&R not just in

---

2. Julian N. Eule, "Judicial Review of Direct Democracy, " 99 *Yale Law Journal* 1503 (1990).

theory but as it's now used—if you like the results—you are likely to be much more restive if the legislature attempts to make access to the ballot more difficult. If you don't like it, you may feel that the courts have been far too obeisant to majority power, not just on single subject, but in their failure to protect minorities against majoritarian assaults on things like affirmative action and bilingual education. Conservative critics who attack judges for overturning voter-approved restrictions on schooling or other public services for illegal aliens as thwarting the will of the people are not quite as certain when it comes (for example) to the wave of successful initiatives legalizing the medical use of marijuana.

Alongside those questions there are still others: As Bruce Cain and Kenneth Miller have pointed out,[3] there is implicit disagreement even among supporters of the process between those who regard it as a progressive safety valve against legislative malfeasance or inertia and those who see it as a populist alternative to all representative government. As technology makes wide-scale interactive politics more feasible and as the internet culture seems to make voters increasingly restive and distrustful of elected officials, both in Washington and in the states, that issue becomes ever more important.

There's not much disagreement in our debates that money—big money—is now as big a factor in I&R as it is in electoral politics. And it seems clear, as Dan Smith points out in this volume, that while money and paid political operatives have played a role in the process almost from the beginning, the process was conceived as an instrument of citizen action. It was to comprise two hurdles: qualifying a measure for the ballot and getting it passed. But in an era when, on the one hand, it's nearly impossible in most states to qualify anything for the ballot without paid petition circulators and, on the other, easy for deep pockets initiative sponsors to qualify almost anything, the first hurdle becomes meaningless as a test of citizen commitment: Instead it becomes a barrier to it. At the same time, it becomes an open invitation to almost anyone who, for reasons of ideology or economic self-interest or political advantage or simple vanity wants to become an instant player. Scholars like Elizabeth Garrett and Elisabeth Gerber contend, correctly, that while a large money advantage is sometimes sufficient to defeat an initiative, it's rarely sufficient by itself to pass an initiative. But without money—the money of self-interested politicians and political parties, or of insurance companies, or Silicon Valley millionaires, or labor unions—initiative proponents can't get to the table at all. In 1998, a coalition of well-heeled gambling interests seeking authority to run electronic slots in reservation casinos, spent $65 million in Cal-

---

3. In a forthcoming paper, "The Populist Legacy: Initiatives and the Undermining of Representative Government."

ifornia to prove they were poor Indians; Nevada gambling interests spent $25 million in their unsuccessful attempt to beat them. It would be hard to describe this battle as anything but a fight between large economic interests. Gerber has found that without other resources, the groups she defines as economic interests can rarely use their financial power alone to prevail at the ballot box. Money often prevails on the negative side, rarely on the affirmative side. But increasingly the definitions become blurred and the groups confused: Is the California Republican Party, which bankrolled the campaign to pass Proposition 209, the measure that banned racial and gender preferences in public education and contracting, a citizens' group? Is U.S. Term Limits? Are the public employee unions?

As the already-large sums spent in initiative campaigns continue to grow—and notwithstanding the debate about the power of money to carry initiatives—there's little disagreement about the desirability over the most commonly proposed reform: requiring greater—and faster—disclosure of campaign contributions to ballot measures. Arthur Lupia[4] has argued cogently that while voters rarely have time to read the texts of initiatives and while initiative fights are dominated by 30-second TV ads and oversimplified mailers, voters get clear enough signals when they know who backs and opposes a measure and that, as others have argued, they rarely regret the votes they've cast. Yet ironically, Humane Society Vice President Wayne Pacelle, in his essay outlining the efforts of hunting organizations to restrict initiatives pushed by animal protection groups, also provides a dramatic illustration of how hunter and gun interests ran highly misleading ads for a successful ballot measure in Utah that now requires a two-thirds majority for any wildlife protection initiative—indicating that you can indeed fool most of the people at least some of the time. Would the voters really have passed that initiative had they known its real purpose and provisions? Pacelle, who strongly supports I&R, clearly implies that they would not. In any case it certainly reinforces the argument for even fuller disclosure: include the names and identities of the principal funders of initiatives in ballot pamphlets and require full disclosure of the names of those who support the pro and no campaigns in paid media ads and all other campaign literature.

But there may be a more significant reform possibility that's gotten a great deal less consideration—a reform that might satisfy some of the concerns on both sides of this debate. Contrary to the complaints of defenders of the process that the courts have become too meddlesome in restricting access to the ballot or in striking down measures, the U.S. Supreme Court has made it clear that any state attempt to prohibit the use of paid

---

4. Arthur Lupia, *The Democratic Dilemma: Can Citizens Learn What They Need to Know?* (1998).

petition circulators is a violation of the First Amendment; similarly, it struck down Colorado's attempts to require petition circulators to identify themselves by name and to require them to be registered voters.[5] (And as suggested above, those decisions have been based on the same principles as the federal court decisions striking down initiatives seeking to impose what the courts have regarded as disproportionately low contribution limits or mandating "blanket" political primaries). But as Paul Jacob correctly points out in this volume, by making it harder for measures to qualify, many reform proposals would simply increase the advantage that moneyed interests enjoy. Given those considerations, could states, in an attempt to reduce the power of money and restore the process to genuine citizen action, create what would, in effect be a second initiative route, requiring significantly fewer signatures, and/or allowing a longer period for proponents to qualify a measure, provided they use only volunteer petition circulators who would, of course be identified as such?

Would the courts permit such a reform? The answer is far from certain; so far it's not even clear whether the courts would tolerate a requirement that required paid signature collectors to wear badges identifying themselves as being paid. In its 1999 *Buckley* decision,[6] the Supreme Court held that petition circulators could not be required to wear badges identifying them by name but left open the question of whether they could be required to indicate whether they were being paid. If the courts did allow such a new process, those citizen initiatives might well serve as reminder to voters and the media that a lot of ballot measures are not brought by the stork of citizen action, thereby imposing a useful constraint on the moneyed sponsors of ballot measures using the conventional system.

But having said all that, we better acknowledge that it's still early days. While I&R have been on the books of many states for a century, and in some cases longer, it's only with the great upsurge of initiatives in the past generation and often only in the past the decade or so, that's it's been generating the intense interest that it's now getting from politicians, scholars and the media.

It's conceivable that with sustained economic prosperity, the social and political pressures that led to the upsurge in initiatives and to the moves to write I&R into the constitutions of non-initiative states like Minnesota, Rhode Island and Texas will subside. Some recent elections have also indicated that there is a sort of natural limit to voters' patience—that when the ballot gets overloaded with issues, especially long, technical issues, people will simply vote no. But what seems more likely is that as the power of our new information technologies increases, as on-line voting

---

5. *Buckley v. American Constitutional Law Foundation* (1999).
6. Ibid.

and (probably) on-line petition signature collection come into practice, and as reliance on unmediated media — talk shows, the Internet, e-mail — grows, they will create still greater public restiveness about the relatively slow and seemingly unresponsive traditional institutions not only in government but in other realms as well. In his recent book, *Democracy Derailed*,[7] *Washington Post* columnist David Broder, among our most sophisticated and thoughtful political journalists, even predicts that we'll soon get some form of direct democracy at the national level. Whether or not that prediction is correct, he's surely right in his finding that in state after state, voters show widespread disdain for their legislatures. In California, one recent survey, by Mark Baldassare of the Public Policy Institute of California, found that when asked about which they trust more fully in making basic policy decisions, the legislature and governor, or the voters through the initiative, the latter won 75 to 21. Broder says that when he asked Oregon voters, who twice balloted on right-to-die initiatives, whether such a fundamental ethical issue should simply be subject to the decision of a 50 percent-plus-one majority, "they looked at me like I was crazy." How else to decide something of this importance?

What could well give the debate even more urgency is the referendum, which has so far been used only rarely at the state level. But if the success of two recent California referenda is any indication — both were put on the ballot by the insurance industry to overturn newly enacted legislation making it somewhat easier for motorists to sue insurers — the process could well attract a lot of other moneyed groups in the future. One of the reasons that, in the view of Gerber and others, money alone has been insufficient to pass ballot initiatives is that when voters are uncertain or confused, they'll vote no. But because a referendum seeks a no vote — the question, essentially, asks whether a particular legislative enactment shall be upheld — confusion and uncertainty play into the hands of the sponsor.

The record of the past generation indicates that once hot-button issues — crime, immigration, abortion, taxes, term limits — have been decided at the ballot box, legislators have been highly reluctant to cross the voters. Still, it's likely that if the wave of the past decade becomes the wave of the future, the debate will intensify. In all probability, legislatures will exert still greater efforts to make it harder to qualify or pass voter-initiated measures, and may invent still more creative devices to curb the process. And as more initiatives move toward the ballot, it's likely that the courts will be seen — correctly or incorrectly — as becoming still more willing to interfere with the right of the voters to make their own decisions. As Kenneth

---

7. Broder, *Democracy Derailed: Initiative Campaigns and the Power of Money* (2000).

P. Miller warned in a recent paper[8] "as courts enforce constitutional norms and invalidate initiatives at a high rate, the public may become increasingly frustrated and may look for ways to undermine the courts' independence." Not being sure of what is supposed to be normative in this area, I can't fully share his conclusion that courts are invalidating initiatives "at a high rate." The courts have struck down initiative-based attempts to write congressional terms into the U.S. Constitution; they have overturned ballot measures in Oregon and Colorado that sought to restrict homosexual rights; they did strike down California's Proposition 187, which sought to deny schooling and other services to illegal aliens and their children and, more recently the voter initiative establishing a "blanket" primary. But most high-profile initiatives — on taxation, on affirmative action, on criminal sentencing, on environmental regulation, on bilingual education — have survived pretty much intact. And when it comes to campaign reform efforts, the courts have given equally strict scrutiny to legislative acts as to those imposed by initiative. *Buckley v. Valeo*, from which most other campaign finance decisions flow, concerned an act of Congress, not an act of direct democracy. Yet here again, how you come down may depend more on your basic attitude about the process and its effects than on some objective balance of how much is too much.

Still Miller's basic point about the potential danger to the independence of the courts is probably correct. There have already been calls for various reforms — requiring three-judge panels, for example, to review challenged initiatives — even in district courts — as well as calls for the impeachment of judges who hand down unpopular rulings. But as I noted above, we should also be mindful of the fact that it was the federal courts that struck down state efforts to prohibit paid signature gatherers, to require them to identify themselves, to require that they be registered voters in the state where they work and to limit contributions to initiative campaigns. And while there remains a lively debate among scholars over whether direct democracy is itself a violation of the federal guarantee clause (guaranteeing each state a republican form of government), the Supreme Court effectively resolved the issue — by ducking it, ruling (in 1912) that this is a political, not a legal issue and thus beyond its jurisdiction.[9] The practical effect was to eliminate what could have been one of the crucial barriers to direct democracy in America. (Interestingly enough, in separate decisions, the Oregon courts ruled that since — in that state — the legislature could amend or repeal statutory initiatives after they pass, the initiative

---

8. Kenneth P. Miller, "Judging Ballot Initiatives: A Unique Role for the Courts," Paper presented at the 2000 Annual Meeting of the Western Political Science Association, San Jose, CA, March 24-26, 2000.

9. Pacific States Telephone and Telegraph Co. v. Oregon 223 U.S. 118 (1912).

process did not violate the guarantee clause, which inferentially begs a question in states like California, where the legislature has no such authority).

I'll avoid the debate about what Madison and most of the other framers of the Constitution really thought about direct democracy, but there seems painfully little evidence, either in the Constitution, the records of the Philadelphia convention, or in the *Federalist* papers (especially Madison's No. 10) that they thought much of it. Certainly the anti-federalists, the real democrats of 1787-88, had no confidence in a document that many believed, in the words of Patrick Henry, "squints powerfully toward monarchy."

And can we really say (as does Jacob) that "the initiative process was the only avenue for citizens to reassert their control over government in the 1990s"? Does that mean that the voters of the 26 states without I&R were disenfranchised? Does it mean that the enormous changes wrought in national politics and policy in the past decade—the Clinton election, the Gingrich revolution, the elimination of the deficit, welfare reform, school reform—came out of thin air? And what virus, we may wonder, infected the legislatures in all the states at the same time that made them all as corrupt, unresponsive and ineffective as the talk-show rhetoric so casually insinuates?

Still there's no doubt that for all the tinkering the legislatures have attempted in recent years, and all the judicial decisions overturning one or another initiative, I&R has become an increasingly important political force, not only in the states that have the formal process, but in the public policy drift of the nation as a whole: The cuts in services even to legal aliens in the federal welfare reform bill were strongly influenced by measures like California's Proposition 187; ditto for the influence of the tax revolt in shaping the Reagan era and for a variety of other things. In the early 1990s, Congress came close to passing a constitutional amendment that would have required a Congressional supermajority to pass the budget and, echoing the state initiatives eliminating race-based affirmative action, to the wholesale elimination of similar federal programs.

Even more certain is the fact that through the past couple of decades, I&R and the policies it's generated has become ever more broadly institutionalized not only in the industries and professions—the petition circulating business, the pollsters, consultants, and media specialists—that have sprung up around it, but in the parties and the conventional political system. Governors and secretaries of state and the same kind of moneyed interests—railroads, insurance companies, public employee unions—that the Progressives once regarded as the special targets of the process now sponsor initiatives of their own. Meanwhile, those same politicians rely increasingly on informal plebescitary devices—the focus group, the overnight poll—to set policy; deep-pockets activists of various stripes increasingly use the threat of ballot measures to drive legislative action. Thus the two seem increasingly to become part of the same continuum: To paraphrase Clausewitz: the initiative has become the extension of politics by other means. All of which seems to reinforce the near-certainty that, regardless of what courts and legislatures may otherwise do, I&R, which was nearly dormant forty years ago, is becoming an increasingly important part not only of policy making but of the public consciousness. If every initiative, especially those impinging on the perks and careers of politicians, tempts those politicians to seek new curbs on the process, each also makes it more likely that there will be still others and that voters will be even more firmly bound to the process. Our technology—indeed our entire civic culture, seems to insure it. How you feel about that depends on a lot of things—maybe your age and your place in the new economy most of all—but does anyone doubt that it's here to stay?

Appendix A: Definition of Terms

Before we can undertake a meaningful discussion of initiative and referendum, we must first agree on what we mean when we use the term initiative and referendum. Almost every academic, reporter and activist has his or her own definition. Nonetheless, the following will provide very simple and easy to understand definitions of what the initiative and referendum process is in the United States.

In many states, citizens have the ability to adopt laws or to amend the state constitution. This is commonly referred to as the initiative process (possible in 24 states—see Appendix C). In many of the same states, as well as others, the citizens have the ability to reject laws or amendments proposed by the state legislature. This process is commonly referred to as the referendum process. There are two types of referendum in this country—popular and legislative. Popular referendum (possible in 24 states) is when the people have the power to refer, through a petition, specific legislation that was enacted by their legislature for the people to either accept or reject. Legislative referendum (possible in all states) is when the state legislature, an elected official, state appointed constitutional revision commission or other government agency or department submits propositions (constitutional amendments, statutes, bond issues, etc.) to the people for their approval or rejection. This is either constitutionally required, as in proposing constitutional amendments, or because the legislature, government official or agency voluntarily chooses to submit the proposal to the people (however, not all states allow their state legislature to place statutes on the ballot for voter approval or rejection). Every state but Delaware requires that constitutional amendments proposed by the legislature be submitted to the citizenry via legislative referendum for approval or rejection. The initiative process is used much more frequently than the referendum process and is considered by many the more important and powerful of the two processes. Additionally, there is no national initiative or referendum process in the United States.

The local initiative process is available in thousands of counties, cities and towns across the country (additional information regarding the local initiative process is available at http://www.iandrinstitute.org) and is utilized far more frequently than statewide I&R. Almost every major city in the country has this process including New York City, Houston, Philadelphia and New Orleans. Many states, like Louisiana and New York, have

261

the initiative process at the local level but not statewide and 356 home rule cities in Texas have the process but the state as a whole does not. Unfortunately, there has been no comprehensive study on the use of the initiative process at the local level but an informal analysis of the process reveals that it has been used on a variety of issues including zoning, prohibition, growth limitation, transportation, and tax related issues.

Appendix B: Important Court Cases Relating to the Initiative and Referendum Process[1]

(Chronological Listing)

Initiative & Referendum Institute v. United States Postal Service

(2000)

The Initiative & Referendum Institute and a coalition of citizen groups and individuals from across the political spectrum filed a legal complaint on June 1, 2000 in the U.S. District Court for the District of Columbia against the U.S. Postal Service (USPS). The suit seeks to overturn the USPS regulation prohibiting citizens from collecting petition signatures on initiative petitions on postal property. The new postal regulation severely limits the ability of citizens around the country to place issues before their fellow voters. The case number is 1:00CV01246 (a copy of the complaint as well as the Institute's press release is available at http://www.iandrinstitute.org/postofficecomplaint.htm).

The Institute also filed a temporary restraining order request due to the urgency in needing to have this prohibition rescinded during the last two months of the 2000 petitioning season. Surprisingly, the U.S. Postal Service voluntarily agreed to not enforce the regulation prior to July 31, 2000 effectively giving initiative proponents the opportunity to utilize postal property during this critical stage in the petition process. As of publication, a final ruling had not been reached.

Initiative & Referendum Institute v. State of Utah

(2-00-CV-837)

This case, filed in the United States District Court for the District of Utah on October 23, 2000, seeks the court to review, declare unconstitutional and enjoin enforcement of Proposition 5, the 1998 legislatively sponsored amendment to the Utah Constitution, Article VI, Section 1. The

---

1. This information compiled from the "Texas Senate Interim Committee Report on Initiative and Referendum" and original research by the Initiative & Referendum Institute.

amendment to the Utah Constitution requires any citizen ballot initiative involving wildlife to pass with a two-thirds supermajority vote of the Utah electorate.

Initiative & Referendum Institute v. State of Idaho
(Case No. 00-668-SMHW)

This case, filed in the United States District Court for the District of idaho on November 12, 2000, seeks the court to review, declare unconstitutional and enjoin enforcement of the state's requirement that signatures for inititative petitions must be obtained from every one of Idaho's Counties as well as other provisions of Idaho's initiative regulations. The plaintiffs argue that these requirements are unnecessary and represent a burden on the citizen's First Amendment right of Freedom of Speech.

On Our Terms '97 Pac, et al., Plaintiffs v. Secretary of State of State of Maine
United States District Court District of Maine
Civil No. 98-104-B-DMC (2000)

In early 1999, the Initiative & Referendum Institute brought a lawsuit in the U.S. District Court of Maine challenging Maine's prohibition on the payment of signature-gatherers on a per-signature basis (instead of by salary). Although the Court ruled that the Institute did not have standing to bring the case (because the Institute was not engaged in any initiative campaigns in that state), the Court did allow two other plaintiffs to remain.

Even though the Initiative & Referendum Institute did not have standing in the case, the Institute was the organization that controlled the legal strategy, coordinated the lawsuit and funded the legal challenge. On December 10, 1999 the U.S. District Court ruled (in *On Our Terms '97 PAC, et al., v. Secretary of State of State of Maine*) that the prohibition was unconstitutional. The remaining plaintiffs, U.S. Term Limits (a group trying to get an initiative on Maine's ballot) and On Our Terms (a group contracted to collect the signatures and run the ballot campaign) argued that the regulation was so restrictive (in that it made it very difficult to collect signatures) that it caused them to stop collecting signatures and cancel their campaign, and was thus an unconstitutional burden on core political speech. Furthermore, they argued that due to the burden of the regulation they would never do an initiative in Maine until the law was changed. The State of Maine argued that the regulation was necessary to prevent fraud because paying petitioners by the number of signatures they gather encourages them to forge signatures. They also argued that while U.S. Term Limits and On Our Terms stopped their campaigns, other groups went on to qualify issues for the ballot and therefore the regulation was not burdensome.

The U.S. District Court ruled, citing *Meyer v. Grant*, that the circulation of an initiative or referendum petition "involves the type of interactive communication concerning change that is appropriately described as core political speech" and citing *Buckley v. ACLF*, that a state may not, consistent with the First Amendment, severely burden such speech unless the regulation at issue is "narrowly tailored to serve a compelling state interest." The Court ruled that although the regulation didn't have the effect of halting all initiative and referendum activity in Maine (and that the proponents probably could have put their initiative on the ballot if they had worked harder and spent more), that the Statute nevertheless severely burdened the plaintiffs' attempt to mount their drive.

Furthermore, because the State of Maine could not provide any proof of rampant fraud in the Maine initiative process through out its history or provide proof that petitioners paid by the signature, instead of salary, were more likely to commit fraud, the State fell short of demonstrating that the Statute was narrowly tailored to meet a compelling state interest. The court added that *Meyer v. Grant* "makes clear that, in the context of strict scrutiny, a state's assumptions cannot be accepted at face value."

The Initiative & Referendum Institute is currently engaged in litigation in North Dakota concerning the same issue litigated in this case.

Boyette v. Galvin

No. 98-CV-10377-GAO filed in the Federal District Court
for the District of Massachusetts (2000)

On March 3, 1998, The Becket Fund filed a lawsuit on behalf of a group of Massachusetts's citizens challenging provisions of the Massachusetts Constitution which forbid citizens from petitioning the legislature for private school funding. Several provisions in the Massachusetts constitution stood in the way: the Anti-Aid Amendment, which barred any portion of the common school fund from going to "sectarian" schools, adopted at the height of anti-immigrant and anti-Catholic fervor during the 1850s; and a 1917 amendment that expanded the earlier amendment to include higher education and non-profit groups, and also created initiative and referendum procedures for the state while explicitly forbidding the use of them to amend the Anti-Aid Amendment. A separate background sheet prepared by the Beckett Fund provides more detail and is available by going to http://www.becketfund.org.

In September 1998, a federal judge signed an order permitting a petition to be circulated for signatures while the court challenge was pending. Nearly 59,000 signatures were gathered, but several thousand were disqualified, leaving the effort just short of the 57,100 needed. Another petition drive was launched in 1999, and this time more than 78,000 were certified, easily surpassing the minimum requirement. But in order for the petition to come before the legislature, and henceforth the voters, the Attorney General must certify that it is proper for the legislators to take it up. In a letter of September 1, 1999, he declared that one of the very constitutional provisions being challenged prohibits him from doing so. And thus, on April 6, 2000, The Becket Fund asked the federal district court in Boston to order the Attorney General to certify the petition so that it can be taken up by legislators before the May 10, 2000 deadline. Unfortunately, the judge decided against the preliminary injunction request. (See the full text of the memorandum in support of a motion for a preliminary injunction by going to http://www.becketfund.org.)

Amalgamated Transit Union Local 587 v. The State of Washington

99-2-27054-1 SEA Superior Court of the State of Washington in and for the County of King (2000)

This case struck down initiative I-695, after being adopted by the voters, as violating the state's single subject requirement for initiatives. The ruling was appealed to the Washington State Supreme Court which affirmed the lower courts decision.

Waremart Inc. v. Progressive Campaigns Inc.

Washington State Supreme Court—67029-3 (2000)

The State Supreme Court ruled that grocery stores do not have to allow initiative petitioning on their property.

Senate of the State of California et al., Petitioners v. Bill Jones, Respondents

California State Supreme Court S083194 (1999)

This 1999 decision struck an initiative off the California primary ballot because it violated the state's single subject provision for initiatives.

Stenberg v. Moore

258 Neb. 199 Filed November 19, 1999. No. S-98-983 (1999)

In *Stenberg v. Moore*, the Nebraska Supreme Court dealt with the constitutionality of a Nebraskan statute that required that the information a voter puts on an initiative petition (signature, address, etc.) be an exact match of what is in the voter registration records in order for the signature to be counted as a valid signature. The Nebraska Supreme Court ruled that this law was facially unconstitutional.

Thomas J. Walsh v. Secretary of the Massachusetts Commonwealth

(1999)

This litigation pertained to the validity of a petition and petition signatures if the petition had been altered in any way. The court ruled that signatures on petitions could be invalidated just because a coffee stain appeared on the petition.

San Francisco Forty-Niners v. Nishioka

San Francisco County Super. Ct. No. 995661-1999

In this case the San Francisco superior court issued a writ of mandate prohibiting respondent San Francisco Director of Elections from qualifying an initiative measure for the ballot. The writ was issued on the grounds that the circulating initiative petition contained false statements intended to mislead voters and induce them to sign the petition.

Joytime Distributors v. The State of South Carolina

(1999)

In this case, the South Carolina Supreme Court ruled that the state legislature did not have the authority to place statutes on the ballot for a general vote of the people.

Buckley v. American Constitutional Law Foundation

(1999)

The *Buckley* case is the latest in a number of supreme court decisions asking how far states may go in regulating the conduct of ballot initiative campaigns. Since the success of term limit and tax limit initiatives, elected officials across the country have been restricting initiative campaigns. In 1988, the Supreme Court struck down Colorado's restriction on paid initiative signature collection, saying that initiative petitions were protected political speech. *Meyer v. Grant*, 486 U.S. 414 (1988). In *Buckley*, Colorado was asking that other restrictions on petitions be upheld.

The question before the court in *Buckley* was whether the State of Colorado may constitutionally regulate the process of circulating initiative petitions by requiring that: (1) petition circulators who verify the signatures of petition signers must be registered electors; (2) petition circulators must wear identification badges; and (3) proponents of an initiative must file reports disclosing the amounts paid to circulators and the identity of petition circulators.

In other words, Colorado attempted to regulate the collection of signatures on initiative petitions by requiring signature collectors ("circulators") to be registered to vote in Colorado and to wear badges with their names and addresses, whether they are paid or volunteer, and, if paid, the name of the person or entity who is paying them, and requiring initiative proponents to file reports disclosing the names of and compensation paid to circulators. The U.S. Court of Appeals for the Tenth Circuit 120 F.3d 1092 (1997) struck down these requirements as unconstitutional infringements on political speech.

Petitioner Colorado claimed that it needed the restrictions to prevent fraud and preserve the integrity of the electoral process, and that the restrictions are permissible under the "flexible standard" applicable to regulation of the ballot. *Burdick v. Takushi*, 504 US. 428, 434 (1992). Colorado was supported by amici briefs from a group of State Attorneys General and by the Council of State Governments and a number of other governmental associations.

The respondents were a conservative legal organization and several individuals who have been involved in initiative campaigns (including Paul Grant, of *Meyer v. Grant*). Respondents contended that the fraud claims were a "facade," that the restrictions violated *Meyer v. Grant* and that the various restrictions violated petition circulators' and signers' free speech rights. Respondents were supported by a variety of organizations from across the philosophical spectrum, including the ACLU, the Initiative & Referendum Institute, and National Voter Outreach, a professional petition circulation firm. One of the amici's points was that Colorado law explicitly placed signature collection outside the electoral process (*Montero v. Meyer*, 861 F.2d 603 (10th Cir. 1988), cert. denied, 492 U.S. 921 (1989); accord, *Delgado v. Smith*, 861 F.2d 1489 (11th Cir. 1988), cert. denied, 492 U.S. 981 (1989)), making the proper standard for review the strict scrutiny applicable to private speech.

The U.S. Supreme Court ruled on January 12, 1999 striking down Colorado's regulation and restrictions on their initiative process as "undue hindrances to political conversations and the exchange of ideas," according to Justice Ruth Bader Ginsburg who wrote for the court.

The decision by the court had two major points: (1) initiative petition circulation is pure political speech and restrictions on circulation, especially at the time of discussions with voters who might potentially sign the petitions, is highly protected and (2) any restrictions on petition circulation must be justified by strong showings that the regulated practices hurt the integrity of the ballot process—in other words, that the restrictions help prevent actual fraud. This was extremely difficult to do considering that no state has ever been able to show convincingly that rampant fraud exists during the petition process.

Canvasser Services, Inc. v. Employment Department
(1999)

In this Oregon case, the courts ruled that signature gatherers cannot be independent contractors and must be paid as employees.

Initiative & Referendum Institute v. Costco
State Court—BC 18052 (1998)

This case was filed in 1998 and seeks to require Costco stores to adhere to existing California law and establish standard and reasonable time, place and manner restrictions for petitioners. The case is pending and waiting a decision.

Initiative & Referendum Institute v. Ralph's
State Court—BC 187162 (1998)

This case was filed in 1998 and seeks to require Ralph's stores to adhere to existing California law and establish standard and reasonable time, place and manner restrictions for petitioners. The case is pending and waiting a decision.

Campbell, Hamilton, Initiative & Referendum Institute et al. v. Buckley
Federal District Court-98B 1022 (1998)

This case was filed in 1998 and challenges Colorado's constitutional, statutory, and administrative procedures for review of initiative measures before they are placed on the ballot. The current regulations violate the First Amendment rights of petition proponents and voters. The lower court ruled against the complaint and has been appealed to the U.S. Supreme Court.

Initiative & Referendum Institute v. State of North Dakota
Federal District Court—A1-98-70 (1998)

This case seeks to overturn North Dakota's prohibition on paying circulators on a per-signature-basis and the requirement that circulators be "electors." The case is pending and waiting a decision.

Bernbeck v. Moore
(1997)

On October 9, 1997, in *Bernbeck v. Moore*, the 8th U.S. Court of Appeals struck down a Nebraska law that required petitioners to be registered voters in Nebraska for at least 30 days before circulating an initiative petition. The court ruled the voter registration requirement violated the First Amendment. The court based its decision on the U.S. Supreme Court decision, *Meyer v. Grant*, which ruled that a ban on paid petitioners violated freedom of expression guaranteed by First Amendment.

The court further stated that nothing in Nebraska law makes it illegal for anyone to hire out-of-state campaign consultants, out-of-state printers, out-of-state canvassers, or out-of-state lobbyists. The state may still require petition circulators to provide, under penalty of perjury, their temporary and permanent addresses, so if they may be located later if necessary. Therefore, Nebraska has no compelling need to require petitioners to be registered voters.

Planning and Conservation League v. Lungren
(1995)

This California case invalidated a legislative attempt to regulate the fashion in which initiatives could qualify for the ballot.

Chemical Specialties Manufacturers v. Deukinejian
(1991)

The California Appellate Court found Proposition 105, which required disclosure in a wide variety of areas (campaigns, hospitals, South African contracts, etc.), to violate the single subject rule of the state constitution.

Missourians to Protect Initiative Process v. Blunt
(1990)

The Missouri Supreme Court rules an initiative off the ballot because it is in violation of the single subject rule.

Finn v. McCuen
(1990)

Since the title of a lottery measure was misleading, the California Supreme Court ruled that the measure should not be allowed on the ballot.

Taxpayers to Limit Campaign Spending v. FPPC
(1990)

The California Supreme Court finds that when two initiatives covering the same topic appears on the same ballot, the one initiative receiving the most votes supersedes the other measure in all respects, even though some of the provisions of the one initiative with fewer voters do not conflict with the provisions of the other measure receiving the higher number of votes.

Meyer v. Grant
(1988)

Colorado had passed a law making it illegal to accept financial reward for signatures collected. The United States Supreme Court overturned this law. Such a law, the Court ruled unanimously, restricts freedom of expression guaranteed by the First Amendment and it restricts access to the most effective fundamental and perhaps economical avenue of political discourse, direct one-on-one communication.

HCHH Associates v. Citizens for Representative Government
(1987)

The California Appellate Court finds that an indoor shopping mall cannot ban petition gatherers but can impose reasonable rules on circulators.

Michigan Chamber of Commerce v. Austin
(1987)

The federal appellate court rules that Michigan's provisions limiting corporate contributions to ballot measure campaigns violates the right of association and free speech guarantees of the First Amendment.

Bilofsky v. Deukmejian
(1981)

California statute upheld as constitutional that prevents the use of names gathered on initiative petitions.

Citizens Against Rent Control v. Berkeley
(1981)

In *Citizens Against Rent Control v. Berkeley*, the U.S. Supreme Court held that a California city's ordinance to impose a limit on contributions to committees formed to support or oppose ballot measures violated the First Amendment. The Court determined that the Berkeley ordinance imposed "...a significant restraint on the freedom of expression of groups and those individuals who wish to express their views though committees," and that "The tradition of volunteer committees for collective action has manifested itself in myriad community and public activities; in the political process it can focus on a candidate or on a ballot measure." In a forceful passage the Court said, "Whatever may be the state interest or degree of that interest in regulating and limiting contributions to or expenditures of a candidate or a candidate's committee there is no significant state or public interest in curtailing debate and discussion of a ballot measure. Placing limits on contributions that in turn limit expenditures plainly impairs freedom of expression. The integrity of the political system will be adequately protected if contributions are identified in a public filing revealing the amounts contributed...."

Pruneyard Shopping Center v. Robins
(1980)

The U.S. Supreme Court rules that state constitutional provisions that permit political activity at a privately owned shopping center does not violate federal constitutional private property rights of the owner.

First National Bank of Boston v. Bellotti
(1977)

In *First National Bank of Boston v. Bellotti*, the U.S. Supreme Court invalidated a Massachusetts statute prohibiting business corporations from making contributions or expenditures "... for the purpose of ... influencing or affecting the vote on any question submitted to the voters, other than one materially affecting any of the property, business or assets of the corporation." In reviewing the Massachusetts law, the Court said, "If the speakers here were not corporations, no one would suggest that the state could silence their proposed speech. It is the type of speech indispensable to decision-making in a democracy, and this is no less true because the speech comes from a corporation rather than an individual. The inherent worth of the speech in terms of its capacity for informing the public does not depend on the identity of its source?" The Court rejected Massachusetts' claim that the statute preserved the integrity of the electoral process and public confidence in democratic government with this often quoted passage: "The risk of corruption perceived in cases involving candidate elections ... simply is not present in a popular Vote on a public issue. To be sure, corporate advertising may influence the outcome of the vote; this would be its purpose. But the fact that advocacy may persuade the electorate is hardly a reason to suppress it ... Moreover, the people in our democracy are entrusted with the responsibility for judging and evaluating the relative merits of conflicting arguments. They may consider in making their judgment, the source and credibility of the advocate."

Hardie v. Eu
(1977)

The California Supreme Court finds unconstitutional the Political Reform Act's cap on expenditures for qualifying ballot measures since it violates First Amendment rights.

Citizens for Jobs and Energy v.
Fair Political Practices Commission
(1976)

The California Supreme Court declares that the Political Reform Act may not limit expenditures by ballot measure committees.

Stanson v. Mott

(1976)

The California Supreme Court rules that the use of public funds for election campaigning to promote or oppose a ballot measure is illegal.

Bernzen v. Boulder

186 Colo. 81, 525 P.2d 416 (1974)

In this case, the court ruled that recall, as well as initiative and referendum, were fundamental rights of a republican form of government which the people have reserved unto themselves.

State ex. rel. Nelson v. Jordan

(1969)

The Arizona Supreme Court finds that when two initiatives conflict, it is the duty of the court to harmonize both.

Pacific States Tel. & Tel. Co. v. Oregon

223 U.S. 118 (1912)

This case addressed whether Oregon's I&R system violated the Guarantee Clause of the U.S. Constitution. The court sidestepped the issue by holding that whether a state had a republican form of government is a political question, and therefore non-justiciable. The court was motivated in part by reluctance to conclude that adoption of the initiative and referendum destroyed all government republican in form in Oregon. The Court stated "[t]his being so, the contention, if held to be sound, would necessarily affect the validity, not only of the particular statute which is before us, but of every other statute passed in Oregon since the adoption of the initiative and referendum." Any such determination should, the court concluded, be made by Congress. This seemed to settle the issue at the federal level.

Hartig v. City of Seattle

53 Wash. 432, 102 P. 408 (1909)

In 1909, the Washington Supreme Court considered whether I&R violated the Guarantee Clause of the Federal Constitution. The Washington court did not think the question of representative government was relevant at all to the question of whether a form of government was republican. They stated: "[I]t can scarcely be contended that this plan is inconsistent with a republican form of government, the central idea of which is a government by the people. Whether the expression of the will of the people is made directly by their own acts or through representatives chosen by them is not material. The important consideration is a full expression."

In re Pfahler
150 Cal. 71, 88 P. 270 (1906)

In this case, the California Supreme Court upheld a local initiative law against a Guarantee Clause challenge while implying that similar measures on the state level would be constitutional as well. The court stated: "In saying this, we do not wish to be understood as intimating that the people of a state may not reserve the supervisory control as to general state legislation afforded by the initiative and referendum, without violating this provision of the federal Constitution."

Kadderly v. City of Portland
44 Or. 118, 74 P. 710 (1903)

In this case, the Oregon Supreme Court sustained I&R against a Guarantee Clause attack. The court stated, "The purpose of this provision of the Constitution is to protect the people of the several states against aristocratic and monarchical invasions, and against insurrections and domestic violence, and to prevent them from abolishing a republican form of government. Cooley, *Const. Lim.* (7th Ed.) 45; 2 Story, *Const.* (5th Ed.) § 1815. But it does not forbid them from amending or changing their Constitution in any way they may see fit, so long as none of these results is accomplished. No particular style of government is designated in the Constitution as republican, nor is its exact form in any way prescribed."

The court acknowledged that James Madison had described republican government as representative, but stated, "Now, the initiative and referendum amendment does not abolish or destroy the republican form of government, or substitute another in its place. The representative character of the government still remains. The people have simply reserved to themselves a larger share of legislative power, but they have not overthrown the republican form of the government, or substituted another in its place. The government is still divided into the legislative, executive, and judicial departments, the duties of which are discharged by representatives selected by the people. Under this amendment, it is true, the people may exercise a legislative power, and may, in effect, veto or defeat bills passed and approved by the Legislature and the Governor; but the legislative and executive departments are not destroyed, nor are their powers or authority materially curtailed."

Appendix C: List of States with Initiative and Referendum Process

States with Direct (DA)[1] and In-direct (IDA)[2] Initiative Amendments;
Direct (DS)[3] and In-direct (IDS)[4] Initiative Statutes and Popular (PR)[5] Referendum[6]
(Legend: X = process available; O = process not available)

States where some form of Initiative or PR is available	Date process was adopted[7]	Type of process available		Type of Initiative process available		Type of Initiative process used to propose Const. Amend.		Type of Initiative process used to propose Statutes (laws)	
		Initiative	PR	Const. Amend.	Statute	DA	IDA	DS	IDS
Alaska	1956	X	X	O	X	O	O	O	X
Arizona	1911	X	X	X	X	X	O	X	O
Arkansas	1910	X	X	X	X	X	O	X	O
California[8]	1911/1966	X	X	X	X	X	O	X	O
Colorado	1910	X	X	X	X	X	O	X	O
Florida	1972	X	O	X	O	X	O	O	O
Idaho	1912	X	X	O	X	O	O	X	O
Illinois[9]	1970	X	O	X	O	X	O	O	O
Kentucky	1910	O	X	O	O	O	O	O	O
Maine	1908	X	X	O	X	O	O	O	X
Maryland	1915	O	X	O	O	O	O	O	O
Massachusetts	1918	X	X	X	X	O	X	O	X
Michigan	1908	X	X	X	X	X	O	O	X
Mississippi[10]	1914/1992	X	O	X	O	O	X	O	O
Missouri	1908	X	X	X	X	X	O	X	O
Montana[11]	1906/1972	X	X	X	X	X	O	X	O
Nebraska	1912	X	X	X	X	X	O	X	O
Nevada	1905	X	X	X	X	X	O	O	X

State	Date							
New Mexico	1911	O	X	O	O	O	O	O	O
North Dakota [12]	1914	X	X	X	X	X	X	X	O
Ohio	1912	X	X	X	X	X	O	O	X
Oklahoma	1907	X	X	X	X	X	X	X	O
Oregon	1902	X	X	X	X	X	X	X	O
South Dakota [13]	1898/1972/1988	X	X	X	X	X	X	X	X
Utah	1900/1917	X	X	O	X	O	O	X	O
Washington	1912	X	X	O	X	O	X	X	O
Wyoming	1968	X	X	O	X	O	O	O	O
TOTALS	27 states	24 states	24 states	18 states	21 states	16 states	2 states	16 states	7 states

1. Direct Initiative amendment (DA) is when constitutional amendments proposed by the people are directly placed on the ballot and then submitted to the people for their approval or rejection.

2. In-direct Initiative amendment (IDA) is when constitutional amendments proposed by the people must first be submitted to the state legislature during a regular session.

3. Direct Initiative statute (DS) is when statutes (laws) proposed by the people are directly placed on the ballot and then submitted to the people for their approval or rejection.

4. In-direct Initiative statute (IDS) is when statutes (laws) proposed by the people must first be submitted to the state legislature during a regular session.

5. Popular Referendum (PR) is the power to refer to the ballot, through a petition, specific legislation that was enacted by the legislature for their approval or rejection.

6. This list does not include the states with Legislative Referendum (LR). Legislative Referendum is when a state legislature places an amendment or statute on the ballot for voter approval or rejection. Every state but Delaware requires state constitutional amendments to be placed on the ballot for voter approval or rejection.

7. This date represents the date that the citizens of the state voted to adopt the process.

8. In 1966 California repealed indirect Initiative for statutes.

9. In Illinois, the subject matter of a proposed constitutional amendment is severely limited to legislative matters. Consequently, Initiatives seldom appear on the ballot.

10. Mississippi first adopted initiative and referendum in 1914 but a court ruling nullified the vote. The voters then adopted it again in 1992.

11. In 1972 Montana adopted a provision that allows for directly initiated constitutional amendments.

12. In North Dakota prior to 1918, constitutional amendments could be initiated only indirectly.

13. In 1972 South Dakota adopted a provision that allows for directly initiated constitutional amendments. In 1988 South Dakota repealed In-direct Initiative for Statutes.

Appendix D: List of Requirements to Place an Initiative on the Ballot

Signature, Geographic Distribution, and Single-Subject Requirements for Initiatives

State	Type	SS[1]	Net Signature Requirements for Const. Amends	Net Signature Requirements for Statutes	Geographic Distribution	Deadline for Sign. Submission	Circulation Period
AK	DS	No	Not allowed by state constitution	10% of registered voters	4% in 3/4 of Election Districts	Prior to the convening of the legislature[2]	1 year
AZ	DA/DS	Yes	15% of votes cast for Governor	10% of votes cast for Governor	No geog. distribution	4 mos. prior to election	20 mos.
AR	DA/DS	No	10% of votes cast for Governor	8% of votes cast for Governor	5% in 15 of 75 counties	4 mos. prior to election	unlimited
CA	DA/DS	Yes	8% of votes cast for Governor	5% of votes cast for Governor	No geog. distribution	To be determined by state each year[3]	150 days
CO	DA/DS	Yes	5% of votes cast for SOS	5% of votes cast for SOS	No geog. distribution	3 mos. prior to election	6 mos.
FL	DA	Yes	8% of ballots cast in the last Presidential election	Not allowed by state constitution	8% in 12 of 23 Congressional districts	90 days prior to election[4]	4 years
ID	DS	No	Not allowed by state constitution	6% of registered voters	6% in each of the 22 counties	4 mos. prior to election	18 mos.
ME	IDS	No	Not allowed by state constitution	10% of votes cast for Governor	No geog. distribution	To be determined by state each year[5]	1 year
MA	IDA/IDS	No	3% of votes case for Governor	3.5% of votes cast for Governor[6]	No more than 25% from a single county	To be determined by state each year[7]	64 days
MI	DA/IDS	No	10% of votes case for Governor	8% of votes cast for Governor	No geog. distribution	Const. Amend.[8] Statute[9]	180 days
MS	IDA	No	12% of votes case for Governor	Not allowed by state constitution	20% from each Congressional district	90 days prior to the convening of the legislature	1 year
MO	DA/DS	Yes	8% of votes case for Governor	5% of votes cast for Governor	5% in 6 of 9 Congressional districts	8 mos. prior to election	18 mos.

1. This column denotes whether or not a state has a requirement that every Initiative or Referendum be limited to one subject.

2. In Alaska, signatures must be submitted prior to the convening of the legislative session in the year in which the initiative is to appear on the ballot. The lieutenant governor shall place the initiative on the election ballot of the first statewide general, special, or primary election that is held after (1) the petition and any supplementary petition have been submitted, (2) a legislative session has convened and adjourned, and (3) a period of 120 days has expired since the adjournment of the legislative session.

3. In California, each year the Secretary of State will set a complete schedule showing the maximum filing deadline and the certification deadline by the counties to the Secretary of State. There is a recommended submission date for "full check" and "random check". These dates are only recommended. Notwithstanding any other provision of law, no initiative shall be placed on a statewide election ballot which qualifies less than 131 days before the date of the election.

4. In Florida, certification must be received by the Secretary of State from the county supervisors stating the number of valid signatures submitted by the initiative proponent no later than 90 days prior to the general election ballot for the initiative to be considered for that ballot. However, there are several additional criteria that must be met prior to the certification of an initiative for the ballot. This includes the requirement that the proposed initiative has been approved for the ballot by the state supreme court. An initiative can only be submitted to the court for review after 10% of the required number of signatures have been collected and certified to the Secretary of State by the county supervisors. The court is under no statutory time frame to render a decision. Therefore, there is no precise date in which the signatures must be submitted in order to insure that you qualify for any specific general election ballot.

5. In Maine, signatures must be submitted on or before the 50th day after the convening of the Legislature in the first regular session or on or before the 25th day after the convening of the Legislature in the second regular session.

6. In Massachusetts, the initial petition must include three percent of the total votes cast for Governor. If the legislature has not passed an initiated statute by the first Wednesday in May, petitioners must file a supplementary petition with petitions equal in number to one-half of one percent of the total votes cast in the previous gubernatorial election to place the issue on the ballot.

7. In Massachusetts, the initial petition signatures shall be submitted no later than the first Wednesday in December in the year in which the Initiative was submitted. If the legislature has not passed the initiated statute by the first Wednesday in May, petitioners must file a supplementary petition with petitions equal in number to one-half of one percent of the total votes cast in the previous gubernatorial election no sooner than the first Wednesday in June and no later than the first Wednesday in July in order for the initiative statute to be placed on the ballot.

8. In Michigan, signatures for constitutional amendments must be submitted not less than 120 days prior to the general election.

9. In Michigan, signatures for statutes must be submitted ten days prior to the start of the legislative session.

Signature, Geographic Distribution, and Single-Subject Requirements for Initiatives (cont.)

State	Type	SS[1]	Net Signature Requirements for Const. Amends	Net Signature Requirements for Statutes	Geographic Distribution	Deadline for Sign. Submission	Circulation Period
MT	DA/DS	Yes	10% of votes cast for Governor	5% of votes cast for Governor	Statute: 5% in 34 of 50 Legislative Districts Amend.: 10% in 40 of 50 Legislative Districts	2nd Friday of the 4th month prior to election	1 year
NE	DA/DS	Yes	10% of registered voters	7% of registered voters	5% in 38 of 39 counties	4 mos. prior to election	1 year
NV	DA/IDS	No	10% of registered voters	10% of registered voters	10% in 13 of 17 counties	Const. Amend.[10] Statute[11]	CA: 11 mos.[12] S: 10 mos.[13]
ND	DA/DS	No	4% of population	2% of population	No geog. distribution	90 days prior to election	1 year
OH	DA/IDS	Yes	10% of votes cast for Governor	6% of votes cast for Governor[14]	Statute: 1.5% in 44 of 88 counties; Amend.: 5% in 44 of 88 counties	Const. Amend.[15] Statute[16]	Unlimited
OK	DA/DS	Yes	15% of votes cast for Governor	8% of votes cast for Governor	No geog. distribution	8 mos. prior to election[17]	90 days
OR	DA/DS	Yes	8% of votes cast for Governor	6% of votes cast for Governor	No geog. distribution	4 mos. prior to election	Unlimited
SD	DA/DS	No	10% of votes cast for Governor	5% of votes cast for Governor	No geog. distribution	Const. Amend.[18] Statute[19]	1 year
UT	DS/IDS	No	Not allowed by state constitution	DS: 10% of votes cast for Governor; IDS: 10% of votes cast for Governor[20]	10% in 20 of 29 counties	Direct Statute[21] In-direct Statute[22]	Unlimited
WA	DS/IDS	No	Not allowed by state constitution	8% of votes cast for Governor	No geog. distribution	Direct Statute[23] In-direct Statute[24]	DS: 6 mos. IDS: 10 mos.
WY	DS	No	Not allowed by state constitution	15% of votes cast for Governor	15% of total votes cast in the last election from at least 2/3 of the counties	1 day prior to the convening of the legislature[25]	18 mos.

10. In Nevada, signatures for constitutional amendments must be submitted 90 days prior to the election.

11. In Nevada, signatures for statutes must be submitted 30 days prior to the convening of the legislature.

12. In Nevada, petition language for constitutional amendments can be filed no sooner than September 1 of the year preceding the election and all signatures are due 90 days prior to the election.

13. In Nevada, petition language for statutes can be filed no sooner than January 1st of an even number year and signatures must be submitted no later than November 1st of that same even numbered year.

14. In Ohio, the initial petition must include three percent of the total votes cast for Governor. A supplementary petition containing an additional three percent is required in the event the proposed statute is defeated, amended or left idle by the legislature.

15. In Ohio, signatures for amendments must be submitted 90 days prior to the election.

16. In Ohio, signatures for statutes must be submitted 10 days prior to the convening of legislature.

17. In Oklahoma, an initiative must be submitted to the state Supreme Court for review before it can be certified for the ballot by the Secretary of State. Due to the fact that there is no statutory deadline for the court to make this determination, the state recommends that you submit your signatures eight months prior to the election that you desire the measure to be considered for.

18. In South Dakota, signatures for amendments must be submitted at least one year prior to the election.

19. In South Dakota, signatures for statutes must be submitted by the first Tuesday in May in the general election year.

20. In Utah, direct statutes require signatures equal in number to 10 percent of the votes cast for all candidates for Governor in the next preceding gubernatorial election for the statute to be placed on the ballot. In-direct statutes must contain signatures from five percent of the votes cast for all candidates for Governor in the next preceding gubernatorial election. If the legislature rejects or does not enact the proposed statute, a supplemental petition contacting additional signatures equal in number to 5 percent of the votes cast for all candidates for Governor in the next preceding gubernatorial election for the statute to be placed on the ballot.

21. In Utah, signatures for direct statutes must be submitted at least four months prior to the election.

22. In Utah, signatures for in-direct statutes must be submitted at least 10 days before the commencement of the annual general legislative session.

23. In Washington, signatures for direct statutes must be submitted four months prior to the election.

24. In Washington, signatures for in-direct statutes must be submitted ten days prior to the convening of the regular session of the legislature.

25. In Wyoming, signatures must be submitted prior to the convening of the legislature. The state constitution states that the legislature shall convene at noon on the second Tuesday in January.

Appendix E: Major Initiative and Referendum Legislation Since 1998

1998 Legislation

- *Mississippi*: Passed legislation requiring that only a person who is a resident of the state may circulate an initiative petition or obtain signatures on an initiative petition.
- *Missouri*: Changed the deadline for submitting initiative petitions from four months prior to the election to six months prior — effectively decreasing the circulation period by two months.
- *Utah*: Amended constitution to require a two-thirds vote of the people in order to adopt by initiative any state law allowing, limiting, or prohibiting the taking of wildlife or the season for or method of taking wildlife.
- *Wyoming*: Required initiative proponents to not only gather signatures equal to 15% of the number of voters in the last general election, but to gather signatures equal to 15% of the number of voters in the last general election in 2/3 of Wyoming counties — making petitioners have to collect an impossible number of signatures in very sparsely populated areas.

1999 Legislation

- *Arkansas*: Legislation requires the reporting of state funds in excess of $100 used to support or oppose a ballot measure.
- *Arkansas*: Gives the Arkansas Supreme Court original jurisdiction to determine the sufficiency of initiative and referendum petitions and proposed constitutional amendments.
- *Arizona*: Required that all petition circulators must be qualified to be registered to vote (i.e. a resident of the state, etc.)
- *Idaho*: Required that all petition circulators be a resident of the state.
- *Missouri*: Required that all petition circulators must be residents of the state. Also required that all signature-gatherers register with the state and provided that all signatures gathered by unregistered circulators be declared invalid.

- *Montana*: Required that employers of paid signature gatherers file financial disclosure reports.
- *Montana*: Gave Attorney General the authority to deny certification of an improper ballot measure.
- *Nebraska*: Passed legislation providing that in order for a constitutional amendment to become law it must be approved twice by the voters in separate elections. Also requires that initiative petitions be filed with the Secretary of State eight months prior to an election, rather than the existing requirement of four months. (Defeated by voters on November 7, 2000.)
- *Oregon*: Passed legislation increasing the number of signatures needed to get a constitutional amendment on the ballot from eight to twelve percent. (Defeated by voters on May 16th, 2000.)
- *Oregon*: Passed legislation extending the time period for the Secretary of State to verify signatures on petitions from 15 to 30 days. (Adopted by voters on May 16th, 2000.)
- *South Dakota*: Provided a procedure for opponents of an initiative to contest the validity of signatures.
- *Utah*: Required that political issues committees for initiatives and employers of paid signature gatherers file financial disclosure reports.
- *Utah*: Required that circulators must be a resident of the state.

2000 Legislation

- *Alaska*: Prohibits initiatives that permit, regulate or prohibit the taking or transportation of wildlife, or prescribes seasons or methods for the taking of wildlife. (Defeated by voters on November 7, 2000.)
- *Arizona*: Requires a supermajority vote of the people for all future wildlife and hunting initiatives. (Defeated by voters on November 7, 2000.)
- *Arizona*: Allows a person to withdraw their signature from a petition.
- California: Requires approval by 2/3 of voters for constitutional initiatives. (Pending in Senate)
- *Minnesota*: Senate Committee kills legislation passed by the House in 1999 allowing the citizens to vote on the establishment of initiative and referendum at the state level.
- *South Dakota*: Changes South Dakota's circulation period for collecting signatures by not allowing collection time to roll over to future ballots. For example, South Dakota's current circulation period is one year. It use to be that if you started collecting signatures in January and the deadline to make the upcoming ballot was May and you didn't have enough signatures by then, you could keep petitioning until

your one year time limit was up—and the measure would go on the next available ballot. Now you still have one year, but no matter when you start you only have until the deadline for the closest election ballot to gather signatures.

- *Wyoming*: Requires petition circulators be registered voters and citizens of the state.

Contributors

Anne Campbell is an Associate Professor of Political Science at the United States Air Force Academy. Her dissertation at the University of Colorado at Boulder, "Setting the Initiative Agenda: the Not-So-Silent Majority," examined the initiative agenda-setting process in Colorado. She has presented several papers on various aspects of the citizen's initiative process at Western Political Science Association annual meetings.

Jennie Drage is a policy specialist in the Legislative Management Program at the National Conference of State Legislatures. She focuses on the areas of campaign finance reform, initiative and referendum, term limits, legislative ethics and lobbying. She holds a Bachelor's degree in political science and Latin American studies, and a Master's degree in linguistics from the University of Kansas.

Elizabeth Garrett is a Professor of Law and Deputy Dean at the University of Chicago Law School. Her primary scholarly interests are legislative process, the law of democratic institutions, direct democracy, the federal budget process, and administrative law. She has just published, with William N. Eskridge, Jr. and Philip N. Frickey, *Legislation and Statutory Interpretation* (Foundation Press Concepts and Insights Series, 2000).

Elisabeth R. Gerber is Associate Professor of Political Science at the University of California, San Diego. She is the author of two recent books on I&R: *The Populist Paradox* (Princeton University Press, 1999), which examines the role and influence of money and organized interest groups; and *Stealing the Initiative* (Prentice Hall, 2000, with A. Lupia, M. McCubbins, and D.R. Kiewiet), which considers the implementation of ballot measures by state government actors. Her numerous articles on the initiative and referendum process are published in such journals as the *American Journal of Political Science* and *Political Research Quarterly*. She is currently working on a major new project on local land use initiatives.

Paul Grant is a Colorado attorney specializing in criminal defense, First Amendment, and other constitutional law. Grant was the lead plaintiff in the first Supreme Court case dealing with initiative petition rights under the First Amendment, Meyer v. Grant, 486 U.S. 414 (1988), the case in which the Supreme Court struck down Colorado's criminal prohibition against paid petition circulation. He was both a witness at trial and co-counsel in the follow-up Supreme Court case, Buckley v. American Constitutional

Law Foundation, Inc., 119 S.Ct. 636 (1999). Today, Grant is building his "Bill of Rights" trial and appellate practice in state and federal courts.

Paul Jacob is the National Director of U.S. Term Limits, the nation's most vocal term limits group. Through his writings and media appearances as well as his weekly radio commentary, "Common Sense," Jacob has become a leading advocate of term limits and the citizen initiative process.

Bill Jones was elected California's Secretary of State in 1994. In 1998 he was re-elected, helped by the unanimous endorsement from every major newspaper in the state. He has aggressively implemented the latest electronic technology in the Secretary of State's Office and promulgated a model comprehensive e-Government plan for all of California's state government. As California's Chief Elections Officer, Bill Jones has worked to increase voter participation, which rose dramatically to a 20-year high in the March 7, 2000 primary election. Bill Jones served in the State Assembly, authoring the immensely successful "Three-Strikes and You're Out" law, the nation's toughest anti-crime legislation that has been a major factor bringing California's crime rate to a 35-year low. Bill Jones is a native California rancher.

Kris Kobach is a Professor of Law at the University of Missouri (Kansas City) School of Law, where he teaches constitutional law, legislation, and legal history. A graduate of Harvard College (1988) and Yale Law School (1995), Professor Kobach also holds a doctorate in politics from Oxford University (1992). He is the author of *The Referendum: Direct Democracy in Switzerland* (Dartmouth Publishing, 1993), a landmark study of Swiss referendums and initiatives. Professor Kobach has also published numerous articles in law reviews and political science journals regarding direct democracy in the United States and Europe. Professor Kobach was extensively involved in defending the constitutionality of Missouri's instruct-and-inform law in the U.S. Supreme Court case of *Cook v. Gralike*.

Rob Natelson is Professor of Law at the University of Montana, where he teaches legal history, property law, and other subjects. He also has been involved in various initiative and referendum campaigns, both a proponent and opponent of ballot measures.

Wayne Pacelle is senior vice president for communications and government affairs for The Humane Society of the United States, the nation's largest animal protection organization. A graduate of Yale, he has conceived of, directed, and helped to pass more than a dozen statewide ballot initiatives on subjects ranging from trapping to hound hunting to cockfighting. Recently, *Campaigns & Elections* magazine named him a "Rising Star in Politics."

Angelo Paparella is the President of Progressive Campaigns, Inc. (PCI), a nationwide petition management firm based in Los Angeles, California. In addition to petition management services, Angelo also acts as a consultant to political candidates and initiative campaign committees on field strategy and operations. After graduating from the University of Notre Dame in 1982, Angelo worked as a field operation specialist for non-profit political organizations before forming Progressive Campaigns, Inc. in 1992.

Dennis Polhill has been Chairman of the Board of directors of the Initiative & Referendum Institute since it was founded in 1998. Educated as an engineer, he became an expert by working in city government and as a consultant. Dennis was a proponent of successful term limits petition drives in Colorado in 1994, 1996, and 1998 and has written, spoken, and testified extensively on initiative and referendum.

Mads Qvortrup is Research Director of IRI Europe. He was educated at University of Oxford, and was awarded his doctorate at Brasenose College, Oxford. He has held research positions at University of London and a professorship at the University of Copenhagen. His articles have appeared in peer-reviewed journals, such as *Representation, History of Political Thought, Political Studies* and *Electoral Studies*. Dr Qvortrup has been described as "a world expert on international referenda," by Israel's leading newspaper *Ha'aretz*.

Peter Schrag is a lifelong journalist. For 19 years he was the editor of the editorial pages of the *Sacramento Bee*, for which he still writes a weekly column. He also writes frequently for national magazines on education and political issues, and is the author of *Paradise Lost: California's Experience, America's Future* (1998).

Daniel A. Smith is Associate Professor of Political Science at the University of Denver. His book, *Tax Crusaders and the Politics of Direct Democracy* (New York: Routledge, 1998), examines the financial backing and the populist-sounding rhetoric of three anti-tax ballot initiatives in the U.S. Smith has published scholarly articles in *Social Science History, Social Science Journal, State Politics* and *Policy Quarterly, Economic Development Quarterly*, and *Presidential Studies Quarterly*. His chapter, "Campaign Finance of Ballot Initiatives in the American States" is being published in *Dangerous Democracy? The Battle over Ballot Initiatives in America* (Lanham, MD: Rowman and Littlefield, edited by Larry Sabato, et al.).

Don Stenberg is Attorney General for the State of Nebraska. He was elected in November 1990. He is the first Attorney General from Nebraska in over 40 years to successfully argue and win a case before the U.S. Supreme Court. He graduated cum laude from Harvard Law School.

Caroline Tolbert is an Assistant Professor of Public Policy and Political Science at Kent State University. She is co-editor of *Citizen as Legislators: Direct Democracy in the United States* (Ohio State University Press, 1988), and author of three chapters in this volume. Her research on direct democracy and public policy has appeared in the *American Journal of*

Political Science, the *Journal of Politics*, *Women and Politics*, and *Comparative Political Studies*. Her recent projects focus on the role of the initiative process in health care reform and governmental reform, such as Internet voting and open primary systems.

M. Dane Waters is a leading authority on the initiative and referendum process and has been personally involved in over forty initiative and referendum campaigns. He has provided information to numerous groups, individuals and governments around the world on how to organize initiative and referendum campaigns. Dane has authored numerous articles on the initiative and referendum process and has lectured to groups around the world on the importance of the initiative and referendum process. He has provided commentary on initiative and referendum to newspapers, radio talk shows and television stations around the world.

Index